D1601161

Immigrant Women in the U.S. Workforce

Immigrant Women in the U.S. Workforce

Who Struggles? Who Succeeds?

Georges Vernez

LEXINGTON BOOKS
Lanham • Boulder • New York • Oxford

LEXINGTON BOOKS

Published in the United States of America
by Lexington Books
4720 Boston Way, Lanham, Maryland 20706

12 Hid's Copse Road
Cumnor Hill, Oxford OX2 9JJ, England

British Library Cataloguing in Publication Information Available

Library of Congress Cataloging-in-Publication Data

Vernez, Georges.
    Immigrant women in the U.S. workforce : who struggles? who
succeeds? / Georges Vernez.
        p.   cm.
    Includes bibliographical references and index.
    ISBN 0-7391-0039-4 (cloth : alk. paper)
    1. Women alien labor—United States.   I. Title.
HD6057.5.U5V47   1999
331.4'086'91—dc21   99-34554
                                                           CIP

Printed in the United States of America

♾️™ The paper used in this publication meets the minimum requirements of American
National Standard for Information Sciences—Permanence of Paper for Printed Library
Materials, ANSI/NISO Z39.48–1992.

Contents

Contents

Figures

Tables

Acknowledgments

I am grateful to Stephanie Bell-Rose of the Andrew Mellon Foundation in New York for recognizing that it was time to pay as much attention to the contributions of immigrant women as has been given to immigrant men and for providing support for this study. At RAND, I want to thank Robert F. Schoeni, who contributed most of the econometrics included herein, and Richard Krop who developed the analytical files from the Surveys of Income and Program Participation that form the basis of chapter 9. I also thank the many policymakers, researchers, and program staff who answered our questions about what information they thought this study ought to generate. Finally, I appreciate the excellent secretarial and administrative assistance provided by Karla McAffee who typed the original draft and the professional expertise of RAND's Publications Department, particularly that of Betty Amo and Sally Belford, who, respectively, edited and formatted the manuscript for printing.

Chapter 1

Introduction

It should come as no surprise that the United States is currently home to more immigrant women than men. Family reunification, the cornerstone of U.S. immigration policy since the 1920s, has ensured that this pattern remains constant to the present day—despite significant increases in immigration and frequent shifts in the predominance of primary countries of origin. What may be surprising is that the United States is one of only a handful of nations in which immigrant women outnumber immigrant men. What certainly is surprising is that to date, no efforts have been made to systematically describe the work experiences of those women.

Immigration flows have increased particularly rapidly since 1970, more than tripling the current peak of more than one million new immigrants every year. Today, immigrant women contribute more than 15 percent to the growth of the country's labor force—up from less than 3 percent in the 1960s. Moreover, although in 1960, 75 percent of immigrant women originated from Europe, today they are almost evenly divided among North America (mostly from Mexico); Latin America and the Caribbean; Asia; and Europe, Africa, Oceania, and the Middle East as regions of origin.

Despite the growing presence of immigrant women in the national labor force, little is known about the role they play in the national economy, their performance in the workforce, and their economic mobility. Until now, analysts and policymakers have directed their attention almost exclusively to immigrant men, even though immigrant women are perceived to face more cultural and social barriers than men in the U.S. labor market. Women are also believed to be more vulnerable to exploitation and to have less access to services that might facilitate entry into and success in the labor market.

This book represents a first effort to systematically describe the experience of immigrant women in the U.S. labor market over the past 30 years. To review this history, the author prepared a profile of the changing origin and characteristics of immigrant women; a description of what they do, where they work, and how they fare in the U.S. labor market; and an account of what use they make of public services to support themselves. Our goal is to provide a better understanding of immigrant women in the labor force, thereby adding a heretofore neglected dimension to our understanding of the immigration phenomenon.

This introduction first briefly establishes the unique dominance of women in immigration flows to the U.S. It then reviews what is known about the experience of immigrant women in the U.S. labor market and the factors that affect this experience, and it outlines the information prominent experts and policymakers told us is needed to assist them in their respective areas of policy and professional interests. Finally, it presents the purpose of the study and its approach.

Women Dominate Immigration Flows to the United States

Throughout the history of the United States, women have constituted a significant share of the immigrants who have settled within the country's expanding borders. From the mid-1800s to the 1920s, two out of every five immigrants were women. And since 1930, more than half of immigrants have been women (Houston et al., 1984). In recent years, a majority of the 800,000 legal immigrants admitted for permanent residence in the United States has been women.

The United States, along with Canada and Britain, is unique among nations to have more immigrant women than men.[1] Other Western countries with a relatively large number of immigrants have experienced a reverse pattern. For instance, in Australia, 49 percent of immigrants are women; in France, Germany, and Switzerland, 47 percent or less of all immigrants are women (United Nations, 1995). In developing countries, typically fewer immigrants are women than men. But, even in these countries, female immigrants typically exceed 40 percent of all immigrants. Notable exceptions include South Africa, Kuwait, and Saudi Arabia, where one out of three immigrants is a woman (United Nations, 1995).

Immigration policy is a major determinant of the share of women in the immigration flows to a specific country (Boyd, 1989; Houston et al., 1984; Tyree and Donato, 1986; United Nations, 1995). Nations such as the United States whose immigration policies emphasize permanent settlement and family reunification are likely to equalize the flow of male and female immigrants over time. And nations that emphasize temporary immigration for labor-shortage reasons are more likely to have immigration flows dominated by men (Houston et al., 1984).

In the United States, the disproportionate share of female immigrants over male immigrants can be traced to the end of unrestricted—mostly labor related—migration from Europe. The 1921 and 1924 quota laws were effective in reducing the large influx of predominantly male immigrants from Southern and Eastern Europe that had dominated migration flows since the 1890s. The 1921 law also gave preference for permanent immigration to alien wives of U.S. citizens, and in 1928 this preference was extended to wives and children (but not husbands) of permanent legal residents. The priority given to family reunification in U.S. immigration policy was further expanded in 1952 by exempting spouses and children of U.S. citizens from its immigration quotas. Spouses of permanent alien residents were also given preference over employment-related immigrants. Family reunification has remained the cornerstone of U.S. immigration policy ever since.

The unique dominance of women in immigration to the United States since World War II has been further fueled by the large number of predominantly male military personnel stationed throughout the world who married abroad and brought their brides home with them. The United States has no limit on the number of foreign-born spouses and children of U.S. citizens who immigrate in any given year. Hence, two-thirds or more of immigrants from countries where the United States has had a large military presence— Germany, Japan, Korea, and the Philippines—have typically been women.

Regardless of motivation for entry and marital status, immigrant women have played an important role in the development and growth of the U.S. economy throughout its settlement history. According to historians, immigrants provided an "abundant, docile, and cheap" labor force that contributed to the rapid growth of factory-made goods and services throughout the 1880 to 1930 time period (Ewen, 1985). As early as 1910, women made up more than 70 percent of the garment industry workforce, most of whom were Jewish and Italian immigrants.[2] In recent decades, the proportion of immigrant women in the national female labor market has steadily increased from 6 percent in 1960 to 9 percent in 1994.

Because immigrants are heavily concentrated in a few states, their increased importance in the labor market of states such as California is significantly greater. In that state, immigrant women have increased their share in the female labor force from 10 percent in 1960 to 23 percent in 1990. Today, about one out of every six workers in California is an immigrant woman, compared to one in 20 in the nation.

In spite of their disproportionate presence in immigration flows to the United States and their growing importance in the labor force of the nation, female immigrants have been nearly invisible in studies of the effects of immigration and performance of immigrants in the labor market. The overwhelming majority of studies of how immigrants perform in the labor market has focused on men. This bias does not result from a lack of appropriate data, because the information available for immigrant men is also available for immigrant women. Rather, it continues to reflect a long-standing scholarly and policy bias developed at a time when women—foreign and native-born— constituted a relatively small share of the labor force.[3] Today, however, more than two out of five immigrant workers are women and there are nearly as many native-born women in the labor force as there are men (47 percent), rendering this bias not only untenable, but undesirable from the perspective of policy formulation.

There are many a priori reasons to believe that the reasons immigrant women enter the labor market and the experience and skills they bring to it may differ from those of immigrant men. Many of the cultures from which immigrant women originate have kept them in traditional homemaking and childbearing roles, thus limiting their access to education and the labor market in their country of origin. A large sociological and ethnographic literature emphasizes the unique sociocultural and language-adjustment difficulties women encounter after coming to the United States and the limited niches they appear to occupy within the U.S. economy, in which they may be subjected to "exploitation" by employers.

Past Research

To the limited extent that research has focused on immigrant women, it has focused on the stresses of adjusting to a new culture and language and to the loss of social and community support. The few studies that have examined the decision of immigrant women to enter the U.S. labor market and their experience in that market have been limited in scope. They typically have focused on a small sample of immigrant women from a specific country of origin. Moreover, the more comprehensive statistical studies have examined the experience of women in a given year—but not over time. Finally, we found no study that examined how immigrant women progress economically from the day they entered the country throughout their lifetimes here.

Still, several findings emerge from existing studies. First, the intent to work in the United States is a primary reason for many women to immigrate in the first place—not only for single, but for married women as well—often as part of a strategy to improve their families' well-being. Predominantly female migratory movements to the United States have also been periodically generated because of particularly unfavorable conditions in various countries of origin. Such was the case for Irish women fleeing famine and their subordinate status in Ireland at the turn of the century (Diner, 1984) and for Jamaican women fleeing the lack of financial support they were receiving from males marginalized by the economic system of that country in the 1960s and 1970s (Ho, 1993). And sometimes immigrant women may be sought out, as in the 1960s and 1970s when Central American immigrant women were recruited by American families in need of child and household care (Repak, 1994).

Second, immigrant women are more likely to work in the United States than they were in their countries of origin, either out of economic necessity, desire to improve their families' economic welfare, or desire for self-realization (Grasmuck and Pessar, 1991; Pedraza, 1991; Perez, 1986; Piore, 1979; Reichert and Massey, 1980). This increase in the economic activities of immigrant women over time seems to reflect economic necessity. It also reflects a desire for economic independence and the adoption of U.S. norms regarding gender equality and the rejection of traditional female roles (Ley, 1981; Morokvasic, 1984; Schwartz-Seller, 1981).

Third, immigrant women are more likely than native-born women to be concentrated in low-skill occupations and industries. Two studies (Boyd, 1996; Tienda et al., 1984) have examined the distribution of working immigrant women across major industries and occupations in 1970 and in 1980. They found an overall similarity in the distribution of immigrant women and native-born women by industry, with a few noteworthy differences. Immigrant women were more likely to work in manufacturing industries (27 versus 18 percent in 1980) and less likely to work in social services (27 versus 36 percent). Immigrant women were also somewhat less likely to work in the retail industry.

A high concentration of female immigrants is found in a few specific industries, including the textile and garment, electronic manufacturing, and domestic services industries. This finding suggests that immigrant women are not doing well in the U.S. labor market (Boyd, 1996; Gilbertson, 1995; Morokvasic, 1984; and Pedraza, 1991). Workers in these industries are low-skilled, receive low wages, and are offered few if any opportunities for advancement. Indeed, the theme of a disproportionate vulnerability of immigrant women to exploitation and discrimination on basis of gender, immigration status, and/or class is a theme that cuts across many of the ethnographic and descriptive studies of the experience of immigrant women in the labor market (Boyd, 1989 and 1992; Brettell and Simon, 1986; Katz, 1982).

These studies, however, typically focus on a small segment of the labor market and on few observations so that generalizations cannot readily be drawn. Furthermore, these judgments by American researchers may not be shared by the immigrant women themselves who may believe they have no real options and may report to be relatively satisfied with what they have (Simon and DeLey, 1984).

Fourth, several factors appear to influence the decision of immigrant women to enter the labor market and their earnings in the labor market. A key factor is level of education: higher educational attainment was found to be consistently associated with higher earnings (Stier, 1991; Stier and Tienda, 1992; Sullivan, 1984) and somewhat less consistently with higher labor-force participation (Huang, 1993; Stier and Tienda, 1992). Previous work experience (in the home country) and older ages (a proxy for experience) are other factors that have been associated with higher labor-force participation, but typically not with earnings (Duleep and Sanders, 1982; Gilbertson, 1995; Nakamura and Nakamura, 1985; Ranney and Kossoudji, 1984; Stier, 1991; Stier and Tienda, 1992).

In addition to these individual factors, a few family factors were also found to be associated with participation in the labor-force. The presence of extended family members in the household increases labor-force participation (Stier, 1991; and Stier and Tienda, 1992), whereas the presence of children below the age of six lowers it (Duleep and Sanders, 1982; Huang, 1993; Ranney and Kossoudji, 1984; Stier, 1991; Stier and Tienda, 1992). For married women, the effect of the husband's earnings on labor-force participation is ambiguous: Stier (1991) and Stier and Tienda (1992) found no effect of this factor on labor-force participation, although Huang (1993) found that higher earnings by the husband were associated with higher labor-force participation. None of the above factors was found to influence earnings of immigrant women.

A number of factors specific to immigrant women may also affect their decision to work and their performance in the U.S. labor-market. Higher English proficiency (Stier, 1991) and the availability of a kinship network (Hondagneu-Sotelo, 1994) were found to lead to higher labor-force participation, while following a husband to the United States had a negative effect (Huang, 1993). And residing in an enclave (Gilbertson, 1995) and illegal status (Simon and DeLey, 1984) were also found to lead to lower earnings.

Finally, the number of years an immigrant woman remains in the United States has been found to be associated with increased labor-force participation (Duleep and Sanders, 1994; Huang, 1993; MacPherson and Stewart, 1989; Reimers, 1985; and Stier, 1991). Generally, entry into the labor market is made relatively rapidly, within the first five or so years in the United States, even for married women (Huang, 1993; Reimers, 1985).

Whether immigrant women experience an increase in their earnings relative to native-born women the longer they work in the United States—as has been documented for most immigrant men in the market—remains to be examined systematically. A few cross-sectional studies have found a positive association between length of stay in the United States and earnings (Huang, 1993; Stier, 1991; and Stier and Tienda, 1992). However, these findings may reflect the effect of different cohorts of immigrants rather than upward economic mobility. Indeed, Long (1980) found that immigrant women have about 13 percent higher annual earnings shortly after arriving in the United States, but that their earnings advantage over native-borns diminishes the longer they are in the United States. Moreover, the one study that has used a cohort longitudinal approach also found that immigrant women commanded higher earnings than native-born women initially, but that this earnings advantage diminished over time (Reimers, 1985). Finally, Chiswick (1980) suggests that the earnings experience of immigrant women may vary across countries of origin. All of these studies pertain to immigrants who have come prior to the large increase in immigration and labor-force participation of women over the past 25 years.

In brief, past studies suggest that the labor-force participation of immigrant women increases over time, but that they are not necessarily economically mobile. They also suggest that there may be significant differences in the labor-market performance of immigrant women from different countries of origin that may in turn reflect differences in their individual and family sociodemographic characteristics. However, the studies are often focused on a specific group of immigrants from a specific country of origin, marital status, or community in a specific year. Hence, these findings cannot be generalized for all immigrants nor for those immigrants who have come in increasing numbers since 1970.

Experts Say More Information Is Needed

In addition to reviewing the available literature, we interviewed 30 prominent researchers, policymakers, advocates, service providers, and representatives of women's associations to guide us in the design and the scope of this study. We asked their views about the status of research on immigrant women, what they needed to know about immigrant women's performance in the labor market, and the issues they were most concerned with regarding the economic mobility of these immigrants.

Our respondents indicated that more needs to be known about a number of topics, and they identified several concerns requiring analysis. In addition to measuring and analyzing the extent to which immigrant women actually progress economically over their lifetimes in the labor market, most respondents indicated that research was needed on factors—including family-related and social/cultural factors—influencing women's decisions to join the labor force. They suggested that traditional attitudes held by immigrant women and men alike against women working outside the home posed a major barrier to the participation of immigrant women in the labor force. Such attitudes were perceived to be stronger among Hispanic and African cultures but were also perceived to be a factor in some Asian cultures as well. At the same time, some respondents pointed to the high degree of cooperation between family members, particularly in family businesses. Different processes and values may be at play across different groups of immigrants and in different circumstances.

A related topic that our respondents thought needed research concerns the availability of child care. This is a topic of concern to all women but of particular relevance to immigrant women, given their relatively high fertility rates and low incomes.

The perceived concentration of immigrant women in the lower end of the labor market prompted our respondents to want to know more about the dynamics of this market and about the performance of immigrant women relative to that of native-born women. The latter reflects a concern—also widespread in the literature noted above—that immigrant women may be more vulnerable to exploitation in this sector of the economy, particularly in the garment and personal-service industries.

At the higher end of the labor market, there was the perception among our respondents that professional immigrant women were often unable to work in their fields of expertise because they lack appropriate certification in the United States. The extent of this problem has not been assessed, however.

Perceived limited access of immigrant women to federal and state programs that may facilitate their integration into the labor market—vocational education, training, job search assistance—is yet another concern expressed by our respondents. No programs exist that are specifically targeted to immigrants, apart from a few job-placement and training programs offered by local offices of Refugee Resettlement that serve refugees exclusively.

Finally, the perception of our respondents was that English language acquisition was seen as a prerequisite to economic and occupational mobility, although not necessarily a prerequisite to obtaining a job. That perception has yet to be corroborated empirically.

Purpose and Main Research Questions

The study is designed to provide quantitative and qualitative information about the work experience of immigrant women in the United States since 1960 and to assess the need for public- or private-policy interventions to enhance the economic mobility of immigrant women. To this end, this study focuses on the following questions:

- What have been the trends in female immigration and why?

- How have the socioeconomic characteristics of immigrant women varied over time and across countries of origin?

- What role do immigrant women play in the U.S. labor force?

- How successful are female immigrants in today's labor market?

- How rapidly do immigrant women progress economically over their lifetimes in the United States?

- To what extent do immigrant women make use of employment-related support programs, and how does that use compare with that of native-born women?

Approach

This study primarily focuses on immigrant women in the labor force from a national perspective. However, since immigrants tend to concentrate in a few states—California, Florida, Illinois, New Jersey, New York, and Texas—we also contrast the characteristics of female immigrants residing in these various states.

Throughout the study we distinguish between female immigrants along two main dimensions. We distinguish between immigrants from different countries or regions of origin. The categories are used to capture differences not only in origin but in socioeconomic characteristics. Generally, we distinguish among immigrants from (1) Europe and Canada; (2) five regions of Asia—China, Japan, and Korea; the Philippines; Indochina; West Asia; and the rest of Asia; (3) three Hispanic regions—Mexico, Central America, and South America; (4) the Caribbean Islands; (5) the Middle East; and (6) all other immigrants. Occasionally, we disaggregate origins in even greater detail.

We also distinguish immigrants by years of education: fewer than 12 years, 12 years; 13 to 15 years; and college graduates. As we shall see, this distinction is particularly important to an understanding of the economic performance and progress of female immigrants.

This study also takes a long-term view, focusing on 1960 to 1997—a 37-year span. We believe this is important for several reasons. First, the origins and characteristics of immigrants have changed over time. Second, the number of immigrants has steadily increased over this period of time, reaching a significant proportion of the labor force in some industries. And third, the environment that immigrant women enter has been changing in the following two significant ways: the cultural bias against women working has eroded and women have entered the labor force in increasing proportions; and the economy has increasingly filled its newly created jobs with college-educated labor, leading to a growing discrepancy between the earnings of noncollege- and college-educated labor.

The study relies primarily on data from the decennial censuses and the Current Population Surveys.[4] However, we complement these data with data from other sources that address specific issues at hand. These data and sources are identified in the chapters in which they are used.

We employ a variety of analytical techniques in our analysis—including time-series and multivariate techniques—as is appropriate with the issues we address and the data we employ. The special features of these techniques are described in the appropriate chapters.

The study has several limitations. First, we lacked reliable data on the legal status of immigrants. Hence, we do not distinguish between legal and illegal female immigrants in the labor force—an issue that recently has been at the center of the immigration debate. However important this distinction is from a legal and value perspective, it is of lesser import when discussing the role and performance of immigrants in the labor market. Whether legal or illegal, workers are workers. Also the status of an illegal immigrant is often one that is temporary (DaVanzo et al., 1994).

Second, we describe the experience of female immigrant labor, but we do not assess its effect on female native-born labor. We do, however, compare the experiences of native and immigrant women in the labor market over time.

Finally, other than briefly in chapter 8, we focus on the integration of immigrant women in the labor market and do not explore the integration of immigrant women in other aspects of American life, including its cultural, social, and linguistic dimensions.

Organization

The remainder of this section is divided into nine chapters. Chapter 2 reviews the trends since 1960 in female immigration into the United States by country of origin. Chapter 3 then describes the changing sociodemographic profile of the female foreign-born population and compares that profile to that of female natives. Chapter 4 examines the changing role of women, especially immigrant women, in the United States labor market, whereas chapter 5 examines what immigrant women do and chapter 6 examines where they work. Chapter 7 assesses trends in performance of immigrant women in the labor market. Chapter 8 examines the lifetime economic mobility of immigrant women in the United States. Chapter 9 analyzes the use immigrant women make of a broad range of federal and state programs designed to facilitate access to the labor market. Finally, chapter 10 summarizes our findings and discusses their implications for public- and private-sector policies.

Notes

1. At their respective last censuses, the share of immigrant women was 51.3 percent in the United States, 50.6 percent in Canada, and 50.5 percent in Britain (United Nations, 1995).

2. Today, the labor force of the apparel and textile industry remains two-thirds female, most of whom (two-thirds) are immigrants.

3. Indicative of this continuing tendency is that all recent studies of the performance of immigrants in the U.S. labor markets have focused on men (Schoeni et al., 1996).

4. We employ data from the Public Use Micro Samples (PUMS) from 1960, 1970, 1980, and 1990 and from the 1997 Current Population Survey of the U.S. Department of Commerce.

Chapter 2

Immigration Policy and Female Immigration

Women have always had a significant presence in immigration flows to the United States. But it was not until the late 1920s that they became the majority of new immigrants entering the country. Ever since, they have dominated immigration flows to the United States, although in varying proportion over time.

This chapter begins with a description of the historical trends in female immigration to the United States since the mid-nineteenth century and shows how immigration policy has affected both the aggregate numbers and share of women in immigration flows. Next, it examines the changing origin of recent female immigration since the passage of the 1965 Immigration Act, which abolished the national origin quota system. It then examines in greater detail how and why the share of women varies by country of origin and over time within the same country of origin.

Brief History

Changes in immigration policy have played a key role in determining the volume of legal immigration to the United States and the share of women in that immigration. In the nineteenth century, unrestricted and primarily economically motivated immigration to the United States was male-dominated. In the 1920s, restrictions placed on the annual number of immigrants and a preference given to family reunification—first to alien wives of U.S. citizens and then to spouses and children of U.S. citizens and legal immigrants—tipped the balance toward female-dominated legal immigration. Illegal immigration, which has increased in recent decades, however, has remained male-dominated.

Legal Immigration

During the second half of the nineteenth century, unrestricted migration from Europe was primarily male-dominated (see table 2.1).[1] The country needed labor to settle and develop its vast expanses of land to the south and west. But even during this labor-induced immigration, two out of every five immigrants were women. During this period of time, two-thirds of the immigrants originated from just five Northern European countries: Germany, Ireland, Norway, Sweden, and the United Kingdom.

The first two decades of the twentieth century saw the largest number of new immigrants entering the country for many decades to come. During that period of time, the share of women in immigration flows dropped to a low of one-third. One reason for this decline was a marked shift in the origin of

Table 2.1

Legal Immigration to the United States by Gender and by Decade, 1860–1996 (Thousands)

Decade	Total	Women	Men	Percent Women
1860–69	2,123	845	1,278	39.8
1870–79	2,742	1,069	1,673	39.0
1880–89	5,249	2,037	3,212	38.8
1890–99	3,694	1,419	2,275	38.4
1900–09	8,202	2,492	5,710	30.4
1910–19	6,348	2,216	4,132	34.9
1920–29	4,296	1,882	2,414	43.8
1930–39	700	387	313	55.3
1940–49	856	524	332	61.2
1950–59	2,499	1,341	1,158	53.7
1960–69	3,213	1,786	1,427	55.6
1970–79	4,336	2,300	2,036	53.0
1980–89[a]	5,853	2,909	2,944	49.7
1990–96[b]	5,476	2,910	2,566	53.1
1990–96[c]	7,681	3,599	4,082	46.9

Sources: Houston et al. (1984), table A-3, pp. 960–963; and the U.S. Immigration and Naturalization Service (INS) Statistical Yearbook, 1980 to 1996.

[a]Excludes 478,814 previously undocumented immigrants amnestied under the Immigration Reform and Control Act of 1986 (IRCA).

[b]Excludes 2,206,078 previously undocumented immigrants amnestied under IRCA.

[c]Includes 2,206,078 previously undocumented immigrants amnestied under IRCA.

immigrants toward the less industrialized regions of Europe. During that period of time, two-thirds of the new immigrants originated from just three major regions in Europe: the Soviet Union and the Austro-Hungarian empire to the east and Italy to the south.

In the 1920s, a significant decline in the volume of immigration was accompanied by a shift in the gender composition of immigrants as a result of the Provisional Quota Law of 1921 and then the Nationality Act of 1924.[2] The latter instituted the national origin system that limited annual immigration from Europe to about 150,000 and set a quota for each nationality on the basis of the national origins of the 1920 U.S. population. In addition, preference in allocating the annual slots of visas was given to alien wives of U.S. citizens (in 1924), and eventually to wives and children (but not husbands) of permanent resident aliens. Immigrants from the Western Hemisphere were exempted from the quotas.

The reasons for these "threshold" changes in the nation's immigration policy appear to have been similar to the measures that have recently led to similar "threshold" changes in the treatment of immigrants enacted in the Personal Responsibility and Work Opportunity Act of 1996 and in the Illegal Immigration Reform and Immigration Responsibility Act of 1996. These changes, just as in the 1920s, were made in the wake of a period of economic slowdown and uncertainty combined with higher levels of immigration and significant shifts in the origin of immigrants.

Restrictions placed on immigration and the new priorities put in place in the 1920s had two immediate and significant effects. First, immigration stopped in its tracks. Annual immigration flows declined nearly tenfold from an average 635,000 in the 1910–1920 decade to 70,000 in the 1930 decade (table 2.1). Second, the share of female immigrants in these flows doubled from one of every three to two of every three immigrants as a result of the preference given to wives (but not husbands) and children of both U.S. citizens and aliens granted permanent residence.

The changes in immigration laws made in the 1920s remained unchanged until 1952, when Congress eliminated discrimination between the sexes with respect to immigration and established a new four-tier preference system that gave priority to immigrants with special skills and to various kinds of relatives of U.S. citizens and permanent-resident aliens. The 1952 act reaffirmed the exemption from the numerical quotas of immigrants from the Western Hemisphere and of spouses (now both men and women) and children of U.S. citizens. Women continued to dominate the flows of immigrants, but in lower proportion, as the number of immigrants began to increase.

The 1950s and early 1960s saw a threefold increase in the number of immigrants over the previous decade. This increase was primarily a result of the resumption of immigration flows from the Western Hemisphere that had been slowed by the Second World War. Although immigration from the

Western Hemisphere had always been open (i.e., unrestricted) it was not until the 1920s that Canada became a significant sending country; and it was not until the 1950s that legal permanent immigration from Mexico began to increase steadily. In these flows, the share of women exceeded 50 percent.

Also during that period, large numbers of postwar refugee families from Europe were allowed to enter the country on an adhoc basis and eventually legalized by successive exceptional acts of Congress (Vernez, 1993). For instance, under the Displaced Persons Act of 1948, and in the space of four years, some 400,000 persons were admitted into the country—a number almost as large as the 500,000 persons admitted under "normal" channels. Three out of four of those admitted came from Poland, Germany, and the Baltic countries (Keely, 1995, p. 79). Similarly, large numbers of refugees came to the United States when the Soviet Union repressed the upheaval in Hungary in 1956 and on the heels of the 1959 change of government in Cuba. From 1959 to 1980, the United States eventually admitted 750,000 Cubans (Zucker and Zucker, 1991, p. 227).

In 1965, yet another major change in legal immigration policy was enacted. The national-origin quota system was abolished, but the primacy of family reunification as the leading principle of immigration to the United States was reaffirmed. Immigration from the Eastern Hemisphere was now numerically restricted to 170,000 annually, the annual number of immigrants from any one country or origin was capped at 20,000, and a new seven-category system of preferences strongly favoring family reunification was put in place. And in 1968, immigration from the Western Hemisphere, which heretofore had been unrestricted, was also put under a numerical cap of 120,000 yearly. Parents, spouses, and children of U.S. citizens regardless of origin continued to be exempt from numerical limitations.[3]

These changes in immigration policy—combined with lagging development in Western Hemisphere countries and large flows of refugees from the Soviet Union, Eastern Europe, Cuba, and eventually Southeast Asia—had a long-term effect on both the size and origin of immigration flows. The volume of legal immigration increased steadily from an annual average of 320,000 in the 1960s to 433,000 in the 1970s; 580,000 in the 1980s; and eventually 770,000 in the first half of the 1990s.

In spite of the large increase in the volume of immigration, women continued to dominate the flow of legal immigration to the United States through the end of the 1970s, when their dominance began to be eroded in part because of a shift in country of origin. In the 1980s, many countries—including Mexico, El Salvador, and Vietnam—were sending increasing numbers of male immigrants to the United States for the first time. And for the first time in six decades, women ceased to dominate the immigration flows. But, as families, initially separated, became reunited over time, the proportion of women in immigration flows increased once again, and by the 1990s women were dominating immigration flows to the United States once again.[4] In 1995 and 1996, women constituted 57 percent of legal immigrants who entered the country.

Illegal Immigration

In contrast to legal immigration, illegal immigration has been male-dominated. Illegal immigration has been a constant in American immigration history ever since the country began to control and restrict immigration. In 1929, the Immigration and Naturalization Service (INS) conducted its first reported crackdown when an estimated 100,000 or more undocumented immigrants yearly were crossing the southern border with Mexico (Cardoso, 1980). After World War II, illegal immigration resumed in spite of the existence of a temporary worker program, the *bracero* program, which had been established in 1942 in response to war-induced labor shortages in the agricultural industry. Perceived competition with that program led to another crackdown on illegal immigration in the 1950s. As a result, more than 1 million undocumented immigrants were deported in 1954 (Galarza, 1964). Following the termination of the bracero program in 1964, illegal immigration increased steadily over the next decades from some 50,000 a year in the late 1960s to some 200,000 to 300,000 yearly in the 1980s and early 1990s (Fernandez and Robinson, 1994; INS, 1996; and Johnson, 1996).[5]

In 1986, Congress legislated an amnesty for illegal immigrants who had resided in the country continuously since 1982 (the Legally Authorized Workers [LAW] program), or who had worked for at least three months in agriculture in the three years preceding the legislation (the Special Agricultural Worker [SAW] program). Eventually, 2.7 million previously illegal immigrants were legalized under these programs.

Only about 900,000 of these 2.7 million legalized immigrants were women: they constituted 44 percent of amnestied illegal immigrants under the LAW program and 17 percent under the SAW program. Eighty-seven percent of the amnestied immigrants were from Mexico, 9 percent from Central America, and the remaining 4 percent from countries all over the world. Table 2.1 shows that with the inclusion of these predominantly male immigrants, women made up an unusually low 47 percent of the flows of immigrants granted permanent resident visas during the early 1990s. However, by 1993, most amnestied immigrants had been legalized and the share of women in legal immigration flows reverted to more than 55 percent of annual entries as noted above.

Along with the amnesty programs, Congress also sought to curtail illegal immigration by prohibiting employers from hiring undocumented immigrants and by allocating additional resources to the border patrol. This effort failed to curtail illegal immigration, which has continued at an estimated 200,000 to 300,000 illegal immigrants a year since then (Bean et al., 1989; Crane and Asch, 1990; INS, 1996; Johnson, 1996; Vernez, 1994). With illegal immigration becoming a leading issue in the 1994 campaign for governor in California and then in the 1996 campaign for president of the United States, Congress responded with yet a new legislative initiative, the Illegal Immigration Reform and Immigrant Responsibility Act of 1996 (IIRIRA), designed to increase border control and the enforcement of laws against illegal immigration. The IIRIRA calls for 5,000 more border patrol agents and 1,500 additional support personnel over five years; requires the construction of 14 miles of triple fencing near San Diego; and increases penalties for smugglers of immigrants and for forgers of documents. It facilitates the administrative deportation of illegal immigrants and bars illegal aliens from adjusting their status until they have remained outside the United States for ten years. The law also requires citizens and resident aliens who sponsor a family member for admission to meet an income level of at least 125 percent of the federal poverty level.[6]

It is too early to assess the net effect that these new measures will have on the size and composition of immigration flows and hence specifically on the aggregate immigration flows of women. On the one hand, if illegal immigration is effectively curtailed, the volume of immigration will be lowered and the share of women will increase as family reunification in legal immigration remains unaffected by these new changes. On the other hand, the newly established minimum income threshold for sponsorship of family members may make it more difficult for low-income immigrants to bring their spouses and children here. Because a significant share of immigrants have low incomes, this new measure may indeed result in a decline in female immigration in the years to come.

Gender Differentials by Legal Categories of Immigrants

The laws governing the six-category system of preferences given to would-be immigrants have not changed significantly since 1965. In this subsection, we take a closer look at the dominance of family reunification in this preference system and within it, to women. Table 2.2 shows the breakdown of immigrants by gender and by broad classes of admission for the period 1972 to 1979.[7] As expected, women dominate the exempt categories of spouses, children, and parents of U.S. citizens that represent more than one-third of the total number of immigrants during that 1972–1979 period. Two out of three spouses reuniting with their family were women, possibly reflecting two factors. The first was the tendency of U.S. military men stationed abroad (e.g., in Germany, Japan, Korea, and the Philippines) to marry and to bring their brides to the United States when they returned. Generally, 70 percent of immigrants from Germany were women and more than 60 percent of immigrants from Japan, Korea, and the Philippines were women, a pattern

Table 2.2

Share of Immigrant Women by Class of Admission, 1972–1979

Class of Admission	Percent Women	Percent of Total
Exempt Categories		
Relatives of U.S. Citizens		
Spouses	62.1	22.7
Children	48.6	5.9
Adopted orphans	60.9	1.6
Parents	66.9	5.6
Refugees	49.8	16.4
Nonexempt Categories		
Family Preferences		
1. Unmarried sons/daughters of U.S. citizens	43.8	.6
2. Spouses and unmarried children of resident aliens	53.1	17.3
4. Married sons/daughters of U.S. citizens	48.6	2.0
5. Brothers and sisters of U.S. citizens	47.5	19.7
Occupational Preferences		
3. Highly skilled	49.9	3.8
6. Skilled and unskilled	45.6	4.2
Total	53.0	100.0
N (millions)	NA	2.6

Source: Houston et al. (1984), figure II, p. 923.

Note: NA means not applicable. The number preceding some items in the first column indicates the "order of preference." Column totals may have been rounded.

that has prevailed. Although the departure of military personnel from these areas over the past decade may have affected this pattern, immigrant wives from these countries have become a source of "new seed" of immigration as they, in turn, sponsor their own family members. A second factor has been the tendency for foreign-born naturalized citizens to bring in their families and/or to marry and to bring brides from their home countries.

Whereas parents are less likely to reunite with their children than are spouses who have individually immigrated to the United States and become naturalized citizens, their numbers and share in immigration flows have increased from an average of 25,000 yearly, or 4 percent of total immigration in the late 1970s, to 62,000 yearly in the early 1990s, or about 8 percent of total immigration. Women represent the overwhelming majority, two-thirds, of these flows. This trend most likely reflects the disproportionate share of widowed mothers—the longer life expectancy of women is nearly universal—reuniting with their children.

The domination by girls in orphans adopted by U.S. citizens (typically less than 2 percent of total flows) reveals the preference of U.S. adoptive parents for girls, combined with the greater availability of girls for adoption. Typically about 60 percent of adopted children from abroad are girls.

Among nonexempt categories, wives have dominated the second preference category of spouses and unmarried children of permanent resident aliens. Almost two-thirds of the spouses were women. However, females accounted for only 45 percent of minor and adult children in this category, reflecting the fact that more boys are born than girls and the higher likelihood of unmarried male children to migrate. Women have a tendency to marry at a younger age than men. Still, more than half (53 percent) of all immigrants in this category were women.

Women constituted less than 50 percent in all other categories of immigrants, with some variations in share. The third-preference category of immigrants—highly skilled members of the professions—were about evenly divided between women and men. Even though women accounted for 43 percent of all principal immigrants in this class, female spouses and children outnumbered males in this category.

Refugees also displayed an almost even share between women and men during this period of time, because refugees, primarily those from Cuba, were typically admitted as a nuclear family. In the 1980s, men dominated the flows of refugees from Indochina. Women accounted for about 45 percent of these flows. As the origin of refugees shifted once again—this time toward countries from the former Soviet Union during the early 1990s, the share of women in these flows increased again to 49 percent in 1993 and 1994.

The sixth-preference category for skilled and unskilled labor had the lowest proportion of women at 46 percent. Even so, the dominance of family reunification in American immigration policy is illustrated in this category as well by the fact that only 25 percent of the principals in this category were women. This male dominance in employment-related immigration is almost entirely offset by wives who immigrate at the same time as their husbands.

Changing Origins of Recent Female Immigration

As alluded to in the previous section, the 1965 abolition of the national-origin quota system and the strengthening of family reunification in U.S. immigration combined with postwar recovery in Europe and political turmoil in Southeast Asia and Central America led to a dramatic shift in the origins of immigrant women (as well as immigrant men), in addition to producing a steady increase in their numbers. These changes are dramatically illustrated in figure 2.1, which shows how the number of women immigrants from four major regions of the world (Europe and Canada, Latin America, Asia, and the rest of the world) has increased from 1960 to 1997.[8]

Figure 2.1 portrays the substantial shifts in the origin of female immigrants since 1960. Prior to 1960, immigrants came primarily from Europe and, in 1960, 90 percent of all female immigrants had come from that region of the world. Over the subsequent decades, their numbers declined 36 percent—from 4.2 million in 1960 to 2.7 million in 1997—for two reasons. First, having arrived primarily during the first two decades of the century, these European immigrants are now reaching old age and are dying in increasing numbers. To date, about one-third of European female immigrants are aged 65 or more and we can expect this downward trend in the number of European women immigrants to continue, if not accelerate during the next decade. New arrivals from Europe have been too few to compensate for this aging process of an older generation of immigrants.

By contrast, immigration from other regions of the world began in earnest only in the 1960s and has accelerated ever since. In 1960, there were less than three-quarters of a million female immigrants from all other parts of the world. Even Mexico, which is often thought to have always sent a steady stream of immigrants to the United States, had fewer than 300,000 female immigrants residing in the United States in 1960. But by 1997, four out of

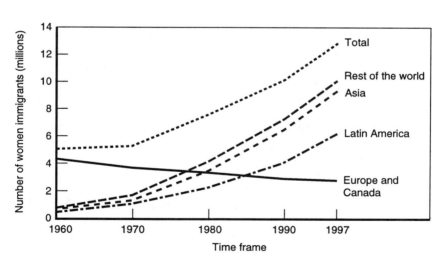

Sources: 1960, 1970, 1980, and 1990 PUMS and the 1997 Current Population Survey of the U.S. Bureau of the Census.

Figure 2.1—Number of Immigrant Women by Region of Origin, 1960–1997

every five immigrants had come from non-European countries—primarily Latin America and Asia. Overall, the number of immigrant women from Latin America has increased from 450,000 in 1960 to 6.2 million in 1997 and today half of women immigrants are of Latin American origin.

Similarly, the number of immigrant women from Asia has increased from 200,000 in 1960 to more than 3 million in 1997. Their share, 25 percent of the female immigrant population, now exceeds the share, 21 percent, of immigrant women from Europe.

The pattern of female immigration within these two main regions of the world has also been changing (table 2.3). Within Latin America, the largest numerical increase has occurred among women immigrants from Mexico, who now number more than 3 million and account for one out of every four female immigrants in the country. And in that region, the area of fastest-growing immigration has changed every decade: in the 1960s, the fastest-growing immigrant flows originated from the Caribbean—most specifically Cuba. During the 1970s they came from Mexico, and during the 1980s and 1990s they came from Central America (including El Salvador). The number of immigrants from the latter region nearly tripled during the 1980s, while the number of women immigrants from other Western Hemisphere countries merely doubled.

A similar origin shift has occurred in the rapidly growing immigration from Asia. In the 1960s, the Philippines and China contributed most of the growth in the number of female immigrants from Asia, and during the 1970s, the number of immigrants from those two countries tripled. Still, during the latter decade, it is Korea that saw its immigration increase most rapidly—more than six times. From the Asian continent during the 1980s, it was the flow of refugees and then immigrants from Southeast Asia—including Vietnam, Laos, and Cambodia—and from South Asia—including India and Pakistan—that grew the fastest. During the 1990s, immigration from Japan and Korea virtually stopped, while immigration from China and South Asia continued to increase at a high rate.

Immigration from other parts of the world, most particularly Africa and the Middle East, has grown as well, although not nearly as rapidly as that from Asia and the Western Hemisphere.

Finally, the number of female immigrants from all parts of Europe has decreased every decade since 1960 with the exception of Eastern Europe and the former Soviet Union. After nearly three decades of decline during which the number of immigrants from this part of the world was cut in half from 1.2 million to 650,000, the number once again increased during the 1990s thanks to the collapse of the Berlin Wall and the end of the Cold War.

Given the consistency of the primacy of family reunification policy since 1965, what other factors might account for these rapid shifts in the origins of immigrants over the past three decades? The answer is that different factors

Table 2.3

Immigrant Women by Country of Origin, 1960–1997 (Thousands)

Region/Country of Origin	Year				
	1960	1970	1980	1990	1997
Asia					
China	43	79	219	463	730
Indochina[a]	—	—	27	147	176
Japan	64	90	139	186	182
Korea	4	29	178	324	327
Philippines	31	76	289	521	620
South Asia	14	28	110	272	431
Vietnam	—	4	111	266	369
Others	35	57	10	150	261
Canada	552	532	489	433	333
Europe					
Eastern Europe/USSR	1,198	886	777	648	870
Northern Europe	1,144	982	899	767	669
Southern Europe	692	639	672	516	437
U.K. and Ireland	666	587	540	480	426
Latin America					
Caribbean	95	369	680	1,027	1,441
Central America[b]	25	61	150	347	589
El Salvador	4	8	54	226	301
Mexico	278	410	1,038	1,944	3,093
South America	45	141	295	545	782
Rest of the World					
Africa	9	20	88	152	213
Middle East	31	54	136	219	332
Oceania	20	26	49	62	104
Others	40	206	476	390	145
All	4,989	5,283	7,522	10,094	12,832
Percent Female	51.1	54.1	53.3	51.3	49.8

Sources: 1960, 1970, 1980, and 1990 PUMS and the 1997 Current Population Survey of the U.S. Bureau of the Census.

[a]Excludes Vietnam.

[b]Excludes San Salvador.

Note: Individual items may not add because of rounding.

account for having initiated these large immigration flows from different parts of the world. Armed conflicts or the collapse of regimes friendly to the United States were the genesis for migratory flows—originally in the form of refugee flows—from Central America (e.g., El Salvador, Guatemala, and

Nicaragua); from the Caribbean (e.g., Cuba, and to a lesser extent Haiti); from the Middle East (e.g., Iran, Palestine, and Lebanon); and from Indochina (e.g., Vietnam, Laos, and Cambodia). These countries contributed about one-third of the growth in the number of non-European female immigrants from 1960 to 1997.

The post–World War II United States military presence was the genesis of migration flows from other Asian countries including Japan, Korea, and the Philippines. As noted earlier, immigration from these countries has declined over time and practically ceased during the 1990s. Similarly, national security interests and human rights considerations were the genesis of migration flows from China, including Taiwan. These countries have accounted for 20 percent of the growth in the number of "new" immigrants during the past 37 years.

The reasons for increased migration to the United States from Mexico and South Asia (India and Pakistan) differ only in degree. In the case of Mexico, increased immigration followed the end of the temporary worker bracero program in 1964. As the demand for labor in the U.S. and most particularly California's—economies continued to increase, this temporary labor was replaced by an increasingly large flow of low-educated illegal and eventually legal immigrants.[9] And in the case of South Asia increased migration resulted from job opportunities available in the United States for a surplus of highly trained technicians and professionals from that region.

Once started, immigration flows become self-sustaining as migrant networks develop between places of origin and places of destination in the United States, even after the original motivation for immigration has disappeared. These networks lower the financial, psychological, and other risks of migration (Massey et al., 1994). The preference given to immediate and extended family members, including parents and sisters and brothers, facilitates and encourages this process. As shown in table 2.3, all countries or areas of the world that had few immigrants residing in the United States in 1960 have generated increasingly larger flows of immigrants in every decade since then. This pattern holds regardless of the reason(s) for migration flows and regardless of the region of the world in which the countries are located. For example, fewer than 10,000 immigrants from countries as diverse as El Salvador in Central America and Vietnam in Asia were residing in the United States in 1960 and even in 1970. But by 1980, 50,000 immigrants had come from El Salvador and 100,000 from Vietnam, and those numbers had more than doubled by 1997. A similar trend took place from regions whose flows originated earlier—in the 1960s—including countries from Central America, the Caribbean, Korea, South Asia, and even Africa and the Middle East. In every case, the number of female immigrants has at least doubled every decade since 1960, as has immigration from countries with more mature flows of immigrants, including Mexico, China, Japan, and the Philippines.

The 1990 increases in immigration quotas all but ensure the continuation of, if not an increase in, these trends.

Share of Women in Immigration Flows Varies
By Origin and over Time

Just as the number of female immigrants varies across countries of origin, the share of immigrant women varies across countries of origin. And this share also varies over time within the same country of origin. The various factors that account for initiating migration flows in different countries also generally appear to account for variations in the share of women in immigration flows from various countries. Refugee flows generated by armed conflict or collapse of friendly regimes are either gender-balanced or female-dominated, at least initially, as are flows from countries with a large U.S. military presence. In contrast, primarily economically motivated immigration flows have been steadily male-dominated. There are significant exceptions, however, as noted below.

The changes in the share of female immigrants who have entered the country in each decade since 1960 by major countries of origin are documented in table 2.4. Immigration from then war-torn Indochina has been generally equally divided between men and women. In contrast, immigration flows from civil conflict–torn Central American countries and Cuba were initially primarily female-dominated, with this dominance diminishing over time as family reunification has taken place.

Marriage of U.S. military personnel to native women is the main reason that women initially dominated migration flows from Japan, Korea, and the Philippines. Although the share of women in immigration from these countries has declined from a high two-thirds in the 1960s, women continued to dominate these flows until the late 1980s when net immigration from Japan and Korea all but stopped (see table 2.3). Although immigration from the Philippines is continuing, it became male-dominated in the 1990s.

Immigration from most other regions of the world, singled out in table 2.4, including Mexico, South Asia, Africa, the Middle East, and Oceania, has been primarily motivated—at least initially—by economic reasons. Hence, these flows have been dominated by men rather than women. Women have accounted for less than 45 percent of immigration from these areas, with little variation over time, even as levels of immigration from these countries/regions has increased.

Among these countries, Mexico stands out not only for the larger size of its migrant flows, but also because a large share of those first entering the United States do so illegally. As noted above, illegal migration from Mexico during the 1970s and 1980s was disproportionately male. In contrast, legal

Table 2.4

Increase in the Number of Immigrants Who Are Female by Region/Country of Origin and by Decade, 1960–1997
(Percent)

Region/Country of Origin	1960–1970	1970–1980	1980–1990	1990-1997	1997
Asia					
China	54.7	52.8	51.3	47.9	49.8
Indochina[a]	NA	45.8	50.2	110.8	54.3
Japan	110.5	57.3	59.8	-46.3	59.8
Korea	66.9	59.5	52.9	17.3	55.3
Philippines	69.9	59.3	60.7	46.1	54.7
South Asia	39.1	45.5	46.4	41.1	42.8
Vietnam	58.3	46.9	49.2	48.2	47.9
Others	52.5	61.2	47.7	57.4	53.7
Canada	-44.0	-52.8	-51.5	-54.2	61.0
Europe					
Eastern Europe/USSR	-45.2	-42.5	-70.1	65.6	55.6
Northern Europe	-36.8	-41.9	-47.9	-53.8	62.8
Southern Europe	-23.6	(+255.7)	-49.3	-50.4	50.3
U.K. and Ireland	-40.5	-55.0	-74.7	NA	53.4
Latin America					
Caribbean	56.5	54.0	52.7	47.6	51.8
Central America[b]	63.6	58.1	49.9	49.2	51.5
El Salvador	60.3	56.7	45.8	54.9	49.6
Mexico	43.0	44.8	42.8	42.4	44.1
South America	53.8	51.5	54.8	46.9	51.1
Rest of the World					
Africa	48.1	37.9	37.2	34.0	38.1
Middle East	38.2	37.6	41.5	57.6	44.9
Oceania	45.5	54.8	43.3	69.7	59.4
All	680.7	51.4	46.1	45.0	49.8

Sources: 1960, 1970, 1980, and 1990 PUMS and the 1997 Current Population Survey of the U.S. Bureau of the Census.

Note: NA means not available. The numbers represent the portion of immigrant women in the total increase in number of immigrants in the decades considered. For example, immigrant women from El Salvador accounted for 60.3 percent of the increase in immigrants from that country in the 1960–1970 decade. A negative percent means that the total number of immigrants from the country decreased and the female immigrants accounted for a percent of that decrease. When the share exceeds 100 percent, the number of female immigrants increased by a number greater than the total number of immigrants.

[a]Excludes Vietnam.

[b]Excludes El Salvador.

immigration from that country has become increasingly female-dominated as previously illegal male immigrants are legalized and reunited here with their spouses and children.

The trends in the share of female immigrants from Europe reflect those of a matured immigrant population that has not been replenished by new arrivals in several decades. Through deaths (and possibly returns to the regions of origin), the number of European immigrants residing in the United States has declined, with women contributing less than half of the decline— reflecting their longer life span than men. As a result, the share of European female immigrants has increased from 51 percent in 1960 to 58 percent in 1990 to 60 percent in 1997. The increase in the share of European women immigrants in the 1990s is a result of a renewal of a predominantly female immigration flow from Eastern Europe and the former Soviet Union.

These variations in the share of women across countries of origin and over time, combined with significant shifts in the relative share of total immigrants from these various parts of the world, has led to an overall decline in the share of female immigrants over time.

During the 1960s, when the total number of immigrants remained constant at 9.8 million, the number of female immigrants increased by 300,000 while that of men decreased by the same amount. The reason for the difference is that during that decade the European male immigrants who came at the end of the nineteenth century died in greater numbers than women, while more new immigrant women came during that decade than men. During the 1970–1980 decade, 51 percent of the net 4.4 million increase in the number of immigrants were women. As immigration flows became increasingly more economically motivated in the subsequent two decades, that share declined to 46 and 45 percent, respectively.

The net results of these dynamic trends are shown in the last column of table 2.4. By 1997, immigrant women ceased to be more numerous than men, their share having decreased to 49.8 percent from a high of 54 percent as late as 1970.

Conclusions

Policy plays a major role in determining both the number of people who immigrate to the United States annually and the share of women among them. Until the 1920s, unrestricted immigration produced large numbers of predominantly male immigrants. But even then, two out of every five immigrants were females. The Nationality Act of 1924 put an end to unrestricted immigration, severely limiting the number of people allowed to immigrate annually. It also made family reunification the cornerstone of the nation's immigration policy. The rules governing the number of people who could immigrate annually have periodically been changed—in 1952, 1965, and 1990—allowing increasingly larger numbers of immigrants to settle in the United States, but the primacy of family reunification has remained consistent to this day. As a result, women have consistently dominated immigration flows since the end of World War II, even as the volume of immigration steadily increased, reaching its current peak of about 800,000 a year.

Ever since immigration to the United States has been restricted, legal immigration has been accompanied by flows of illegal immigrants that at their peak, in the 1980s and 1990s, represented as much as 20 percent of annual immigration flows into the United States. In contrast to legal immigration, illegal immigration has been male-dominated. But over time, the gender balance of this immigration is restored as previously illegal immigrants have been amnestied or are being legalized through regular procedures and eventually sponsor family members. Hence, the share of immigrants who are women has consistently exceeded 50 percent in post–World War II United States.

The primacy of family reunification has consistently produced female-dominated immigration even though the primary origin of immigrants has shifted from Europe to Asia and Latin America. Today, in excess of 80 percent of all immigrants—female or male—come from Asia or Latin America.

The share of women in immigration flows differs markedly across countries of origin, and to a lesser degree, over time within a country of origin. By and large, these variations appear to be a by-product of the factors that motivated the emigration in the first place. Refugee flows initiated by armed conflict or the collapse of countries friendly to the United States have been either gender-balanced or female-dominated. Immigration from countries with a large U.S. military presence have also been female-dominated. By contrast, economically motivated immigration has been male-dominated, at least initially. Over time, family reunification balances the share between genders.

Notes

1.   Immigration to the United States was open until 1875, when federal legislation barring convicts and prostitutes was enacted. Subsequent legislation excluded Chinese laborers (1882) and eventually, in 1917, Asians and illiterates as well as various other classes of aliens, including paupers, persons with dangerous diseases, contract laborers, and anarchists.

2.   The Quota Law of 1921 limited the number of aliens of any nationality entering the United States to 3 percent of the foreign born of that nationality who lived in the United States in 1910. About 350,000 such aliens were permitted to enter each year as quota immigrants. The 1924 law made the quota system permanent and further limited the number of quota immigrants. All provisions of this first comprehensive and permanent overhaul of U.S. immigration policy were not fully implemented until 1929.

3.   In 1978, the separate ceilings for the two hemispheres were combined into a worldwide ceiling of 290,000.

4.   In 1990, Congress increased the annual immigrant ceiling from 500,000 to about 675,000 worldwide and doubled the number of visas made available for employment-based immigration. These changes have had no significant effect on the share of women in immigration flows as family reunification remains the cornerstone of our immigration policy.

5.   About 60 percent of these immigrants are estimated to enter the country illegally without inspection and another 40 percent violate the limited time of their visas.

6.   Members of the armed services petitioning for a spouse or child must meet a lower income standard of 100 percent of the poverty level.

7.   This subsection is derived from a special analysis of INS records by Houston, et al. (1984).

8.   Unlike the previous discussion which focused on changes in the gross flow of immigrants entering the country over a specified period of time, the number of immigrants displayed in figure 2.1 reflects net changes in the number of female immigrants—both legal and illegal—from one decennial year to the next, that is, the number of both legal and illegal immigrant women having entered the country during a decade minus those who left or died during that same decade.

9.   Including 2.6 million illegal immigrants legalized under IRCA.

Chapter 3

Profile of Immigrant Women

Women who immigrate to the United States not only come from all over the world, they also come with varied human capital endowment and sociodemographic characteristics. And just as the origins of immigrant women have changed over time, so have their characteristics. This chapter begins with a comparison of the sociodemographic characteristics of immigrant women from different national/regional origins. For ease of exposition, we group them into twelve categories, each representing a sizable share of the foreign-born population and displaying considerable similarity across characteristics. Then, we show how the characteristics of immigrant women differ from those of native-born women and how these have changed over time. We conclude with an examination of the significant differences in the profile of immigrant women across states. Throughout this chapter, we focus primarily on characteristics of immigrants that have been found to be associated with the decision of women immigrants to enter the labor market and with their eventual performance in that market (see chapter 1). Such characteristics include length of residence in the country, age, education, English proficiency, and family responsibilities.

A Heterogeneous Population

In debates over domestic social policies, we often distinguish among different groups of native-borns by class, ethnicity, location, or other traits that are relevant to an issue at hand. In public debates over immigration policy, however, immigrants are often lumped together, suggesting that they, unlike native-borns, have similar sociodemographic characteristics and behaviors. Nothing, of course, can be further from reality. Indeed, we might expect even more variations among immigrants than among native-borns because immigrants come from countries as different in culture and economic development as Haiti and Japan. In turn, we should not necessarily expect fewer variations among immigrants from the same country of origin than we expect among native-borns.

Women immigrants from different regions of the world differ in the amount of time they have been here, their age structure, family responsibilities, and education. Tables 3.1 and 3.2 present an overall picture of how these characteristics vary among immigrant women from different origins; the first table focuses on length of stay, age, and family characteristics, and the second table focuses on education and English proficiency.

European and Canadian immigrant women are significantly older, with half of them having been here an average of at least 30 years. More than one-third of them are aged 65 or older. Their family characteristics resemble those of native-born women, although they are somewhat more likely to be married than their native-born counterparts. Their educational characteristics also resemble those of their native-born counterparts. The fact that 10 percent of these immigrant women still speak English poorly reflects the recent arrival of a new wave of immigrants from the former Soviet Union and from Eastern Europe on the heels of the political changes that have rocked this region of the world since the mid-1980s.

Immigrant women from the Caribbean countries—including Cuba, Santo Domingo, and Jamaica—also form a distinctive group of older immigrants. More than half have been in the United States for more than 20 years, with an increasingly higher share reaching retirement age. They typically have fewer children and smaller households than other immigrant women. They also have had more schooling than other Hispanic immigrant women. Even so, a significant proportion speaks English poorly.

In contrast to the above two groups, half or more of the immigrant women from other parts of the world have been in the country for fewer than ten years and are typically younger. What distinguishes them from each other are their respective family responsibilities and education. At the low end of family responsibilities and high end of the educational distribution are Asian immigrant women from China, Japan, Korea, and the Philippines. Half of the Filipinas and one-third of the Chinese, Japanese, and Korean immigrant women are college graduates, a share significantly greater than that of any other immigrant group and even of native-born women. Their family structures resemble those of native-born women, but they are more likely to be married. Filipinas also live in larger households than immigrant women from China, Japan, and Korea. Filipinas distinguish themselves from other Asian immigrant women by their high proficiency in English. Only 4 percent speak English poorly compared to 30 percent of immigrant women from the other three Asian countries.

At the other end of the spectrum are immigrant women from Mexico. They live in significantly larger households, have more children, and have less education than any other group of immigrant women. By ages 40 to 44, they will have raised nearly twice as many children as most other immigrant and native-born women. And more than two-thirds of these immigrants have fewer than 12 years of education and more than half speak English poorly.

Indochinese and Central Americans, two of the newest groups of immigrant women—more than two-thirds have entered the country during the

Table 3.1

Demographic Characteristics of Immigrant Women by Country of Origin, 1990

Origin	Length of Stay			Age			Family Responsibilities			
	Share of Total Immigrants (Percent)	Immigrants Who Entered After 1980	Years in the U.S. (Median)	Mean	0–17 (Percent)	>65 (Percent)	Married (Percent)	Number of Children (Mean)	Number of Persons in Household (Mean)	No. Children Born to Married Woman 40–44
Canada	9.1	18	32	54	3	35				
Europe	19.1	22	29	54	4	35	72ᵃ	1.9ᵃ	3.1ᵃ	2.207ᵃ
Asia										
China/Japan/ Korea	9.6	48	10	39	9	9	71	1.5	3.6	1.980
Philippines	5.2	51	10	40	8	10	67	1.8	4.3	2.158
Indochina	4.1	68	8	33	18	4	61	2.3	5.2	3.504
Other Asia	6.4	59	8	35	12	5	76	1.7	4.0	2.170
Latin America										
Mexico	19.3	47	11	33	16	6	65	2.6	5.4	3.798
Central America	5.6	64	8	35	15	7	52	2.0	4.8	2.895
Caribbean	10.2	38	21	42	9	14	64ᵇ	1.7ᵇ	3.7ᵇ	2.067ᵇ
South America	5.4	52	12	38	11	8	57ᶜ	1.8ᶜ	3.9ᶜ	2.419ᶜ
Africa, Oceania, and Other	6.0	50	11	37	11	11	52	1.8	4.0	2.589
All Immigrants	100.0	41	11	42	10	16	65	2.0	4.1	2.544
Native-borns	NA	NA	NA	36	25	15	59	1.8	3.2	2.196

Source: 1990 PUMS of the U.S. Bureau of the Census.
ᵃIncludes Canada.
ᵇCuban only.
ᶜAlso includes Caribbean, except Cuba.

Table 3.2

Education and English Proficiency of Immigrant Women by Origin, 1990

Origin	Mean Years	Percent 12 Years or Fewer	Percent 16 Years or More	Percent Who Speak English Poorly
Canada/U.K./Europe	12.4	18	21	9
Asia				
China/Japan/Korea	12.6	18	33	30
Philippines	13.8	11	50	4
Indochina	8.9	47	9	42
Other Asia	13.3	16	46	12
Latin America				
Mexico	7.6	69	3	53
Central America	9.4	49	7	48
Cuba	11.4	29	16	39
Other Latino	11.2	30	15	31
Africa, Oceania, and Other	10.6	39	14	25
All	11.1	31	20	27
Native-borns	12.8	14	20	1

Source: 1990 PUMS of the U.S. Bureau of the Census.

1980s—have remarkably similar characteristics. They both have higher fertility rates and live in larger households than other immigrant women, with the exception of Mexican immigrants. They are also much less likely to be married than other immigrant women, although their marriage rates compare to those of native-born women. Finally, both groups have a relatively high share—one-half—of immigrant women with fewer than 12 years of education and a similarly high share of those who speak English poorly.

Immigrant women from the above groups account for 82 percent of all immigrant women in the country in 1990. The remaining 18 percent are immigrant women who came from areas as disparate as South Asia, South America, Oceania, Africa, and the Middle East. They generally have characteristics that resemble those of immigrant women as a whole, with two exceptions. South Asians are the most educated and the most likely to be married of any group of immigrant women. And all three groups have few children living with them.

Changing Profile of Immigrant Women

The previous section showed that in 1990, the profile of immigrant women varied broadly depending on their country of origin. As the origins of immigrant women have been changing over time (chapter 2), their characteristics also have been changing. This section examines the nature of these changes and compares them with changes in the characteristics of native-born women whose characteristics have been changing as well. We first compare changes in the sociodemographic characteristics between immigrants and native-born women in the aggregate. These aggregates, however, mask a convergence in the age distribution of immigrant and native-born women, and a divergence in the educational distribution and in the fertility rates between these two groups.

How the sociodemographic profiles of immigrant and native-born women have changed since 1960 is displayed in table 3.3. Several changes stand out. First, the length of time that the average immigrant woman has been in the country has steadily declined, reflecting the increasing flows of immigrant women in the 1970s and 1980s. In 1970, the average immigrant woman had been in the United States for 23 years, but by 1990, the average immigrant woman had resided in the country for only 13 years and 40 percent had been here for 10 years or less. The average age of working female immigrants has also declined: by 6 years since 1960, compared to only one year for native-born women. In 1997, there was no difference in average age (39 years old) between immigrant and native-born women of working age.

Second, the average years of education of immigrant women increased dramatically from 1960 to 1980 gaining on the average one year in each of the 1960 and 1970 decades. Their education has continued to increase, but at a slower pace since then. In the meantime, native-born women have also upgraded their education and just as rapidly. The net result is little change in the average gap in education between immigrant and native-born women from 1960 to 1997.

Third, in 1960 as in 1970, most immigrants had resided in the country for 20 years or more and, after that much time, spoke English relatively well. With the large number of new immigrants arriving in the 1970s, 1980s, and 1990s, mostly from non-English speaking regions of the world, however, this pattern has changed. By 1980, one out of every four immigrants reported speaking English poorly or not at all, and this share has increased since then. The ability to communicate in English is an immediate and visible sign of assimilation in this country. Hence, it is not surprising that many among the native-borns have become concerned that the new immigrants are not assimilating as previous immigrants are perceived to have done. Native-borns who experience casual encounters with immigrants in shops or other public places cannot distinguish between those who have been here long enough to have mastered the language and the many who have been here for only a few years and are still struggling with the English language. By the time one wave of immigrants has learned English, a new and larger wave of immigrants has arrived, fueling the perception of a lack of assimilation in the English language.

Table 3.3

**Selected Characteristics of Women Aged 18 to 64
by Immigration Status, 1960–1997**

Characteristics	Immigrants					Native-Borns				
	1960	1970	1980	1990	1997	1960	1970	1980	1990	1997
Median years in U.S.	—	23	15	13	13	NA	NA	NA	NA	NA
Mean age (18–64)	46.2	41.7	38.8	38.5	38.8	39.1	38.6	37.7	38.1	38.9
Mean years of education	8.6	9.9	10.9	11.1	11.8	10.4	11.1	12.1	12.8	13.4
English spoken poorly or not at all	—	—	23	27	—	—	—	1	1	—
Family responsibilities										
Married	75	74	70	65	65	75	71	63	59	57
Mean number of children	2.3	2.0	2.0	2.0	—	2.4	2.1	1.9	1.8	—
Mean number of persons in household	3.3	3.6	3.7	4.1	3.8	3.8	3.6	3.3	3.2	3.1

Sources: 1960, 1970, 1980, and 1990 PUMS and the 1997 Current Population Survey of the U.S. Bureau of the Census.

Note: "—" means not available; NA means not applicable.

As we shall show in chapter 6, however, assimilation in the English language takes place relatively rapidly for most immigrants.

Fourth, both immigrant and native-born women have been increasingly less likely to be married. This change in marital status has taken place more rapidly among native-borns than among immigrant women. Whereas in 1960, 75 percent foreign- and native-born women were married, by 1997, this share had declined to 57 percent among native-born women and to 65 percent among immigrant women.

Immigrant and native-born women have also increasingly diverged in the number of children they are responsible for at home and in the average size of the households in which they live. The mean number of children living at home with immigrant women has remained constant at two per immigrant woman after a 15 percent dip—from 2.3 to 2.0—in the 1960s. By contrast, the average number of children living with native-born women has steadily declined from 2.4 children in 1960 to 1.8 in 1990. In that year, the mean number of children living with an immigrant woman was 10 percent higher than that for a native-born woman.

The most dramatic divergence in behavior between immigrant and na-tive-born women, however, has taken place in their living arrangements. The first are living in increasingly larger-size households while the second are liv-ing in increasingly smaller households, reflecting both the extended family reunification process among immigrants and the lower earnings of immi-grants relative to native-born women and men, as we shall document later in chapter 7.

Converging Age Distribution

The age structure of immigrant women has been largely shaped over the past 30 years by the aging of the pre-WWII European immigrants and by the ar-rival of a new, younger wave of immigrants from Latin America and Asia beginning in the late 1960s. Thus in the 1960s, the age structure of female immigrants was heavily tilted toward the elderly, as one out of three immi-grant women was aged 65 or older. By 1997, new arrivals had caused the share of elderly women among immigrants to drop to one out of seven. At the same time, the share of school-age and college-age female immigrants had doubled by 1980 and has remained relatively constant since. Finally, the share of working age immigrant women has increased from one-half in 1970 to two-thirds in 1990 (figure 3.1, top half).

At the same time that the age structure of immigrants has become younger, that of the nation's native-born women has become older because of the aging of the post-WWII "baby boomers" (figure 3.1, bottom half). In the 1960s, the age structure of native-born women was heavily weighted toward children and adolescents, with one-third aged 17 or younger. Over time, these "baby boomers" became new entrants in the labor force in the 1970s and 1980s, and their parents began to retire. The result of this aging process has been a doubling of the share of native-born elderly from 8 percent in 1960 to 15 percent in 1990 while the share of school-age children has declined from one-third to one-fourth.

Children born in the United States of immigrant parents are typically considered a component of the natural increase of the native-borns and were so included in the previous discussion.[1] If they are excluded, however, the 1997 share of children in the native-born population drops by 2 to 3 percent-age points from 28 to 26 percent.

Whether they are foreign- or native-born, the children of immigrant par-ents are being raised and supported economically and otherwise by them and, hence, should be so accounted for when it comes to considering dependency rates. Accounting for native-born children of immigrants in this way has a dramatic effect on the age structure of immigrants. For instance, in 1997, it increases the share of school-age children in the immigrant population from 10 percent to 26 percent and makes the age structure of immigrants and na-

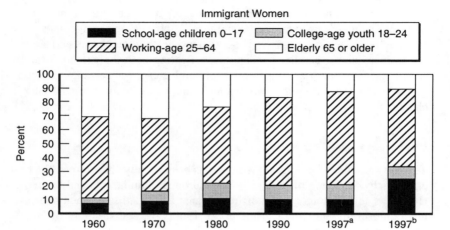

^aFemale children born in the United States of immigrant parents are included with the native-born women.

^bFemale children born in the United States of immigrant parents are included with immigrant women.

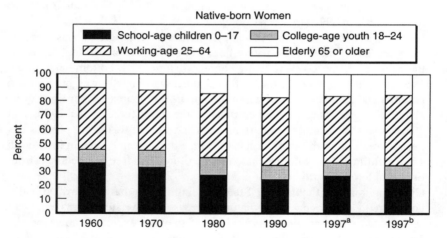

^aFemale children born in the United States of immigrant parents are included with the native-born women.

^bFemale children born in the United States of immigrant parents are included with immigrant women.

Figure 3.1—Age Distribution of Women by Immigration Status, 1960–1997

tive-born women look virtually identical (last bars in figure 3.1). This reality undercuts the often heard argument that diverging age distributions between immigrant and native-born communities will inevitably lead to diverging relative needs for education, training, and other services for the younger age groups on the one hand and the needs of the growing elderly population on the other hand. Indeed, in 1997 both immigrants and native-borns had virtually the same share (about 40 percent) of dependents: children aged 17 or younger and the elderly. This overall dependency rate has decreased over time for both groups: from 45 percent in 1960 to 40 percent in 1997 for native-born women and from 50 to 38 percent for immigrant women. At the same time, the share of elderly of the dependent population has converged between these two groups. Among native-borns, the elderly have been doubling their share of the dependent population from 17 percent in 1960 to 35 percent in 1997. Among immigrants, the elderly have decreased their share of the dependent population from 62 percent in 1960 to 31 percent in 1997.

Diverging Educational Distribution

Disparate trends between immigrant and native-born women have taken place at the lower end of the education distribution and at the "some college" level. At the lower end of the educational distribution—less than 12 years of education—both immigrant and native-born women have seen their share decline steadily, but at sharply different rates (table 3.4). Whereas the proportion of immigrants with fewer than 12 years of education was cut in half from about two-thirds in 1960 to one-third in 1990, the share of native-born women was cut nearly five times from 52 percent in 1960 to 11 percent in 1997. For immigrants, the decline in that share slowed significantly in the 1990s. And at the "some college" level, native-born women have increased their share relative to immigrant women with most of this increase taking place during the 1980s decade.

At the highest levels of education, however, trends have been similar for both immigrant and native-born women. The share of college graduates has increased equally sharply for both groups. In 1997, one out of every four immigrant and native-born women was a college graduate, up from one in 20 in 1960.

Increases in the share of high school graduates have also been relatively similar for both groups, although the proportion of immigrants with 12 years of education remains 10 percentage points lower than that for native-borns.

Overshadowing these trends, however, has been a dramatic upgrade in the overall education of women. Figure 3.2 compares the 1970 and 1990 educational distribution of adults aged 25 to 64 for the nation; the dark portion of the bars represent the immigrant women's share of that population at each educational level. First, there has been a dramatic increase in the share of

Table 3.4

Educational Distribution of Working-Age Women (25–64) by Immigration Status and Level of Education, 1960–1997

Years of Schooling	Immigrant					Native-Born				
	1960	1970	1980	1990	1997	1960	1970	1980	1990	1997
0–11	68	52	40	31	32	52	41	26	14	11
12	21	30	31	28	26	32	39	43	37	36
13–15	7	10	15	21	19	10	11	17	29	29
16+	4	8	15	20	24	6	9	14	20	25
Total	100	100	100	100	100	100	100	100	100	100
Average (Years)	8.6	9.9	10.9	11.1	11.8	10.4	11.1	12.1	12.8	13.4

Sources: 1960, 1970, 1980, and 1990 PUMS and the 1997 Current Population Survey of the U.S. Bureau of the Census.

Note: Individual columns may not add to 100 because of rounding.

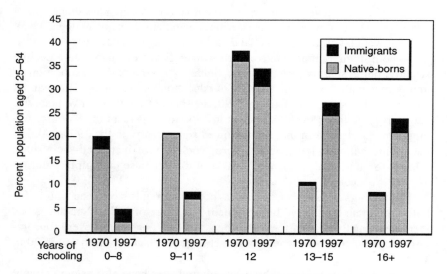

Sources: 1970 PUMS and the 1997 Current Population Survey of the U.S. Bureau of the Census.

Figure 3.2—Changes in Educational Distribution by Immigration Status and Level of Education

women with a college education in this short 20-year period: whereas 9 percent of those 25 to 64 years old were college graduates in 1970, 25 percent were college graduates in 1997. An equally large increase occurred in the share of adult women with "some college"—from 10 percent to 28 percent. Second, there was a simultaneous decline in the share of women with fewer than 12 years of education: from 41 percent in 1960 to 13 percent in 1997.

Female immigrants have contributed to this increase at all levels of education, although in varying degrees across the various educational levels. Most noteworthy is the quintupling—from 10 to 53 percent—in the share of female immigrants among those with fewer than eight years of education, even though, the total number of women with less than eight years of education has been more than halved from 9.4 million women in 1970 to 3.5 million in 1997.

Diverging Family Responsibilities

Earlier, we noted the diverging trend in rates of marriage and average number of children between immigrant and native-born women. Because even small changes in fertility rates can have important long-term effects on the number of new births and, eventually, on the demand for child care, education, and other services, we explore changes in these rates in greater details below.

The fertility rate of successive cohorts of women (rows in table 3.5) has declined since 1970 for both immigrant and native-born women, but the decline has been more rapid among native-born than among immigrant women. These trends are best illustrated by focusing on the cohort of those aged 25 to 29. For women in this age group, the number of children ever born per native-born married woman has declined 34 percent—from 1.997 in 1970 to 1.313 in 1990 compared to a decline of 15 percent for native-born women—from 1.691 to 1.441 children per married immigrant woman. The net result of these trends has been a reversal in the relative fertility rate of immigrant and native-born women: whereas, the fertility rate of immigrant women aged 25 to 29 was 14 percent lower than that of native-born women in 1970, it was 10 percent higher by 1990. These trends are apparent at all ages and any given marital status. The fertility rate of married immigrant women aged 40 to 44 in 1970 was 15 percent lower than that of native-born women in 1970, but was 16 percent higher in 1990.

Profile of Immigrant Women Varies across States

It is well documented that immigrants (both men and women) from a specific country, and even region or town of that country, tend to congregate at their

Table 3.5

Cumulative Fertility Rates by Age and Immigration Status

Age	Immigrant				Native-born			
	1960	1970	1980	1990	1960	1970	1980	1990
Married Women								
18–21	.786	.710	.764	.775	1.015	.794	.671	.779
22–24	1.319	1.095	1.053	1.073	1.581	1.149	.946	.939
25–29	1.645	1.691	1.495	1.441	2.282	1.977	1.398	1.313
30–34	2.211	2.323	2.086	1.966	2.671	2.830	1.997	1.786
35–39	2.344	2.680	2.503	2.315	2.732	3.193	2.547	2.021
40–44	2.340	2.673	2.842	2.544	2.601	3.130	3.040	2.196
45 and older	2.409	2.394	2.842	2.925	2.461	2.605	2.963	2.927
Other Women[a]								
18–21	1.474	.108	.102	.142	1.247	.133	.142	.166
22–24	1.172	.332	.284	.313	1.702	.481	.372	.412
25–29	1.296	.585	.635	.658	2.238	1.144	.733	.737
30–34	1.674	1.066	1.098	1.251	2.363	1.914	1.306	1.118
35–39	2.078	1.526	1.651	1.616	2.337	2.243	1.996	1.400
40–44	2.103	1.725	2.085	1.904	2.318	2.259	2.611	1.706
45 and older	2.722	1.981	2.410	2.636	2.490	2.005	2.543	2.655

Sources: 1960, 1970, 1980, and 1990 PUMS of the U.S. Bureau of the Census.

Note: The fertility rate in this table is the number of children born per woman in the age group specified.

[a] Other women include never-married, divorced, separated, and widowed women.

migratory destinations (Massey et al., 1994). The net result of this migratory behavior is that immigrant women not only concentrate in a handful of states, but their sociodemographic characteristics also differ significantly between states, with important implications for population growth and demand for public services.

Residential Concentration of Immigrants of Same Origin

Immigrant women reside primarily in just six of the 52 states in the nation: California, Florida, Illinois, New Jersey, New York, and Texas. In 1990, 72 percent of female immigrants compared to 36 percent of all women resided in these states (figure 3.3). Three of these states are major ports of entries: California for immigrant women from Asia; Florida for immigrant women from the Caribbean and Central and South America; and New York for immigrant women from Europe. Two states are interior border states: Illinois bordering Canada and Texas bordering Mexico. In addition to being a major port of entry, California is a border state with Mexico. The state of

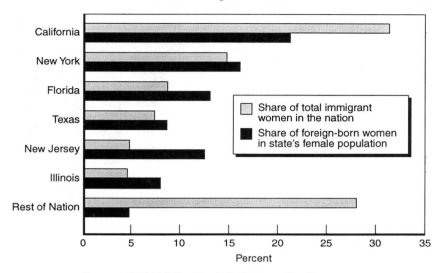

California
New York
Florida
Texas
New Jersey
Illinois
Rest of Nation

Share of total immigrant
women in the nation

Share of foreign-born women
in state's female population

0   5   10   15   20   25   30   35
Percent

Source: 1990 PUMS of the U.S. Bureau of the Census.

**Figure 3.3—Percent of Total Immigrant Women and Percent
Foreign-Borns by State, 1990**

New Jersey is neither, but its close proximity to New York makes it part of
the New York–New Jersey metropolitan area where immigrants in these two
states mostly reside. As we shall see below, these different geographical
positions and roles have conditioned the residential patterns of immigrants
within the United States.

Overall, immigrant women have tended to locate in states that are the
closest to their home countries (figure 3.4). For immigrants, this residential
pattern reduces both their monetary and nonmonetary costs of adjusting to a
new environment as they receive subsistence, housing, job-search, and other
forms of support from the relatives and acquaintances who have preceded
them. They also can continue to benefit from the social and cultural affinity
they share with their countrymen, thereby helping to minimize the "shock" of
entering a new culture through the initial maintenance of cultural rituals and
social practices such as the celebration of special holidays, playing soccer on
weekends, and the daily social interactions and communications that are
embedded in specific national and/or regional cultures and in the sharing of a
"new experience."

Immigrant women from Mexico are the most highly concentrated of any
immigrant group. They are concentrated in that region of the United States
that has historical ties with Mexico: California, where more than half of Mex-

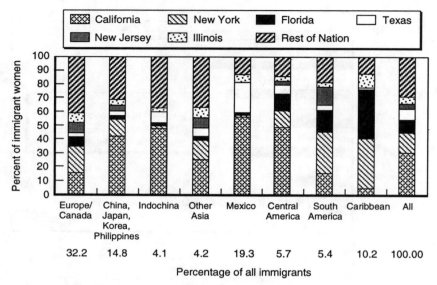

Source: 1990 PUMS of the U.S. Bureau of the Census.

**Figure 3.4—Percent Distribution of Immigrants by State and by
Country/Region of Origin, 1990**

ican immigrants reside, and Texas, where another 22 percent of all Mexican immigrants in the country reside.

  Nearly half of immigrant women from West Asia—China, Japan, Korea, and the Philippines—and from Indochina and Central America also reside in California: 43 to 49 percent. The other half of these immigrants are evenly distributed throughout the rest of the United States, although some notable exceptions exist. Indochinese have practically no presence in Florida, Illinois, New Jersey, and New York. But, they have the highest presence of any immigrant groups (with the exceptions of European immigrants) outside the six high-immigration states. This finding reflects governmental efforts to distribute refugees throughout the country, to minimize the "burden" on any one area. The current concentration of Indochinese refugees into California is the result of secondary migration into a state where the largest share of such refugees had located in the first place. The California share of these refugee women increased from 25 percent in 1960, to 35 percent in 1980, to 40 percent in 1990. By contrast, a disproportionate share of immigrants from Central America reside in Florida and in New York, in addition to California: three-fourths of these immigrants reside in these three states.

  Immigrant women from the Caribbean countries are concentrated primarily in just two states: Florida, where the majority of Cuban immigrants reside, and New York, where the majority of Haitian and Jamaican immigrants reside.

European immigrant women are the least concentrated of any immigrant group, reflecting the effects of secondary migration within the country for this group of immigrants who primarily came prior to 1960. Today, less than 20 percent of European immigrants continue to reside in New York, their traditional port of entry and often first residence. And more than 40 percent, the highest share of any group, reside outside the six "high" immigration states.

Immigrants from South America display yet a different pattern of residential settlement across states. They concentrate primarily in the East Coast in New York (30 percent), Florida (16 percent), and New Jersey (15 percent).

Dominant Immigrant Groups within States

The tendency toward residential concentration of immigrant women from the same country or region of origin has, in turn, resulted in the dominance of one or two groups of immigrant women within a given state (figure 3.5).

No other state is more dominated by immigrant women from any single country than the State of Texas, where three out of every five immigrants originated from Mexico. In this state, immigrants from no other countries or region exceed a share of more than 10 percent of all immigrants.

In California, Mexican immigrant women also constitute a significant share of the immigrant population (one-third) as do immigrant women from West Asia (one-fifth). California is also unique in having a higher share of refugees from Indochina and immigrant women from Central America than any other state and the lowest share of immigrant women from Europe and the Caribbean.

In New York—the state with the second largest number of immigrants— European immigrant women continue to dominate (one-third). New York also has a disproportionate share of immigrant women from the Caribbean (16 percent) and from South America (13 percent). Indeed, New York has been the preferred destination of immigrant women from countries of South America—one out of three reside there—much ahead of Florida, which is often referred to as the port of entry to the southern part of the Western Hemisphere. In contrast to California, less than 1 percent of New York's immigrant women are refugees from Indochina or immigrants from Mexico.

At the southern end of the East Coast of the United States, immigrant women from the Caribbean constitute the largest share (43 percent) of immigrants in Florida. The second largest share of immigrants (25 percent) is from Europe. As in California, a disproportionate share of Central American immigrant women resides in Florida and, as in New York, Florida has few immigrants from Indochina and Mexico.

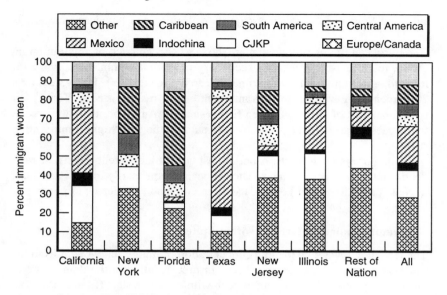

Source: 1990 PUMS of the U.S. Bureau of the Census.

Figure 3.5—Percent Distribution of Immigrants by Country/Region of Origin and by States, 1990

In both New Jersey and Illinois, European immigrant women constitute the largest share (about 40 percent) of their immigrant women. But they differ in their respective second largest group: Caribbean immigrant women in New Jersey (16 percent) and Mexican immigrant women in Illinois (25 percent). Both of these states have few immigrant women from Indochina and from Central America.

Implications of Variations in the Residential Patterns of Immigrant Women

Since immigrant women from different countries differ in their educational and sociodemographic characteristics, differences in their residential patterns lead to significant differences between states in the sociodemographic characteristics of their respective immigrant women population.

Table 3.6 illustrates the differences in age, family responsibilities, education, and English proficiency of the immigrant populations in the six states with the highest concentration of immigrant women. It also highlights differences in time of arrival of women immigrants in different states. The latter is an important indicator of the degree of assimilation that may be expected to already have taken place. Key differences are highlighted below.

Table 3.6

Selected Sociodemographic Characteristics of Immigrant Women in High-Immigration States, 1990

State		Percent Entering Since 1980	Median Years in the U.S.	Age			Percent Married	Mean Number of Children	Mean Number of People in Household	Number of Children Born to Women 40–44	Education[a]			Percent Who Speak English Poorly[a]
				Mean 18–64	0–17	>65					Mean	<12	>16	
California	(I)	48	11.0	36.9	13	11	64	2.1	4.8	2.727	10.5	39	18	35
	(N)	—	—	37.7	29	13	54	1.6	3.1	2.019	13.2	9	24	1
Florida	(I)	37	17.0	40.5	8	23	64	1.8	3.6	2.175	11.5	27	15	26
	(N)	—	—	39.0	23	20	59	1.8	3.0	2.068	12.7	14	18	1
Illinois	(I)	37	14.3	38.9	9	17	70	2.0	4.0	2.492	11.3	32	21	27
	(N)	—	—	38.1	26	15	57	1.8	3.2	2.231	12.9	11	22	1
New Jersey	(I)	38	15.4	39.7	8	19	69	1.8	3.8	2.207	11.9	24	24	23
	(N)	—	—	38.6	24	15	56	1.6	3.3	2.075	13.0	11	25	1
New York	(I)	39	15.0	39.4	8	19	59	1.8	3.8	2.356	11.6	27	20	23
	(N)	—	—	38.2	26	15	52	1.6	3.2	2.129	13.0	12	25	1
Texas	(I)	45	11.5	36.8	13	9	70	2.4	4.4	3.039	9.3	51	13	39
	(N)	—	—	37.5	29	12	61	1.8	3.2	2.257	12.6	16	20	1
Total	(I)	41	13.5	38.5	10	16	65	2.0	4.1	2.544	11.1	31	20	27
	(N)	—	—	38.1	25	15	59	1.8	3.2	2.196	12.8	14	20	1

Source: 1990 PUMS of the U.S. Bureau of the Census.

Note: "I" means immigrants and "N" means native-born; "—" means not applicable.

[a]Immigrants aged 18–64 only.

At one extreme are immigrant women residing in California and Texas. Immigrant women in these two states are 26 percent more likely than immigrants in other states to have come within the past ten years, 40 percent more likely to be children, 20 to 60 percent more likely to have fewer than 12 years of education, and 30 to 70 percent more likely to speak English poorly or not at all. They also are less likely than in other states to hold a college degree, more likely to live in larger households, and more likely to have higher (from 9 to 40 percent higher) fertility rates. As we shall see in chapter 9, these characteristics are associated with higher use of safety net public services and a disproportionate increase in enrollment of students in the educational institutions of these two states.

Immigrant women in these two states also differ most from their native-born counterparts. For instance, the average educational gap between immigrant and native-born women in California and Texas is about twice as large as that in other states (2.7 to 3.3 years versus 1.1 to 1.6 years). The fertility rate of immigrant women in California is 35 percent higher than that of native-borns compared to less than 10 percent higher in other states. And the size of immigrants' households in these two states is some 40 percent larger than that of native-borns (4.4 and 4.8 versus 3.2 and 3.1) compared to 25 percent or less in other states. Such differences, compounded by the fact that the share of immigrant women in California's population is from 33 percent to more than 100 percent larger than in other states, are bound to exacerbate perceived differences between immigrant and native-born women as well as to result in a more visible impact in California than in any other state. (Also see McCarthy and Vernez, 1997).

Immigrant women in the East Coast states of Florida, New York, and New Jersey, have generally similar sociodemographic characteristics—even though their origins differ as was noted above. The average years of education of immigrant women in these three states vary within a small range from 11.5 years in Florida to 11.9 years in New Jersey, as does their fertility rate, which varies between a low 2.175 in Florida and a high 2.356 in New York for women aged 40 to 44. There are a few notable differences among these three states. Florida has a low share of immigrant women with a college degree and New Jersey has the highest share of such immigrant women of any state. Florida also has the highest share of elderly in its immigrant female population (about one in every four immigrant women compared to less than one in five immigrant women in other states). Finally, New York's immigrant women are significantly less likely to be married than are immigrant women in other states: from 8 to 20 percent less likely.

Immigrant women in these three states also differ from their native-born counterparts, but they do so once again in a generally similar fashion. For instance, the average educational gap between immigrant and native-born women in these three states varies within a small range: from 1.1 years in Florida to 1.4 years in New York. Fertility rates of immigrant women relative to native-born women are 5 percent higher in Florida and 11 percent higher in New York, with New Jersey fertility rates falling in between.

Notable differences relative to native-borns in these three states are few. The differential in marriage rate between immigrant and native-born women in New Jersey is twice as large as that in New York and Florida. And New York's immigrant women are much less likely than their native-born counterparts to have a college degree than in Florida and New Jersey.

Driven by its sizable share of immigrants from Mexico, the overall education, fertility, and household-size characteristics of immigrant women residing in Illinois are in between those observed in California and Texas on the one hand and Florida, New Jersey, and New York on the other hand. The only departure from this "in between" pattern is the higher marriage rate of Illinois immigrants relative to native-borns (23 percent higher), which is higher than in any other state. Illinois also has a smaller share of immigrant women in its population than the five other states considered here.

Conclusions

Generalizations about the sociodemographic characteristics of immigrant women cannot readily be made. There is as much diversity in these characteristics among immigrant women as there are among native-born women. For example, striking differences exist between European, Caribbean, and most Asian immigrant women on the one hand, and Mexican, Central American, and Indochinese immigrant women on the other. The former are older, better educated, have fewer children, and live in smaller households than the latter. The differences are often large. For instance, immigrant women from Europe and most of Asia—like more native-born women in general—have on the average five more years of education than immigrant women from Mexico and four more years than immigrant women from Indochina. Also, the latter two groups have fertility rates that are about two-thirds higher than the former group.

The sociodemographic characteristics of immigrant women have changed over time, most frequently in the same direction as those of native-born women. The average number of years of education of immigrant women as a whole has increased an average 2.5 years since 1980, as has the average years of education of native-born women, so that the gap of the average education between immigrant and native-born women has remained constant at 1.7 years. The distribution by education levels of these two populations has, however, diverged over time. Immigrant women have become two times more likely than native-born women to have fewer than 12 years of education and are less likely to have some college. Hence, they face increasingly more difficulties in a labor market that disproportionately rewards some college education or more. The share of college graduates in both groups, however, is the same.

Over the years, there has been a notable convergence between immigrant and native-born women in their respective share of the dependent population: the elderly and children aged 17 or younger. This share (about 40 percent) was about the same in 1997 for both groups, down from 45 percent in 1960 for native-born women and from 50 percent for immigrant women. The relative share of the elderly (one-third) to children aged 17 or less (two-thirds) in this dependent population is also currently about the same for both groups. This convergence in the age distribution between immigrant and native-born women undercuts the often-heard argument that diverging age distributions between these two groups will lead to diverging relative needs for education, training, and other services for the younger age groups on the one hand and the need for health care for the elderly population on the other.

Trends in rates of marriage and fertility have been diverging between the immigrant and native-born female population. Family formation has declined more rapidly for native-born than for immigrant women. And the fertility rates of the latter group, which were once lower than those of native-born women (by 15 percent in 1970), are now 16 percent higher. Higher rates of family formation and higher fertility combined with a growth in the immigrant population exceeding that of the native-born population signal that the children of immigrants will constitute an increasing share of newborn children in the United States for many years to come.

The diversity in the sociodemographic characteristics of immigrant women, coupled with the tendency of immigrants from the same country of origin to concentrate residentially, has resulted in significant variations in the profile of immigrant women across states. For instance, immigrant women residing in California and Texas not only are less educated and have larger families than immigrant women in any other state in the nation, they also differ most on these characteristics compared to native-born women. In contrast, immigrant women in the high-immigration states of Florida, New York, and New Jersey, on the East Coast, have generally socioeconomic characteristics that are closer to those of their native-born counterparts. These differences also imply that the effects of immigrant women will differ among states.

Note

1.   McCarthy and Vernez (1997) have estimated that approximately 70 percent of school-age children living with an immigrant parent in 1990 were born in the United States. We estimate that between 7.5 percent to 10 percent of the 60 million school-age children in the nation in 1990 were native-born children of immigrants.

Chapter 4

The Changing Economy and the Immigrant Female Labor Force

More than five million immigrant women are currently in the labor force in the United States, up from less than two million in 1970. Today, one in every five women added to the labor force is foreign-born compared to one in every 25 in the 1960s. As the number of immigrant women in the labor force has increased, their characteristics have changed (see chapter 3), as have the economic and labor-force environments in which they have been entering.

The next four chapters focus on how immigrant women have been integrated into the labor force and the U.S. economy over time. This chapter examines the increasingly important role immigrant women play in a rapidly changing national economy and labor market and the nature of that role. In turn, chapter 5 examines in greater detail what female immigrants do and chapter 6 examines where they work. Finally, in chapter 7, we compare the labor-force outcomes of immigrant women from different countries of origin to those of native-born women, focusing on labor-force participation, unemployment, earnings, and self-employment.

To set the context, this chapter first reviews how the national economy has changed since 1960, focusing on its increasing diversification, reliance on female labor whether native- or foreign-born, and reliance on college-educated labor. The second section examines the growing role of immigrant women in the labor market and the skills they bring to it. Variations in the role of immigrant women in the economy of high-immigration states are examined in the last section.

Our emphasis throughout this chapter is on long-term trends rather than on year-to-year or short-term fluctuations. We also focus on changes at the margin, that is, changes from one period of time to another. Traditionally, analysts of immigration have looked at the status of immigrants at one point in time or at most at the changes over one decade. This approach often misses the cumulative effects of successive waves of immigration and fails to place the changing characteristics of immigrants in the perspective of changes in the overall labor market.

The Changing National Economy

Since 1960, successive waves of immigrant women have entered an economy that has steadily

- created a significant, but declining, number of new jobs;

- shifted from producing manufactured goods to providing a growing range of financial and professional services;

- relied increasingly on female labor; and

- relied increasingly on college-educated labor.

In recent years, these trends have been associated with the globalization of the world economy and the ensuing competitive pressures on U.S. industries. What the long-term analyses presented below suggest, however, is that these trends have been in motion for decades and have been accelerating. Yearly fluctuations in the growth of the economy since 1960 have included three recessions in the early 1970s, 1980s, and 1990s, respectively. And there have been ups and downs in specific industries across the economy that loom large for the states, localities, and people directly affected. But for the economy at large, these long-term and one-directional sectoral and education shifts have continued unaltered.

Also, the aggregate trends documented here are at odds with views about trends in the economy that are widely held in the research literature. They suggest that the availability of jobs for workers—including new entrants in the labor force—with fewer than 12 years of education has been steadily shrinking over time, in contrast to the widespread belief that "economic restructuring" is leading to an expansion of jobs for low- as well as highly educated workers (Sassen, 1991; Boyd, 1996). Instead, the trends discussed here are generally consistent with the increasing movements "offshore"—to Mexico and Asian countries—of low-skill manufacturing and service jobs. They are also consistent with the well-documented decline in the employment rate of persons with low levels of education. This rate has declined from 72 percent in 1970 to 53 percent in 1990 for native-born male high school dropouts and from 89 to 80 percent for male high school graduates. Employment rates of women have increased during that period of time, but the increase was significantly lower for less-educated women than for more-educated women (McCarthy and Vernez, 1997; Mishel and Bernstein, 1994).

Slowing Employment Growth

The number of persons in the labor force has consistently increased since 1960. Employment grew by 18 percent in the 1960s. It grew even faster during the 1970s, with the number of new jobs created during that period twice as large as the number created during the 1960s. The 1980s were a mirror image of the 1960s as far as the employment rate of growth was concerned (figure 4.1). However, national employment growth slowed down during that decade and further declined in the 1990s, so that by 1997, employment was growing at only three-quarters of the rate of the 1980s. Employment growth has accelerated since the end of the early 1990–1993 recession and national employment is once more growing at roughly the rate it did during the 1980s.

Diversifying Economy

In 1960, three sectors dominated the national economy: manufacturing, wholesale, and retail trade. Together, they employed half of the national labor force. Today, these sectors employ a reduced one-third of the national labor force. This trend reflects a relatively slow but steady shift of employment from these industries toward financial, business, health, and other professional services.

Figure 4.2 shows a remarkable consistency since 1960 between the sectors that led the national economy and those that lagged. Five sectors were consistently among the top leading sectors in every decade since 1960: business/repair; entertainment; FIRE (financial, insurance, and real estate), health, and other professional. As a result, their share of the national employment has

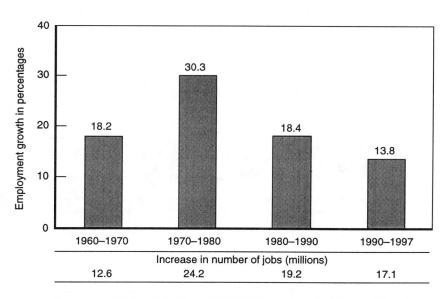

Sources: 1960, 1970, 1980, and 1990 PUMS and the 1997 Current Population Survey of the U.S. Bureau of the Census.

Figure 4.1—National Employment Growth, 1960–1997

Immigrant Women in the U.S. Workforce

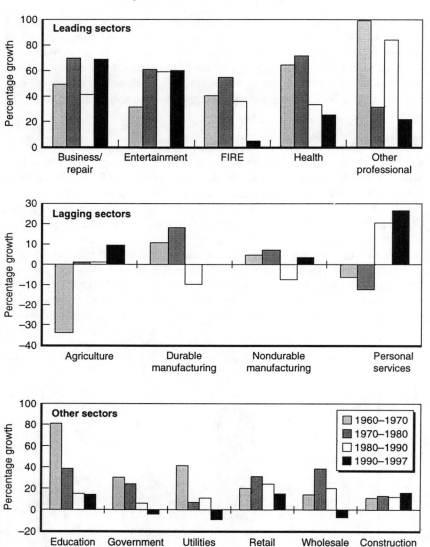

Sources: 1960, 1970, 1980, and 1990 PUMS and the 1997 Current Population
Survey of the U.S. Bureau of the Census.

**Figure 4.2—Employment Growth by Main Sectors of the National
Economy, 1960–1997**

doubled from 15 percent in 1960 to 30 percent in 1997. All but two of these sectors maintained their robust growth rate during the recessionary years in the early 1990s. The exceptions are FIRE, as would be expected, and other professional services, which include engineering, architecture, accounting, and public relations.

Similarly, four sectors have consistently lagged behind other sectors in employment growth. The most important of these sectors are durable and nondurable manufacturing. These two sectors had a relatively low, but positive employment growth during the 1960s and 1970s, eventually turning into a negative growth in the 1980s. Agricultural employment dropped by one-third during the 1960s and remained practically unchanged during the subsequent two decades. Employment in this sector grew in the 1990s, however. Employment in personal services—including private households, hotels and motels, laundry, and various shops—declined for two decades, but recovered during the 1980–1990 decade and continued to grow in the 1990s. Together, the employment share of these four lagging sectors was cut in half from 42 percent in 1960 to 22 percent in 1997.

The remaining sectors may be divided into two groups: sectors whose employment growth has steadily declined since 1960 and sectors whose growth has fluctuated with the overall national economy (figure 4.2). In the first group, education and government experienced vigorous employment growth in the 1960s, only to experience increasingly slower growth in the 1970s, 1980s, and 1990s signifying steady relative disinvestments in these important publicly funded sectors. The reversal in the decline of employment growth in education is mostly a result of a steady increase in enrollment, itself the product of the echo from the baby boom and of international immigration.

Employment in utilities also experienced rapid growth in the 1960s, but its rate of growth has been below the national average ever since and declined in the 1990s.

All three sectors in the second group, retail trade, wholesale trade, and construction have experienced fluctuation in their employment growth that mirror fluctuations in the national economy as a whole. Generally, where the national economy goes these sectors follow: their employment share of national employment has remained roughly constant over time—it was 21 percent in 1960 and 23 percent in 1997.

Growing Role of Women

Since 1960, female labor has played a growing role in the growth of the U.S. economy. Women have consistently contributed nearly two-thirds of the increases in the labor force from 1960 to 1990 and still more than half of the increases in the labor force in the 1990s (figure 4.3).

A major, often overlooked, reason why women have contributed a disproportionate share in the growth in the nation's labor force has been the shift of the economy from manufacturing to services. As early as 1960, women were disproportionately concentrated in those service sectors that, as we have shown, have led employment growth in subsequent decades (table 4.1). In 1960, women constituted nearly half of the labor force in these sectors—including education, business/repair, entertainment, health, FIRE, and other professional. By contrast, the 1960 share of women in other sectors, including those whose share has declined significantly—such as agriculture, durable and nondurable manufacturing, and government services—was significantly lower, 30 percent or less. So, as the demand for services grew, women seized the new opportunities that were offered to them. In the process, their share of the service-sectors labor force grew to nearly two-thirds of their labor force. The share of women increased in other industries as well but still does not exceed 40 percent.

Overall, differences in sectoral growth that has "favored" female labor have contributed to two-thirds of the growth of women in the labor force (table 4.1, right-hand column). Only one-third has been the result of an increase in the share of women throughout the economy.

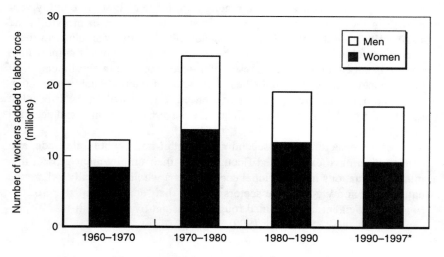

Sources: 1960, 1970, 1980, and 1990 PUMS and the 1997 Current Population Survey of the U.S. Bureau of the Census.

*For comparison with the decennial growth, the figure shown is adjusted to a 10-year period.

Figure 4.3—Workers Added to the Labor Force by Gender and by Decade, 1960–1997

Table 4.1

Share of Total Labor Force and Share of Women in Leading and Lagging Growth Sectors of the Economy, 1960–1997
(Percent)

Sectors	Share of Total Labor Force		Share of Women in Sector		Share of Total 1960–1997 Growth in Women Resulting from:	
					Growth of Sector	Increase in the Share of Women
	1960	1997	1960	1997		
Leading Sectors[a]	35.3	56.1	47.2	58.2	60.1	20.0
Steady Sectors[b]	17.5	17.2	12.7	21.3	3.6	4.8
Lagging Sectors[c]	47.2	26.6	29.9	38.6	4.0	7.5
Total	100.0	100.0	32.9	46.6	67.7	32.3

Sources: 1960 PUMS and the 1997 Current Population Survey of the U.S. Bureau of the Census.

[a]Includes business/repair, education, entertainment, FIRE, health, other professional, and retail.

[b]Includes construction, transportation, communication, utilities, and wholesale.

[c]Includes agriculture, durable and nondurable manufacturing, personal services, and government.

Increasing Share of College-Educated Labor

Although sectoral shifts in the economy have led to a significant increase in women working, they have been a minor contributor to the just as remarkable increase in the educational attainment of the labor force. Surely, the share of college-educated labor in leading sectors was already higher than in other sectors in 1960, 31 percent versus 14 percent. But, more significant has been the large increase in college-educated workers in all sectors of the economy including lagging sectors (table 4.2).

From 1960 to 1997, the share of college-educated labor nearly doubled in the leading growth sectors of the economy, from 31 to 58 percent of the labor force. However, it tripled in lagging as well as steady-growth sectors. In brief, the increase in the educational attainment of the labor force cuts across all sectors and industries of the economy including traditionally "low skilled" sectors as we shall see in greater detail below.

Men and women have contributed roughly equally in the increase in level of education. If anything, the increase has been slightly greater for women than for men. This is particularly the case in those sectors that have maintained their share in the overall economy, including construction, communications, utilities, transportation, and wholesale (table 4.2). The propor-

Table 4.2

**Share of Total and Female Labor Force with Some College Education by
Growing and Lagging Sectors of the National Economy, 1960–1997
(Percent)**

Sectors	Share of Total Labor Force with Some College or More		Share of Women in Labor Force with Some College or More	
	1960	1997	1960	1997
Leading Sectors[a]	30.7	58.0	28.7	56.1
Steady Sectors[b]	14.0	45.3	16.0	55.3
Lagging Sectors[c]	13.5	36.7	8.9	42.8
Total	19.4	53.3	19.1	54.8

Sources: 1960 PUMS and the 1987 Current Population Survey of the U.S. Bureau of the Census.

[a] Includes business/repair, education, entertainment, FIRE, health, other professional, and retail.

[b] Includes construction, transportation, communication, utilities, and wholesale.

[c] Includes agriculture, durable and nondurable manufacturing, personal services, and government.

tion of women with some college in steady-growth sectors has increased in excess of three times from 16 to 55 percent, compared to an increase from 14 to 45 percent in the overall labor force.

The net results of these trends are shown in table 4.3. At the lower end of the educational distribution, the number of jobs filled by labor with fewer than 12 years of education has been nearly halved since 1960, from 36 to 19 million. The number of such jobs has steadily decreased for three decades: by 4.5 million jobs in the 1960s, 5.0 million in the 1970s, and 7.9 million in the 1980s. In the 1990s, this trend was reversed with the number of jobs filled by workers with fewer than 12 years of education increasing slightly from 18 to 19 million. Still this increase constitutes less than 1 out of 10 net new jobs created by the economy during that decade.

The number of net new jobs that have been filled by high school graduates only has also been declining over time, most particularly since 1980. Whereas, two-thirds of the net new jobs created in the 1960s were filled by high school graduates only, less than 50 and 25 percent of net new jobs created in the 1970s and 1990s, respectively, were filled by such workers. Most net new jobs created in the 1970s, and even more so in the 1980s and 1990s, were filled by college graduates.

Table 4.3

Number of Jobs by Educational Attainment, 1960–1997 (Millions)

Years of Education	All Workers					Female Workers				
	1960	1970	1980	1990	1997	1960	1970	1980	1990	1997
< 12	35.8	31.3	26.3	18.4	19.2	10.3	10.8	10.1	7.2	7.5
= 12	18.6	28.0	39.7	40.9	44.0	7.5	12.5	18.8	19.4	20.9
13-15	6.8	10.3	19.6	36.3	37.8	2.5	4.1	8.8	17.9	18.9
16+	6.2	10.0	18.5	27.7	34.2	1.8	3.2	6.8	11.8	15.6
Total	67.6	79.9	104.1	123.1	135.2	22.2	30.7	44.5	56.5	62.9

Sources: 1960, 1970, 1980, and 1990 PUMS and the 1997 Current Population Survey of the U.S. Bureau of the Census.

This progressive upgrading in the education of the national labor force has accelerated over time. Whereas 30 percent of new jobs were filled by college graduates in the 1960s, this share increased to 35 percent in the 1970s. In the 1980s, nearly half of net new jobs were filled by college graduates, as were 55 percent of net new jobs in the 1990s.

Educational trends for women in the labor force have generally mirrored those for the labor force as a whole. However, the number of jobs filled by women with low levels of education has not declined as rapidly as those filled by men. As a consequence, the share of women filling jobs at this low educational level has increased from 29 percent in 1960 to 39 percent in 1997. Still, it is in jobs filled by college graduates that women have increased their share the most, from 29 percent in 1960 to 46 percent in 1997.

The trend toward more and more jobs filled by college-educated labor does not mean there are no job openings for new entrants into the labor force—including immigrant men and women—who are less educated. The labor force is dynamic with older, less-educated workers retiring, more experienced workers upgrading their education and moving into new jobs, and young adults increasingly completing one or more years of college. In this dynamic process, low-educated new entrants into the labor force are for the most part backfilling jobs that are vacated by other workers.

These trends also suggest that projections made about the significant future growth in jobs to be filled by high school dropouts and high school graduates only are somewhat optimistic. In 1993, the Bureau of Labor Statistics (BLS) projected that up to 40 percent of the 26 million net new jobs projected to be created from 1990 to 2005 would be filled by high school dropouts (11 percent) and by high school graduates (29 percent) (Silvestri, 1993). As of 1997, only one-third of 12 million jobs created has been filled by high school dropouts (7 percent) and by high school graduates only (26 percent). The BLS estimates may also be too optimistic in light of the fact that the 1990s departed from a three-decade-long declining trend in the number of jobs filled by low-educated workers. The first half of the 1990s may be a temporary reversal of this long-term trend.

In spite of these trends, a question remains about whether the college education acquired by the workers filling new jobs is actually needed to perform the tasks demanded by employers in our increasingly service-oriented economy. There is evidence that jobs available to less-educated workers require the daily performance of one or more cognitive/social tasks, such as dealing with customers, reading and writing, arithmetic calculations, and the use of computers (Holzer, 1996; Murnane and Levy, 1996). These skills can be taught at the primary and secondary school levels, but often are not (Murnane and Levy, 1996). As a result, employers may require credentials, such as some postsecondary education (or at least specific experience beyond a high school diploma), to screen out potential workers who may lack these necessary cognitive/social skills (Holzer, 1996). In this event, it is not so much that a college education is needed to fill a large share of newly created jobs; rather, cognitive and social skills required by employers need to be taught in and acquired at the secondary educational level. Until requirements change, however, the trends described above mean that at least some college has become a widespread prerequisite for filling new jobs created by the economy, including jobs traditionally labeled as "low skill."

Growing Importance of Immigrant Women in the Economy

In this changing and dynamic economy, immigrant women have become increasingly more important as another source of low- and high-skilled labor. Over time, the general level of education of the immigrant women in the labor force has increased, but so has that of native-born women. And since 1980, immigrant women have been increasingly more likely than native-born women to have low levels of education.

A Growing Component of the Labor Force

New jobs created by the national economy, as well as current jobs vacated by workers retiring or moving to other jobs, can be filled by increases in the native-born population; by increases in labor-force participation; by either women, men, or both; or by immigrants from abroad.

At the national level, the relative contribution to employment growth of these sources of labor has varied in each decade since 1960 (figure 4.4). In the 1960 decade, when the economy grew by 18 percent, the vast majority of new net jobs—two-thirds—were filled by native-born women. Immigrant

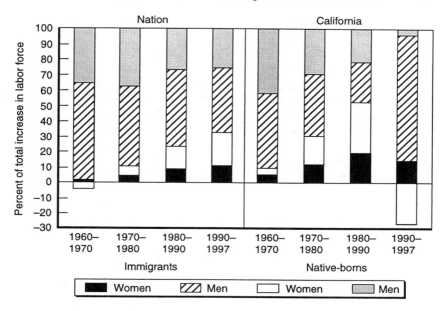

Sources: 1960, 1970, 1980, and 1990 PUMS and the 1997 Current
Population Survey of the U.S. Bureau of the Census.

**Figure 4.4—Distribution of Employment Growth by Immigration Status
and Gender, in the Nation and in California, 1960–1997**

women contributed less than 3 percent in that growth and the share of
immigrant men in the economy actually declined during that decade.

In the three subsequent decades, native-born women continued to
contribute in excess of half of the growth of the national labor force. But
immigrants, both women and men, contributed a rapidly growing share of the
growth of the national labor force. Immigrant women increased their share of
employment growth from 5 percent in the 1970s, to 10 percent in the 1980s,
and to 12.5 percent in the 1990s. And so did immigrant men, at an even faster
pace, from 6 percent in the 1970s to 22 percent in the 1990s. Today
immigrant men and women contribute more than one-third of the growth in
the national labor force, up from one-fourth in the 1980s and 10 percent in the
1970s.

As rapidly as the share of immigrants in the share of the labor force has
increased in the nation as a whole, nowhere has that share grown more
rapidly than in the state of California. There, immigrants already contributed
16 percent to the employment growth of the state in the 1960s. That share
increased to one-third in the 1970s and to more than half (54 percent) in the
1980s, with immigrant women contributing 40 percent of the share of

immigrants and 21 percent of total growth in employment (figure 4.4). By the 1990s, all new net entrants into the California labor force were immigrants with immigrant women contributing one-third of that growth. California suffered a deep and long recession during the first half of the 1990s, so that employment grew uncharacteristically slowly at about half the rate of the national economy after having grown at more than 1.5 times the rate of the national economy in the three previous decades. California's economic woes did not slow down international immigration; however, net in-migration of workers from other parts of the United States to California not only stopped, but it became negative, with more native-born workers leaving than entering the state. This cyclical phenomenon affected most native-born women whose number in the labor force declined by 250,000. Native-born men contributed a modest 3 percent in the growth of the California labor force during that period.

An Educationally Diverse Labor Force

Success in the United States labor market depends largely on education. Much has been written recently about the decline, since the 1970s, in the education of immigrants relative to that of native-borns in the labor market (e.g., Borjas, 1995; McCarthy and Vernez, 1997). From a national perspective, this characterization of recent immigration fits immigrant men more than it does immigrant women, and for both, it applies primarily at the lowest levels of education (table 4.4).

Viewed from a national perspective, the increase in the educational level of immigrant women was more rapid than that of native-born women during the 1960s and 1970s, leading to a decrease in the educational gap between immigrant and native-born women during this period of time. This decline is apparent in the lessening of the gap in mean years of schooling from 1.6 years in 1960 to 1.3 in 1970 to 1.1 in 1980. This favorable trend, however, was briefly reversed in the 1980s when the disparity in educational level of immigrant women relative to native-born increased only to decrease once again in the 1990s. By 1997, the difference in mean years of schooling between immigrant and native women was at its lowest in nearly four decades (at one year).

The gap in average years of education between immigrant and native-born men also declined in the 1960s (from 1.6 years in 1960 to 1.1 years in 1970). In contrast to that of immigrant women, however, it began to increase in the 1970s, and this relative deterioration accelerated in the 1980s so that by 1990, the educational gap between immigrant and native-born men in the labor force had reverted to its 1960 level of 1.6 years. This gap remained constant in the 1990s.

Most apparent for both immigrant women and men has been the increase in their share among low-educated workers, most particularly workers with

Table 4.4

**Educational Attainment of Workers by Gender and Immigration
Status, Nation, 1960–1997**
(Percentages)

Years of Schooling	1960 I	1960 N	1970 I	1970 N	1980 I	1980 N	1990 I	1990 N	1997 I	1997 N
					Females					
< 12	63	44	48	35	35	22	27	12	25	10
= 12	22	34	31	41	31	43	28	35	27	34
13–15	9	11	12	14	18	20	24	33	23	31
16 +	6	8	10	11	16	15	21	21	25	25
Total	100	100	100	100	100	100	100	100	100	100
Mean Years of Schooling	9.3	10.9	10.3	11.6	11.3	12.4	11.7	13.0	12.5	13.5
					Males					
< 12	69	55	52	41	40	26	33	15	36	13
= 12	14	25	21	32	23	36	24	33	21	33
13–15	8	10	11	13	15	18	20	28	17	27
16 +	9	10	11	14	22	20	24	24	26	26
Total	100	100	100	100	100	100	100	100	100	100
Mean Years of Schooling	8.8	10.4	10.3	11.4	11.2	12.4	11.3	12.9	11.9	13.5

Source: 1960, 1970, 1980, and 1990 PUMS of the U.S. Bureau of the Census.
Note: I means immigrant and N means native-born.

fewer than 12 years of education. Whereas immigrant women were one-third more likely than native-born women to have fewer than 12 years of education in 1970, they were twice as likely, by 1990, and 2.5 times more likely by 1997. Again, this differential increased more rapidly for immigrant men relative to native-born men: the first were 26 percent more likely to have fewer than 12 years of education in 1970 but nearly three times more likely in 1997.

A similar, but significantly less pronounced trend has taken place at the high school and some college levels for immigrant men and women, although to a lesser extent for the latter. For instance, immigrant women were 14 percent less likely to have some college education than native-born women in 1970, but 26 percent less likely in 1997.

However, no major changes have occurred at the highest level of education (i.e., college-educated workers). Both immigrant women and men were as likely as their native-born counterparts to be college educated in 1970, and they have continued this pattern in every decade since.

The net outcome of these trends is that immigrant women have increasingly replaced native-born women in jobs typically filled by workers with the lowest levels of education. Table 4.5 shows that while the number of jobs filled by workers with fewer than 12 years of education has declined rapidly over time, immigrant women have filled an increasing number of these jobs. For instance, in the 1970s, when the number of jobs filled by women with fewer than 12 years of education declined by 708,000, immigrant women increased their holding such jobs by 250,000. This pattern was repeated even more dramatically in the 1980s and in the 1990s: all new 250,000 additional jobs filled by women with fewer than 12 years of education were filled by immigrants.

This trend toward replacement of native-born women by immigrant women is also apparent for jobs filled by high school graduates only. In the 1970s, about 6 million such jobs were created, and immigrant women filled a low 6 percent of them. The number of such newly created jobs—less than 1 million—plummeted in the 1980s and immigrant women filled two-thirds of these jobs. In the 1990s, three times as many net new jobs were filled by female high school graduates only and one-fourth of those jobs were filled by immigrants.

Throughout the 1970s and 1980s immigrant women filled a constant share, about one in every ten, of the new jobs filled by college graduates. This share increased significantly in the 1990s so that one in every six new jobs was filled by an immigrant female college graduate.

Although immigrant women are filling an increasing number of jobs available to low-educated workers, and in recent years even to college graduates, one cannot conclude that they are displacing native-born workers from these jobs. Replacement is not the same thing as displacement. As noted in the previous chapter, an increasing share of native-born women are entering the labor force with some college education. Hence, what this pattern suggests is a dynamic labor market within which immigrant women are filling jobs vacated by older native-born female workers lacking a college education, while younger college-educated native-born women fill the increasing number of newly created jobs demanding such an education.

This dynamic process is illustrated in table 4.6, which shows changes in the 1970s and the 1980s in the number of native-born adult women aged 16 to 64 by level of education. The table contrasts these changes with the changes in the number of new jobs and the number and share of these new jobs filled by native-born women, also by level of education. Several observations can be made from this table.

First, it shows (see last column) that the 1970–1980 1.6 million decline in the number of native-born women with less than 12 years of education (holding the labor-force participation rate constant over the period

Table 4.5

Net New Jobs Filled by Women by Level of Education, Nation, 1970–1997

Years of Schooling	1970–1980			1980–1990			1990–1997		
	Net New Jobs Filled by Women (Thousands)	Jobs Filled by Immigrant Women Number (Thousands)	Percentage	Net New Jobs Filled by Women (Thousands)	Jobs Filled by Immigrant Women Number (Thousands)	Percentage	Net New Jobs Filled by Women (Thousands)	Jobs Filled by Immigrant Women Number (Thousands)	Percentage
< 12	−708	249	—[a]	−2,893	252	—[b]	248	255	102.8
= 12	6,288	404	6.4	686	448	65.3	1,480	338	26.2
13–15	4,690	323	6.9	9,127	646	7.1	979	285	29.1
16 or more	3,551	304	8.6	5,038	554	11.0	3,731	603	16.2
Total	13,280	1,279	9.3	11,958	1,900	15.9	6,437	1,481	23.0

Source: 1970, 1980, and 1990 PUMS of the U.S. Bureau of the Census.

[a]Immigrants have replaced native-borns in 3 percent of remaining jobs.

[b]Immigrants have replaced native-borns in 3.5 percent of remaining jobs.

Table 4.6

Changes in Total Number of Jobs and Jobs Filled by Native-Born Women Compared to Changes in Number of Working-Age Native-Born Women, Nation, 1970–1990

Years of Schooling	Net New Jobs Filled by Women (Thousands)	Jobs Filled by Native-Born Women — Number (Thousands)	Jobs Filled by Native-Born Women — Percent of Net New Jobs	Net Increase in Number of Native-Born Women Ages 16–64	Estimated Net Increase in Native-Born Women in Labor Force Holding LFPR[a] Constant
		1970–1980			
<12	−708	−957	—[b]	−4,073	−1,593
=12	6,288	5,884	94	5,763	2,991
13–15	4,690	4,367	93	5,020	2,605
16+	3,551	3,247	84	3,659	2,349
Total	13,820	12,541	91	10,369	6,352
		1980–1990			
<12	−2,893	−3,145	—[c]	−7,516	−3,202
=12	686	238	35	−2,383	−1,477
13–15	9,127	8,481	93	9,476	6,254
16+	5,038	4,448	89	4,567	3,425
Total	11,958	10,058	84	4,144	5,000

Source: 1970, 1980, and 1990 PUMS from the U.S. Bureau of the Census.

[a]Labor-force participation rate is held constant.

[b]Immigrants have replaced native-borns in 238,000 jobs.

[c]Immigrants have replaced native-borns in an additional 252,000 jobs.

considered) exceeded the total loss of jobs filled by such native-borns: the net loss of 957,000 jobs to native-born women with less than 12 years of education was matched by a decline in the number of native-born women with fewer than 12 years of education of nearly double that number. A similar, although less pronounced, pattern is apparent in the 1980s. In that decade the decline in the number of native-born women aged 16–64 in the labor force with fewer than 12 years of education (3.2 million at constant labor-force participation rate) equaled the decline in the number of jobs filled by native-born women with fewer than 12 years of education (3.1 million). This decline suggests that the number of native-born women who retired during these years exceeded the number of jobs filled by immigrant women. The net result has also been an increase in labor-force participation rate among native-born women with less than 12 years of education.

In the 1980s, the number of native-born women with 12 years of education only (holding labor-force participation constant at the level of the beginning of the decade) declined by 1.5 million at the same time as the number of such jobs filled by native-born women increased by 238,000. Again, this reflects a significant increase in labor-force participation among native-born women.

Finally, the number of native-born female college graduates who were entrants in the labor force (again holding labor-force participation constant at the level of the beginning of the period) was always lower than the number of net new jobs filled by native-born female college graduates, reflecting an increase in labor-force participation by these women. For instance, in the 1980s, native-born female college graduates filled 4.5 million net new jobs, but only 3.5 million such women would have been added to the labor force if their participation rate had remained equal throughout the decade to its 1980 level.

Arguably, increases in labor-force participation of native-born women at all levels of education might have been even larger without female immigrants filling some of these jobs. We discuss this possibility briefly in chapter 6.

Variations across States

Viewing the educational trends in immigrant women relative to native-born women with a national lens is generally descriptive of the distributional patterns prevailing in most states including high-immigration states such as Florida, New Jersey, New York, and even Illinois. It does not, however, reflect the highly different characteristics of immigrants to California and Texas as was documented in the previous section. Table 4.7 shows that immigrant women in the latter two states are not only considerably less educated than native-born women in those states, they also are less educated than immigrant women in other states. *In 1990, the gap in mean years of schooling between immigrant and native-born women in these two states was about 3 years, more than twice the gap observed in other states. And immigrants in those states have, on average, more than one year less of education than immigrants in other states.* Hence, we would expect that in these two states, the disproportionate number of low-educated immigrant women would increasingly dominate the low end of the labor market, which indeed they now do.

Table 4.8 compares the changes in the number of net jobs added to the economy with those filled by immigrant women by level of education in California and the rest of the nation. It shows that as immigrant women contributed an increasing share of the growth of the California female labor force—one quarter in the 1970s, nearly one-half in the 1980s, and more than 100 percent in the 1990s—the number of jobs filled by workers with fewer

Table 4.7

**Educational Attainment of Women Aged 16–64 by Selected States
and by Immigration Status, 1990
(Percent)**

Years of	Nation		California		Florida		Illinois		New Jersey		New York		Texas	
Schooling	I	N	I	N	I	N	I	N	I	N	I	N	I	N
<12	31	14	39	9	27	14	32	11	24	11	27	12	51	16
12	28	37	23	29	34	38	27	36	32	39	33	37	21	33
13–15	21	29	21	38	25	31	19	30	19	25	20	26	16	31
16	20	20	18	24	15	18	21	22	24	25	20	25	13	20
Mean	11.1	12.8	10.5	12.2	11.5	12.7	11.3	12.9	11.9	13.0	11.6	13.0	9.3	12.6

Source: 1990 PUMS of the U.S. Bureau of the Census.

Note: I means immigrants and N means native-born.

than 12 years of education has declined much less rapidly than in the rest of
the nation (also see McCarthy and Vernez, 1997). This pattern suggests that
the constant renewal of a supply of low-educated immigrant labor has
contributed to slowing down the long-term decline in the number of low-skill
jobs in California relative to the rest of the nation. Immigrant women in
California have been replacing native-born women in jobs available to the
low-educated at a higher rate than in the rest of the nation. For instance, the
share in jobs of immigrant women with fewer than 12 years of education has
increased from 16 percent in 1970 to 62 percent in 1997, compared to an
increase from 7 to 15 percent in the rest of the nation. In the 1980s and 1990s,
the number of jobs available to women with a high school education declined,
at the same time as immigrant women were filling an increasing share of
these jobs. Their share of jobs filled by high school graduates only has
doubled from 10 percent in 1970 to 26 percent in 1997 compared to an
increase of 4 to 7 percent in the rest of the nation.

California's experience in the 1990s is of particular interest. During that
period, unlike in the three decades that preceded it, California's economy
suffered an unusually long and deep recession that began in 1990. During the
first three years of this recession, California's economy lost in excess of
400,000 jobs, while immigration continued at roughly the same pace adding
an estimated 270,000 immigrants yearly, compared with an average 287,000
during the 1980s (McCarthy and Vernez, 1997). By the end of 1994, the
economy was once again creating net new jobs, but at less than one-third of
the rate that California had been accustomed to for three decades. And it was
not until late in 1995 that employment in California returned to its 1990 level.
Since then, employment growth has increased, adding 909,000 new jobs by
late 1997.

Table 4.8

Net Jobs Filled by Women in California and the Rest of the Nation, 1970–1997

	1970–1980			1980–1990			1990–1997		
	Net New Jobs Filled by Women	Jobs Filled by Immigrant Women		Net New Jobs Filled by Women	Jobs Filled by Immigrant Women		Net New Jobs Filled by Women	Jobs Filled by Immigrant Women	
Years of Schooling	(Thousands)	Number (Thousands)	Percent of Net New Jobs	(Thousands)	Number (Thousands)	Percent of Net New Jobs	(Thousands)	Number (Thousands)	Percent of Net New Jobs
California									
<12	134	169	126.1	-59	174	a	64	98	53.1
12	530	97	18.3	-55		b	-120	44	c
13–15	672	97	14.4	1,132	219	19.3	-152	81	d
16+	441	85	19.3	712	178	25.0	356	170	47.8
Total	1,778	448	25.2	1,729	767	44.4	149	394	164.4
Rest of the Nation									
<12	-842	80	NA	-2,834	57	NA	184	157	85.3
12	5,758	307	5.3	741	274	37.0	1,600	294	18.7
13–15	4,018	226	5.6	7,995	427	5.3	1,131	204	18.1
16+	3,110	219	7.0	4,326	376	8.7	3,375	433	12.8
Total	12,042	831	6.9	10,229	1,133	11.1	6,288	1,087	17.3

Source: 1970, 1980, and 1990 PUMS of the U.S. Bureau of the Census.

Note: NA means not applicable.

[a] Immigrant women have replaced native-born women in 20 percent of remaining jobs.

[b] Immigrant women have replaced native-born women in 10 percent of remaining jobs.

This recovery has not benefited all skill levels equally, underlying California's accelerated structural shift toward an increasingly high-skill economy (Center for Continuing Study of the California Economy, 1996). During the 1990s, the only major growth occurred in jobs filled by college graduates. The total number of jobs held by women with some college or a high school degree declined, while the number of jobs held by women high school dropouts remained relatively stagnant (table 4.8).

As immigration flows continued unaffected by the recession, immigrant labor, including immigrant women, dominated the shifts taking place in the economy throughout the 1990s. Whereas the total number of jobs held by women with some college and a high school degree only declined, immigrant women increased their numbers, and whereas the number of jobs held by female high school dropouts increased slightly, those held by immigrant women increased even more. Even at the college graduate levels, immigrant women filled half of the net new jobs held by women, again underlying the unique dependence of California on immigrant labor. The combination of slow employment growth and continuing high immigration led to the replacement of native-born female labor at all levels of skill in the California economy and eventually to a net out-migration of native-born labor from California to the rest of the nation during the 1990s (Gabriel, Mattey, and Wascher, 1995; Johnson and Lovelady, 1995).

Conclusions

As immigrant women fill an increasing share of the net new jobs created by the economy at all levels of education, the structure of the economy and the demand it places on female labor is changing as well. These changes were set in motion long before analysts began to focus on the effects of globalization on the economy and the competitive pressures it places on U.S. industries, most particularly on low-skill industries. Three changes are particularly important as far as immigrant women are concerned.

First, the rate at which the economy has created net new jobs has been steadily declining, from 30 percent during the 1970–1980 decade to 18 percent during the 1980s and 14 percent during the 1990s. Surely, employment growth in the final years of the 1990s has been more vigorous than in the first half of the 1990 decade, but it remains to be seen whether it can be sustained in the long term. Such a case is unlikely, as it would reverse nearly 30 years of downward trends.

Second, and at the same time, the demand for female labor has increased steadily as the economy has shifted from producing manufactured goods to providing a growing range of financial and professional services. In 1960, women already constituted half of the labor force in the sectors that have been leading the economy since then—business/repair, education, entertainment, FIRE, health, and other professional—and by 1997 they had increased their share to nearly two-thirds. By contrast, the remaining sectors of the economy employed only 25 percent women in 1960 and this share had increased to only 31 percent by 1997.

The third significant long-term trend is that the net new jobs created by the national economy have been increasingly filled by labor with at least some college education. Whereas 59 percent of the net new jobs created by the economy were filled by such labor in the 1960s, in the 1980s all net new jobs and more were filled by workers with some college. In the meantime, the number of jobs filled by workers with fewer than 12 years of education was halved from 36 million in 1960 to 18 million in 1990. Although the 1990s saw a stabilization in the number of jobs filled by low-educated labor, the direction of this trend remained the same. The case may well be, as some have argued, that this trend reflects, at least in part, the increasing supply of college-educated laborers, many of whom remain in traditionally low-skill industries, rather than the education needed to perform the jobs. It may also be that the cognitive/social skills—such as dealing with customers, reading and writing, performing simple arithmetic calculations, and using computers—are not being adequately acquired at the secondary school level. Whatever the reason, however, the fact remains that at least some college has become a widespread prerequisite for filling the new jobs created by the economy.

Trends in the educational characteristics of immigrant women entering the U.S. labor market have generally been consistent with the trends in the demand for labor in the economy, certainly more so than for immigrant men. The share of immigrant women in the labor force with at least some college has increased proportionately to the female labor force as a whole, from 15 percent in 1960 to 48 percent in 1997, compared to an increase of 19 percent in 1960 to 54 percent for the female labor force as a whole.

Since 1980, however, immigrant women have become increasingly more likely than native-born women to have fewer than 12 years of education. Throughout the 1960s and 1970s, immigrant women in the labor force were 50 percent more likely than native-born women to have fewer than 12 years of education—a 35 percent versus a 22 percent share. By 1997, they were 150 percent more likely to have such a low level of education, 25 versus 10 percent.

As a result, immigrant women are playing an increasing and disproportionate role at the lower end of the labor market, increasing their share of the female labor force from 7 percent in 1970 to 21 percent in 1997. This result compares to an increase from 5 to 10 percent among college graduate women in the labor force. As the total number of jobs held by workers with fewer than 12 years of education has declined, immigrant women have been replacing native-born women in these jobs at an accelerated rate since the 1970s. This replacement does not signify a one-to-one displacement of native-born women, however.[1] In this dynamic process, immigrant women are primarily replacing older native-born women who are retiring, whereas increasingly more college-educated female laborers can avail themselves of the increasing number of jobs requiring this level of education.

Nowhere have these long-term processes been more pronounced than in the state of California, which has the distinction of having the largest flow of immigrants in the nation with a disproportionately larger share of them having fewer than 12 years of education. There, immigrant women now hold two-thirds of the stagnant number of jobs filled by women with fewer than 12 years of education. In the 1980s and 1990s, immigrant women began to replace native-born women in jobs held by high school graduates only, and in the 1990s, they began to replace native-born women in jobs held by women with some college only.

Note

1. A number of recent studies have sought to estimate the extent to which immigrant labor may actually displace native-born workers in the labor market (Borjas, 1997; Card, 1996; McCarthy and Vernez, 1997; National Research Council, 1997; Ong and Valenzuela, 1996). Although these studies differ in the magnitude of the displacement effect, the difference is relatively small, averaging around a 1 percent decline in the employment rate (affecting about 1.3 million in a 135-million-strong labor market) for the nation as a whole and around 4 to 6 percent in California. All in all, the estimates translate into the displacement of one native-born worker for every 20 to 30 new immigrant workers. These estimates were made in the context of a growing macroeconomy and may underestimate displacement during periods of slow or negative economic growth. Also, all estimates converge in having a greater impact on less-educated workers, as might be expected given the decline in the number of jobs open to them and given the disproportionate share of immigrants who are low-educated.

Chapter 5

What Immigrant Women Do

As the national economy has shifted from manufacturing to services, the distribution of the labor force by occupations and by industries has changed. In this context, this chapter focuses on changes in the distribution of native-born and immigrant women across occupations. The next chapter will focus on changes across industries.

Changes in the occupational distribution of women have generally mirrored those in the economy as a whole. But, occupational differences between men and women have remained remarkably constant even though women have increased their share in the managerial and professional occupations more rapidly than men. Over time, there has been a remarkable similarity between the occupational distribution of native-born and immigrant women. But, there are some exceptions. The latter are increasing their relative share in the low-skill occupations—especially in occupations where communication skills and English proficiency are not critical to the job. Immigrant women are also less likely to fill occupations requiring certification in the United States. Overall, however, we find no evidence of occupational segmentation between native-born and immigrant women who have similar levels of education.[1]

This chapter first examines trends in the occupational distribution of the labor force as a whole and of the female labor force in particular. The second section, then, describes changes in the occupational distribution of immigrant women and compares them to those of native-born women. The last section analyzes in greater detail the "division of labor" between immigrant and native-born workers.

Occupational Changes in the Nation's Economy

As the national economy has shifted from manufacturing to services, there has been a steady increase in the share of workers in high-skill occupations and a corresponding decrease in the share of workers in low-skill occupations (figure 5.1). The share of managerial, professional, and technical occupations in the labor force increased from one in every five workers in 1960

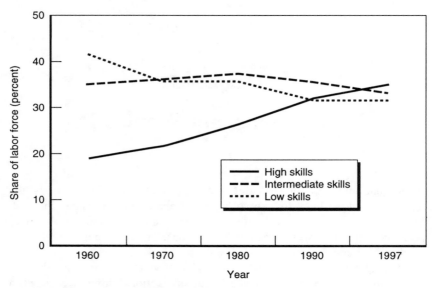

Sources: 1960, 1970, 1980, and 1990 PUMS and the 1997 Current Population Survey of the U.S. Bureau of the Census.
Note: High-skill occupations include executive, administrative, managerial, professional, and technical occupations; intermediate-skill occupations include sales, clerical, administrative support, precision-production and craft occupations, and supervisors; and low-skill occupations include laborers, machine operators, assemblers, personal-service providers, and farm workers.

Figure 5.1—Occupational Distributions by Skills, in the Nation and in California, 1960–1997

to more than one in every three workers in 1997. At the same time, the proportion of operatives, laborers, and farm workers has declined from one in every three to one in every five workers.

Meanwhile, the share of the labor force in intermediate-skill occupations has remained relatively constant at about one-third of the labor force. Within this grouping, there has been a shift from craftspeople and supervisors toward clerical workers. The share of craftspeople and supervisors declined from 14 percent in 1960 to 11 percent in 1997 as technology allowed major productivity gains in these occupations. At the same time, the share of clerical workers increased from 14 to 17 percent, and the share of retail and service workers has remained relatively constant.

On the aggregate, changes in the occupational distribution of women have mirrored those in the economy as a whole. Table 5.1 shows that their share in high-skill occupations has more than doubled; their share in low-skill occupations has declined in the same proportion as in the economy as a whole; and their share in intermediate-skilled occupations has remained relatively constant, at least until 1990. In the slow economic growth of the 1990s, the share of workers in these occupations has declined somewhat. But, women have increased their share in managerial and professional occupations more rapidly than men and decreased their share in low-skill occupations more rapidly than men.

The occupational distribution of women within each of the three major groupings—high-skill, intermediate-skill, and low-skill occupations—differs markedly from that of the economy as a whole, and, hence, from male labor. These occupational differences between female and male workers have remained remarkably constant over time as is shown in table 5.2. Within high-skill occupations, women are more likely to be professionals such as teachers and health specialists than they are to be managers. This differential, however, has narrowed over time. For instance, the share of women in managerial

Table 5.1

Distribution of Labor Force by Major Occupations, Nation, 1960–1997

Occupations	Share of Total Labor Force			Share of All Women Workers			Percentage of Women in the Occupation		
	1960	1990	1997	1960	1990	1997	1960	1990	1997
High-skill occupations									
Executive, professional, technical	19.0	31.7	34.8	16.2	31.4	35.5	28.1	5.4	47.4
Intermediate-skill occupations									
Sales, clerical	21.1	25.1	23.0	37.0	37.8	34.7	57.5	68.9	70.2
Craftsperson/ supervisory	13.7	10.6	10.1	1.2	1.9	1.6	2.9	10.4	9.8
Subtotal	34.8	35.7	33.1	38.2	39.7	36.3	36.1	51.4	50.4
Low-skill occupations									
Service worker	11.2	13.7	14.1	21.2	17.1	18.4	62.9	59.2	60.5
Machine operator, laborer	24.1	16.5	15.8	6.8	8.7	7.7	24.7	30.7	25.0
Farm worker	5.9	1.6	1.7	1.7	.7	.8	9.6	18.8	22.9
Subtotal	41.2	31.8	31.6	39.7	26.5	26.9	31.8	40.2	42.0
All Others	5.1	.8	.4	5.9	2.4	1.3	NA	NA	NA
Total	100.0	100.0	100.00	100.0	100.0	100.00	32.9	45.8	46.5

Sources: 1970 and 1990 PUMS and the 1997 Current Population Survey of the U.S. Bureau of the Census.

Note: NA means not available.

Table 5.2

Distribution of the Labor Force by Occupations and by Gender, Nation, 1970–1997

Occupation/Skills	Women			Men		
	1970	1990	1997	1970	1990	1997
High-skill occupations						
Executive/managerial	3.4	10.6	13.9	10.5	15.1	17.8
Professional	13.3	18.3	19.2	11.5	13.4	13.8
Engineer	.1	.3	.4	2.6	2.5	2.8
Math/computer	.1	.5	.8	.4	.8	1.4
Health specialist	3.1	4.2	4.4	1.1	1.5	1.5
Teacher	7.3	7.2	7.3	2.4	2.6	2.6
Other professional	2.7	5.9	6.1	4.6	5.5	5.0
Technical	1.0	2.5	2.4	2.0	3.5	2.1
Computer programmer	0	.4	.3	0	.7	.6
Subtotal	17.7	31.4	35.5	24.0	32.0	33.7
Intermediate-skill occupations						
Salesperson	6.7	6.3	5.9	6.5	6.6	6.1
Clerical worker	32.3	31.5	28.8	7.1	7.8	6.7
Craftsperson/supervisor	1.7	1.9	1.6	20.0	17.9	17.6
Subtotal	40.7	39.7	36.3	33.6	32.3	30.4
Low-skill occupations						
Machine operator	13.4	7.1	6.1	12.9	9.3	8.7
Laborer	.9	1.6	1.6	6.3	7.3	7.4
Service worker	18.6	17.1	18.4	7.5	10.3	7.9
Private household staff	3.5	.9	1.2	.1	.0	.0
Personal service worker	2.6	3.6	4.1	.8	.7	.8
Cook	1.8	1.8	1.6	.7	1.6	1.9
Food preparer	4.9	4.2	4.2	1.2	1.9	2.1
Health service worker	3.6	3.5	3.6	.3	.4	.4
Janitor	2.0	2.5	2.4	2.6	3.0	2.7
Protective service worker	.2`	.6	1.0	1.8	2.7	2.6
Transportion worker	.4	.9	.8	5.5	5.7	6.0
Farm worker	.8	.7	.8	4.2	2.4	2.4
Subtotal	34.1	27.4	27.7	36.4	35.0	35.0
Others	7.5	1.5	.5	6.0	.7	.9
Total	100.0	100.0	100.00	100.0	100.0	100.0

Sources: 1970 and 1990 PUMS and the 1997 Current Population Survey of the U.S. Bureau of the Census.

occupations has increased more rapidly than for men, from 3 percent in 1970 to 14 percent in 1990 compared to an increase from 10 to 18 percent for men. Women, however, continue to dominate the teaching and health occupations.

Women are more likely than men to work in intermediate-skill occupations and to perform significantly different work, a difference that has persisted over time. In 1970, women were more than four times more likely than men to work in clerical occupations, which was still the case by 1997. About one out of three women work in clerical occupations compared to one in fifteen men. However, men are ten times more likely to be craftspeople and supervisors than are women. Finally, women and men are just as likely to be working as salespersons, and that tendency has remained unchanged over the past 27 years.

Similarly significant differences exist in the distribution of occupations between women and men in low-skill occupations. Typically, women have been performing primarily service work including household work, food preparation, and personal and health services, whereas men have primarily been occupied as laborers and farm workers. The share of women in services occupations and the share of men who are laborers has remained constant over time. However, the share of men working in farming occupations has been cut in half from 4 to about 2 percent of the male labor force. And both men and women have seen their share in machine-operation occupations cut in half over the past 27 years.

Changes in Occupations of Immigrant Women

Over the years, immigrant women have increased their presence in all occupations. Figure 5.2 displays the 1970 to 1997 changes in the share of immigrants in the female labor force by occupations in the nation.

It shows that immigrant women are more highly concentrated in low-skill occupations than native-born women, primarily in the machine-operation, private household, cleaning and service-to-buildings, and farming occupations. The relative concentration of immigrant women in these occupations has increased most particularly in private household, janitorial, machine-operation, and cooking occupations.

The reverse trend has taken place in high-skill occupations where the relative concentration of immigrant women has generally remained constant or has declined over time. For instance, the relative concentration of immigrant women has declined 11 percent among health professionals, 25 percent in management occupations, and 29 percent among teachers. The relative share of immigrant women among engineers has increased, however, as has the concentration of immigrant women in computer related occupations including both hardware and software programming.

In intermediate-skill occupations, the relative concentration of immigrant women has remained constant with the exception of sales occupations where the relative share of immigrant women has declined.

In brief, immigrant women have increasingly filled the slow-growing number of jobs in low-skilled occupations, and native-born women have increasingly filled the fast-growing number of jobs in high-skill occupations.

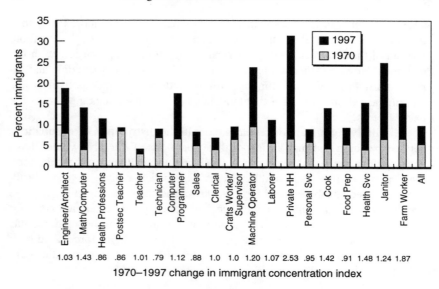

1970–1997 change in immigrant concentration index

Sources: 1970 PUMS and the 1997 Current Population Survey of the U.S. Bureau of the Census.

Figure 5.2—Share of Immigrant Women in the Female Labor Force by Major Occupations, Nation, 1970–1997

Table 5.3 displays the relatively slow growth of low-skilled occupations and the simultaneous acceleration of the growth of high-skill occupations. In the 1960s, 1980s, and 1990s—few jobs in low-skill occupations were added to the economy. There was, however, a more vigorous growth in low-skill jobs during the 1970s, suggesting that the growth of the latter is sensitive to the overall national growth. By contrast, the growth in high-skill occupations steadily accelerated relative to aggregate growth of the economy; it grew one-third more rapidly in the 1960s and eventually more than two times more rapidly in the 1980s and 1990s. Growth in intermediate-skilled occupations has been somewhat less than proportional to overall national growth.

The net result of these trends has been a growing disparity in the occupational distribution between immigrant and native-born women (table 5.4). Whereas, the share of immigrant women in low-skill occupations has remained relatively constant over the past 27 years—at more than 40 percent—the share of native-born women in these occupations has declined from one-third to one-quarter. Both groups, however, have increased their share in high-skill occupations.

Table 5.3

Changes in Occupations by Skill Level, Total and Women, Nation 1960–1997

Occupations	Number (Thousands)					Decennial Growth (Percent)			
	1960	1970	1980	1990	1997	1960–1969	1970–1979	1980–1989	1990–1997
All									
High-skill occupations	12,814	17,177	24,523	39,116	47,124	24.3	60.2	42.1	29.3
Intermediate-skill occupations	23,523	29,028	38,958	43,932	44,296	12.3	34.2	12.8	2.8
Low-skill occupations	27,768	28,375	36,864	39,181	42,699	2.2	29.9	6.3	12.7
Not classified	13,469	5,303	736	1,016	606	—	—	—	—
Total	67,574	79,883	104,081	123,245	134,725	18.2	30.3	18.4	13.8
Women									
High-skill occupations	3,595	5,416	10,514	17,751	22,336	50.7	94.1	68.8	36.9
Intermediate-skill occupations	8,485	12,505	19,026	22,389	22,821	47.4	52.1	17.7	2.7
Low-skill occupations	8,835	10,442	14,529	15,768	17,427	18.2	39.1	8.5	15.0
Not classified	1,327	2,320	434	553	316	—	—	—	—
Total	22,242	30,683	44,503	56,461	62,900	38.0	45.0	26.9	16.3

Sources: 1960, 1970, 1980, and 1990 PUMS and the 1997 Current Population Survey of the U.S. Bureau of the Census.

Table 5.4

**Distribution of Women by Occupations and by Immigration Status, Nation,
1970–1997**

Occupation/Skills	Native-Born			Immigrant		
	1970	1990	1997	1970	1990	1997
High-skill occupations						
Executive	3.4	10.9	14.2	3.3	8.2	10.4
Professional	13.5	18.6	19.5	10.7	14.6	16.1
Engineer	.1	.3	.4	.1	.5	.8
Math/computer	.1	.5	.8	.1	.5	1.1
Health specialist	3.1	4.2	4.3	6.0	4.6	5.0
Teacher	7.5	7.5	7.7	3.9	3.9	3.4
Other professional	2.7	6.0	6.1	2.6	4.8	5.4
Technical	1.1	2.5	2.8	1.3	2.6	2.5
Computer programmer	0	.4	.3	0	.6	.5
Subtotal	17.9	32.0	36.5	15.3	25.4	29.0
Intermediate-skill occupations						
Salesperson	6.7	6.4	6.0	6.5	5.2	4.9
Clerical worker	32.8	32.3	29.8	24.4	23.4	19.8
Craftsperson/supervisor	1.7	1.9	1.6	2.0	2.3	1.5
Subtotal	41.2	40.6	37.4	32.9	30.9	26.2
Low-skill occupations						
Machine operator	12.8	6.4	5.2	23.6	14.8	14.5
Laborer	.9	1.6	1.6	.9	1.8	1.8
Service worker	18.4	16.4	17.0	20.5	22.6	25.4
Private household staff	3.4	.7	.9	4.5	3.0	3.8
Personal service worker	2.6	3.6	4.1	3.0	3.8	3.6
Cook	1.8	1.7	1.5	1.5	2.1	2.2
Food preparer	4.9	4.2	4.3	5.0	3.9	3.9
Health service worker	3.6	3.4	3.4	2.9	4.3	5.5
Janitor	1.9	2.2	2.0	3.5	5.2	5.9
Protective service worker	.2	.6	.8	> .1	.3	.6
Transportation worker	.4	.9	.8	.1	.4	.5
Farm worker	.7	.6	.8	.9	1.5	1.3
Subtotal	33.2	25.9	24.4	46.0	41.1	43.5
Others	7.7	1.5	.7	5.8	2.6	1.3
Total	100.0	100.0	100.00	100.0	100.0	100.0

Sources: 1970 and 1990 PUMS and the 1997 Current Population Survey of the
U.S. Bureau of the Census.

Indeed, there is a remarkable similarity in the share of both immigrant
and native-born women in most of the twenty-two occupations displayed on
table 5.4. For instance, immigrant and native-born women are generally just
as likely to work in occupations as disparate as engineers, health profes-

sionals, and technicians as they are to work as salespersons, craftspeople, cooks, laborers, or providers of personal and health services. A number of notable exceptions exist, however. In 1997, immigrant women were much less likely than native-born women to be teachers, other professionals (including lawyers and social workers), or to work in clerical occupations. The share of immigrant women working as teachers was more than half that of native-born women (3 versus 8 percent) and the share working in clerical occupations was one-third lower (20 versus 29 percent). These differences have remained constant since 1970. On the other hand, immigrant women were typically three times more likely than native-born women to operate machines, to clean and service buildings, and to provide private-household services. These latter differences have increased slightly over time.

"Division of Labor" between Native-Born and Immigrant Women

The relative increase in the concentration of immigrant women in low-skill occupations reflects a higher share of immigrant women with low levels of education compared with native-born women. Table 5.5 shows that the distribution of immigrant women by occupations is remarkably similar after controlling for education. It also shows that within a given education level, immigrant women were consistently less likely to be employed in an occupation requiring communications skills, proficiency in the English language, and/or certification for certain professional services. These differences in "division of labor" within a specific level of education are larger at lower than at higher levels of education.

Consider female workers with fewer than 12 years of education; at this level of education, a higher share of immigrants than native-borns work in low-skill occupations (79 versus 55 percent), whereas the reverse is the case in intermediate-skill occupations (13 versus 34 percent). All of this differential, however, is accounted for by immigrant women being twice as likely as native-born women to work as machine operators (32 versus 12 percent) and, conversely, half as likely to work in clerical and sales occupations (11 versus 32 percent). The first set of occupations are "backroom" occupations that do not require frequent if any contacts with clients, the public, or coworkers, whereas the second set of occupations requires contacts requiring proficiency in English, which immigrant adults with fewer than 12 years of education are less likely to develop even over several years.[2]

Among female workers with fewer than 12 years of education, immigrant and native-born women are just as likely to be working in service occupations. They perform generally different tasks, however. Immigrant women are significantly more likely than native-born women to be working in private households, cleaning and servicing buildings, and farming. By contrast, native-born women are more likely to work as cooks and in food preparation.

Table 5.5

Distribution of Female Workers by Occupation, Education, and Immigration Status, Nation, 1997

Occupations/Skills	Education (Years)							
	<12		12		13–15		16+	
	I	N	I	N	I	N	I	N
High-skill occupations								
Executive	3.4	5.4	9.8	12.1	13.0	15.5	15.7	19.3
Professional	1.8	1.8	3.8	4.7	12.9	14.7	45.6	54.3
Engineer	0	0	0	.1	.7	.1	2.5	1.3
Math/computer	0	0	.3	.3	.6	.7	3.6	2.0
Health professional	.1	.2	.4	.4	4.5	5.7	15.0	9.8
Teacher	.5	.8	1.2	1.4	1.8	3.1	9.8	25.2
Other professional	1.2	.8	1.9	2.5	5.3	5.1	13.2	14.7
Technical	.6	.7	1.0	2.2	4.6	4.9	4.8	2.4
Computer programmer	0	.1		.1	.6	.2	1.4	.7
Subtotal	5.8	7.9	14.4	18.7	30.1	33.7	66.1	75.5
Intermediate-skill occupations								
Salesperson	2.3	5.9	5.9	5.6	8.5	6.8	3.3	5.7
Clerical worker	8.8	25.8	21.8	37.8	32.6	36.0	16.6	12.8
Craftsperson/ supervisor	2.1	2.4	2.3	2.2	1.3	1.5	.3	.4
Subtotal	13.2	34.1	30.0	45.6	42.4	44.3	20.2	18.9
Low-skill occupations								
Machine operator	31.9	11.7	17.5	8.7	5.5	2.8	2.7	.4
Laborer	3.8	3.7	1.7	2.3	1.1	1.0	.5	.4
Service worker	39.6	37.0	33.9	21.9	18.1	14.9	9.3	3.8
Private household	8.5	3.2	3.5	1.1	2.3	.6	1.0	.1
Personal service	4.0	3.9	6.0	5.3	2.5	4.7	1.7	1.7
Cook	4.0	4.6	3.3	2.3	1.4	.7	.1	.1
Food preparer	5.5	12.9	5.2	4.7	3.2	3.6	1.4	.8
Health service	4.6	5.3	8.9	4.8	5.9	3.5	2.6	.5
Janitorial	12.6	6.4	6.6	2.9	2.4	.9	1.9	.1
Protective service	.4	.7	.4	.8	.4	.9	.6	.5
Transportation worker	.8	1.2	.8	1.3	.8	.7	0	.2
Farm worker	3.6	1.7	.2	.9	.8	.6	.5	.4
Subtotal	79.7	55.3	54.1	35.1	26.3	20.0	13.0	5.2
Others	1.3	2.7	1.5	1.6	.7	2.0	.7	.4
Total	100.0	100.0	100.0	100.0	100.0	100.0	100.0	100.0

Source: 1997 Current Population Survey of the U.S. Bureau of the Census.
Note: I means immigrant and N means native-born.

A similar pattern of division of labor is notable among women with a high school education only, that is, 12 years of schooling. In 1997, immigrant women were half as likely to work in clerical occupations and twice as likely to work as machine operators than native-born women. In addition, high school graduate immigrant women were also more likely to work in service occupations than their native-born counterparts (34 versus 22 percent). This is primarily a result of the higher share of immigrant women working in private households, cleaning and servicing buildings, and health services. In turn, native-born women are more likely to work in management and professional occupations although the differential here is not large (15 versus 19 percent).

Now consider college graduates. At this level of education, two-thirds of immigrant women and three-fourths of native-born women are working in high-skill occupations. This differential is mostly because immigrant women are nearly three times less likely than native-born women to be employed as teachers (9 versus 25 percent). Teaching in the United States, as in most other countries, requires not only a college education, it also requires certification, which immigrant women are less likely to acquire after they have arrived here. Certification requires going back to college to take specialized college courses including becoming more familiar with U.S. norms and history, which immigrants may be reluctant to do for economic reasons. As a result, college graduate immigrant women are more likely than native-born women to work in other professions including engineering, technical occupations, and health related occupations, all occupations whose requirements are more universally shared. Also noteworthy is the higher proportion of immigrant than native-born women working as computer programmers.

The large differential in the share of clerical and machine operation noted between immigrant and native-born women who are high school dropouts or graduates only, not only disappears among college graduates, it is reversed. Immigrant female college graduates are more likely to work in clerical occupations than native-born women, providing further support to the view that poor knowledge of English is a main reason why at the lower levels of education immigrant women are less likely to access these occupations than their native-born counterparts.

In our introductory chapter, we noted that organizations that help immigrants and refugees find jobs in the United States were concerned that professionals schooled in foreign countries could not readily transfer their credentials here and hence were finding themselves without opportunities to continue practicing their chosen professions. The data presented in table 5.5 suggests that this problem is not widespread. A majority of college-educated immigrant women can find jobs, if they exist, for which they were prepared in their own country or after acquiring the necessary certification here. The data, however, also lend some support to the view that immigrant women are more likely than native-born women to find themselves unable to find such jobs. Twice as many college-graduate immigrant women (12 percent) work in low-skill occupations as do native-born women (5 percent). These immigrant women are more likely to work as operators or to provide health services than native-born women. Although a relatively small share, the absolute number of such immigrant women is not negligible.

Conclusions

As immigrant women have increased in numbers, they also have increased their presence in all occupations of the national economy. At the same time, their concentration in low-skill occupations has increased more rapidly than in intermediate- and high-skill occupations. As a result, disparities between native-born and immigrant women in their respective distribution across occupations have increased over time.

Still, and after controlling for education, there is a remarkable similarity in the occupational distribution between native-born and immigrant women. This finding portrays a female labor force in which both native-born and immigrant women operate within the context of an integrated labor market. To the extent that one group is more concentrated than the other in some occupations, this reflects their respective educational endowments, the need of certain occupations for certification (i.e., teachers), and the need for face-to-face communications requiring proficiency in the English language.

Although some mostly low-skill occupations have a relatively high concentration of immigrant women, no one occupation is yet dominated by female immigrants. Even in the occupations with the highest concentration of immigrant women, their share did not exceed a third, a finding that undermines the suggestion often found in the popular press that there are jobs that native-borns do not want to perform.

Similarly, we find only weak evidence suggesting that college-educated immigrant women have widespread difficulties because of certification difficulties in finding jobs in the professions they may have been trained for in their home countries. The one piece of evidence pointing in this direction is the slightly higher share of college graduate immigrant women working in low-skill occupations compared with native-born women. Overall, however, the occupational distribution of immigrant women who are college graduates is similar to that of native-born women.

However, the relatively low share of immigrant women who are teachers may reflect either a strong selectivity among immigrants away from this profession or, indeed, difficulties in obtaining certification to pursue this vocation in the United States. The latter instance suggests the existence of a potential pool of would-be teachers that until now has remained untapped. Given the large expected increases in K–12 and eventually in postsecondary enrollments in the next decade—most particularly in the high-immigration states of California, New York, and Florida—and the resulting need to recruit large numbers of new teachers, this potentially untapped supply should be further explored. These college-educated immigrant women have the additional advantage of being fluent in the language and the culture of many of their potential students.

Notes

1. Card (1996), examining occupational differences between native-borns and immigrants, reached a similar conclusion for the nation as a whole, and so did McCarthy and Vernez (1997) for California.

2. Another potential reason for the "division of labor" at the lower end of the educational distribution might be a differential in wages—that is, native-born women having greater access than immigrant women to higher-paying occupations. The data, however, do not support this view. In 1990, a native-born woman earned less in a clerical occupation (an average $6.90 per hour) than as a machine operator ($7.40 per hour). For immigrant women the reverse was true: immigrant women were paid on the average more in clerical ($7.80) than in machine-operation ($7.00) occupations.

Chapter 6

Where Immigrant Women Work

As the share of immigrant women has increased in all occupations, so has their share in all industries of the national economy. Notable variations across industries are examined in this chapter. The first section examines how the distribution of immigrant women across the nation's industries has changed over time. In the second section, we examine the extent to which immigrant and native-born female labor play differing roles within an industry. Some industries—such as textile and apparel, private households, and perishable agriculture—are often portrayed as being predominantly dependent on immigrant labor for their competitive survival. We examine this question in the last two sections: first, by looking at the type of industries in which immigrants are highly concentrated in either share or number, and second, by analyzing in detail their characteristics.

Immigrant Women Work in All Sectors of the Economy

Figure 6.1 shows that the 1997 distribution of immigrant women across the nation's industry has remained relatively the same over time. Where immigrant women were disproportionately represented in 1970, they remained so in 1997. Indeed, in these sectors—which include agriculture, durable and nondurable manufacturing, business/repair, and personal services—immigrant women increased somewhat their concentration as indicated by the ratio of their 1997 to 1970 concentration index of more than one. By contrast, in industries in which immigrant women were underrepresented in 1970—construction, communications, utilities, and government—they continued to be underrepresented in 1997. However, in communications and government, the share of immigrant women has increased more rapidly than in the nation as a whole, whereas in the other two sectors the share of immigrant women has declined.

In all other sectors shown in figure 6.1—including such large sectors as education, health, other professional, and retail—the concentration of immigrant women has remained proportional to the share of immigrant women in the overall female labor force.

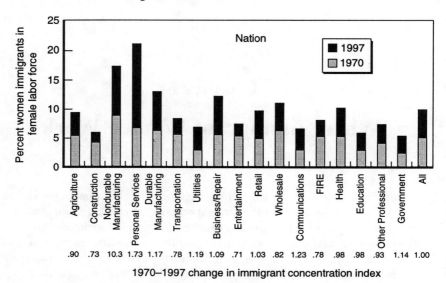

1970–1997 change in immigrant concentration index

Sources: 1990 PUMS and the 1997 Current Population Survey of the U.S. Bureau of the Census.

Figure 6.1—Share of Immigrant Women in Female Labor Force by Industry, Nation, 1970–1997

"Division of Labor" within Sectors of the Economy

In all sectors, immigrant and native-born women and men work side by side, but their role within a sector is all the more differentiated the lower skilled the sector is. In low-skill sectors, immigrant women, as well as men, are more likely to provide the labor force in the "back office," while higher educated native-born women and men are more likely to be in the "front office." This division of labor is consistent with the lower participation of immigrants in occupations that require contacts with the public and/or fluency in the English language. In high-skill industries, in contrast, no apparent differentiation exists between the role of immigrant and native-born labor.

We grouped industries into three groups, low-skill, medium-skill, and high-skill, according to the average years of schooling of the individuals in each labor force (table 6.1). In low-skill sectors—including agriculture, construction, nondurable manufacturing, and personal services—there is a sharp split between immigrant and native-born workers: among women, the first averaged 10.8 years and the latter 12.8 years, or a two-years difference; among men, immigrants similarly averaged 9.8 years and native-borns, 12.7

Table 6.1

Educational Characteristics of the Labor Force by Type of Industry and Immigration Status, Nation, 1997 (Percent)

Industries	Mean Years			>12 Years			<16 Years			Percent of Total Employment	Percent of All Immigrants	Share of Immigrants in Industry
	All	I	N	All	I	N	All	I	N			
Women												
Low-skill[a]	13	11	13	19	41	15	15	18	15	14	22	17
Medium-skill[b]	13	13	13	12	22	11	19	21	18	37	39	10
High-skill[c]	14	14	14	5	9	4	35	46	37	49	38	8
Men												
Low-skill[a]	12	10	13	26	55	19	15	12	15	24	29	15
Medium-skill[b]	13	12	13	15	29	14	21	27	21	51	52	13
High-skill[c]	15	15	15	4	8	4	50	59	49	24	18	10

Source: 1997 Current Population Survey of the U.S. Bureau of the Census.

Note: I means immigrant and N means native-born.

[a]Includes agriculture, construction, nondurable manufacturing, and personal services.

[b]Includes durable manufacturing, transportation, utilities, wholesale and retail trade, business/repair, and entertainment.

[c]Includes communications, FIRE, health, education, other professional, and government.

years of education, an even sharper difference. Immigrants in low-skill industries—both men and women—are also two times more likely to have fewer than 12 years of education than native-born workers. In 1997, one in every six women workers in low-skill industries was an immigrant compared to one in 17 in 1970. These industries accounted for about 22 percent of immigrant women (as well as immigrant men) in 1997.

By contrast, in high-skill sectors—communications, FIRE, health, education, other professional, and government—which account for about 40 percent of immigrant women and 50 percent of native-born women, immigrant and native-born women have the same educational characteristics. In these industries, immigrant women (as well as men) are even more likely to be college educated than native-borns, and there is no difference in the average years of schooling between the two, 14.3 versus 14.2 years for women and 15.3 and 15.0 years for men. In these industries, immigrant women constitute 8 percent of the labor force, up from 4 percent since 1970. As noted in chapter 4, these industries have traditionally employed a higher share of women than men, hence, the higher share of immigrant women working in these industries (38 percent) than the share of immigrant men (18 percent).

The "division of labor" in medium-skill industries—business/repair, entertainment, durable manufacturing, retail, transportation, utilities, and wholesale—falls somewhere in between these two extremes. Immigrant women are just as likely as native-born women to have some college; about 20 percent of both groups do. But immigrant women are more likely than native born women to have fewer than 12 years of education (22 versus 11 percent). These industries employed about 40 percent of both native-born and immigrant women.

Industrial Niches for Immigrant Women

The ten national industries with the highest share of immigrant women in their female labor force in 1997 are listed in table 6.2. These industries, often credited by the popular press as having high concentrations of female immigrants, include such sizeable industries as private households, laundry and cleaning, services to buildings (janitorial services), and textiles and apparel. They also include smaller industries such as food preparation, groceries, and the now fast-growing computer and accounting machine industry. Seven of these ten industries are service industries whereas the other three are manufacturing industries.

As of 1997, none of these industries was dominated by immigrant women. With one exception—shoe repair—the share of immigrant women in these industries did not exceed one-third of their labor force, suggesting that they have not yet come to dominate the female labor force of these industries. However, the share of immigrant women has increased steadily since the 1970s and has particularly accelerated since 1990. For instance, in 1970, 13

Table 6.2

Industries with the Highest Share of Immigrant Women in the Female Labor Force, Nation and California, 1970–1997

Industries	Nation				California			
	Percent Immigrant Women			Number of Immigrants	Percent Immigrant Women			Number of Immigrants
	1970	1990	1997	1997	1970	1990	1997	1997
Shoe repair	7.3	20.7	42.1	2,736	NA	36.7	NA	124
Laundry/cleaning	6.5	18.4	36.8	107,196	19.3	52.2	85.0	38,166
Apparel/fabrics	14.4	23.4	34.6	20,241	16.1	46.3	39.8	3,116
Private households	6.9	26.6	30.0	262,920	17.2	59.9	64.6	115,885
Textile/apparel	12.5	19.5	27.6	289,727	45.1	75.6	83.8	104,663
Services to buildings	15.1	20.6	27.4	129,204	13.6	52.3	85.8	41,570
Hotel/motel	7.9	17.0	23.4	186,208	17.2	43.3	47.3	47,334
Food and food preparation	7.6	16.9	22.9	94,363	19.7	53.0	60.1	24,531
Groceries and related	7.7	12.8	22.5	54,508	14.7	36.5	43.3	14,757
Computers and accounting machines	7.0	14.4	20.6	50,264	9.6	29.3	17.8	10,705
Total				1,197,367				400,727
Percent of total immigrant women	23.3	16.4	18.9		22.0	19.0	20.8	

Source: 1970 and 1990 PUMS of the U.S. Bureau of the Census.

Note: Blank means not applicable, NA means not available.

percent of the textile and apparel industry female labor force was foreign-born; this share increased to 20 percent in 1990 and eventually to 28 percent in 1997. Disproportionate increases in the share of immigrant women have also occurred in the laundry and cleaning, groceries, shoe repair, and computer and accounting machines industries. The ten industries with the highest share of immigrant women continue to account for nearly one out of every five immigrant women compared to only one out of every fifteen native-born women.

A glimpse at how immigrant women are coming to dominate the female labor force of these industries can be gained by examining trends in those same industries in the state of California (table 6.2).

In 1997 in California, immigrant women constituted a majority of the female labor force in six of these ten industries. In three of these industries—laundry and cleaning, textile and apparel, and services to buildings—nearly the entire (85 percent) female labor force is foreign-born. In the private household and food preparation industries, a high two-thirds of the female labor force is foreign-born. As at the national level, the share of immigrant women in those industries has increased steadily since 1970.

As disproportionate as the share of immigrant labor in these industries is, much larger numbers of immigrants work in other industries including high-skill industries such as hospitals, doctors' offices and clinics, educational institutions, banks, and even the government (table 6.3). Although these industries frequently have a less than proportionate share of immigrant women, they are large industries. In 1997, doctors' offices and clinics employed more immigrant women than any other industry and twice as many as the textile and apparel industry or the private household industry. Moreover, although immigrant women were significantly less likely than their native-born counterparts to be teachers, 262,000 immigrant women were employed in the nation's primary and secondary schools and another 364,000 were employed in the nation's libraries, universities, colleges, and preschool educational institutions. Overall, half of all immigrant women were employed in these industries, a decline from about two-thirds in 1970, further underlining the dispersal of immigrant female labor throughout the economy.

Many of the industries with the largest number of immigrants are high-skill industries, reflecting the combination of two trends already noted in previous chapters. The first is simply that the number of college-educated immigrant female laborers has increased, even though their rate of increase has been slower than for less-educated immigrants. And the second is that low-educated immigrants are filling jobs previously held by native-born workers in the low-skill occupations that are still needed by even high-skill industries, although in sharply decreasing numbers.

These trends are illustrated in table 6.4, which shows the number of jobs held by women added or lost from 1980 to 1997, in total and by level of education, and the number of these jobs filled by immigrant women (rows in ital-

Table 6.3

Industries with Highest Number of Immigrant Women, Nation and California, 1970–1997

Industries	Nation				California			
	Percent Immigrant Women			Number of Immigrants	Percent Immigrant Women			Number of Immigrants
	1970	1990	1997	1997	1970	1990	1997	1997
Office/clinic	5.1	7.5	10.9	565,326	9.7	19.4	28.1	130,713
Eat/drink places	5.7	9.5	12.0	454,013	11.8	28.2	43.9	145,650
Hospitals	5.9	9.1	9.5	386,238	10.5	26.6	23.5	102,749
Textile/apparel	12.5	19.5	27.6	289,727	45.1	75.6	83.9	104,663
Private households	6.9	26.6	30.0	262,920	17.2	59.9	64.6	115,885
Schools	2.6	4.4	5.0	262,592	4.4	11.6	14.7	87,380
Business services	5.4	8.0	10.0	246,591	8.6	17.4	20.3	67,612
Education	4.5	7.0	6.9	214,320	6.9	18.6	19.1	59,684
Hotel/motel	7.9	17.0	23.4	186,208	17.2	43.3	47.3	47,334
Banking/credit	5.5	8.7	9.3	181,996	12.5	21.7	24.3	37,526
Food stores	4.7	5.3	8.4	174,957	8.7	21.1	30.4	43,736
Colleges/universities	5.4	8.2	9.0	150,363	8.6	16.9	24.1	31,255
Government	2.6	4.9	5.6	140,542	4.2	12.5	12.0	
Total				3,515,793				1,008,084
Percent of total immigrant women	67.6	52.1	48.7		67.1	47.8	52.3	

Source: 1970 and 1990 PUMS of the U.S. Bureau of the Census.

Note: Blank means not applicable.

ics) in selected high-skill and in selected low-skill industries.[1] These industries account for nearly half (47 percent) of the net number of jobs created by the national economy since 1980 and 54 percent of the increase in the number of jobs filled by immigrant women.

Both high- and low-skill industries have lost jobs filled by female workers with fewer than 12 years of education, in spite of vigorous growth in all but one of these industries. For instance, between 1980 and 1997, high-skill industries such as hospitals lost 380,000 jobs held by persons with fewer than 12 years of education and elementary and secondary schools lost 178,000 such jobs in spite of an increase in net jobs of 570,000 and 1,247,000, respectively. Even some low-skill industries typically viewed as immigrant-dependent industries, such as private households, lost 66,000 jobs held by persons with fewer than 12 years of education and only 11,000 net new such jobs were added to the eat/drink industry in spite of a net increase of more than one million jobs. Also, nearly all of the 535,000 net jobs lost in the textile and apparel industry were lost by female workers with fewer than 12 years of education.

Most of the 1.2 million jobs lost to female workers with fewer than 12 years of education were lost by native-born women. Whereas in the industries listed on table 6.4, the number of jobs filled by immigrant women declined by 62,000, it decreased by 1.1 million for native-born women. The decline in the number of jobs filled by immigrant women is a result of the decline of the textile and apparel industry. Excluding the latter, the number of immigrant women with fewer than 12 years of education increased by 315,000.

The pattern described above reinforces a point we made earlier—that is, that the number of jobs available to low-educated labor in the national economy is declining increasingly rapidly for both native-born and immigrant women alike. The remaining low-skill jobs vacated by an increasingly college-educated native-born labor force are being filled by low-educated immigrant women especially in low-skill industries. Whether this process is demand-driven (i.e., employers need greater skills because of advances in technology) or supply-driven (i.e., a large number of college-educated persons are available) cannot be disentangled. The fact remains, however, that employers are hiring primarily people with a college education to fill the net new jobs they generate. Indeed, the largest increase in net jobs in female high-skill industries listed in table 6.4 have been filled by women with college degrees, followed by women with some college.

Even industries typically viewed as low-skill are not immune to this upward educational process including the textile and apparel, eat and drink places, and the hotel and motel industries. All three industries added jobs filled by persons with some college even in the face of a net overall loss in their number of jobs.

This creeping up of the education of women filling the jobs added to the economy is also leading toward a slowdown, and, most likely in the future, a

Table 6.4

**Change in Total Number of Jobs Filled by Women and by Immigrant Women
by Selected High- and Low-Skill Industries and by Level of Education,
Nation, 1980–1997 (Thousands)**

Industries	Total	Level of Education (Years)			
		<12	12	13–15	16+
High-skill					
Offices/clinics	2,924	−40	873	1,263	827
	432	*47*	*129*	*108*	*147*
Business Services	1,394	108	267	555	463
	179	*37*	*31*	*45*	*65*
Elementary and	1,247	−178	60	328	1,037
secondary schools	*125*	*7*	*24*	*35*	*58*
Hospitals	568	−80	−291	582	656
	127	*−11*	*−6*	*56*	*89*
Colleges/universities	497	−34	−91	260	363
	78	*1*	*5*	*17*	*55*
Banking, savings and	378	−104	−180	398	264
credit	*76*	*−7*	*1*	*37*	*44*
Government	342	−159	−260	374	387
	57	*−1*	*−3*	*20*	*40*
Low-skill					
Eat/drink places	1,030	11	341	548	130
	269	*64*	*111*	*62*	*49*
Private households	192	−66	120	118	20
	180	*90*	*46*	*30*	*15*
Hotels/motels	228	0	76	87	65
	122	*42*	*38*	*15*	*26*
Services to buildings	347	115	155	66	10
	113	*46*	*40*	*13*	*11*
Textile and apparel	−535	−470	−160	67	27
	39	*0*	*16*	*9*	*13*

Sources: 1980 PUMS and the 1997 Current Population Survey of the U.S. Bureau of the Census.

Note: Numbers in the top row of each industry indicate total change in number of jobs held by women between 1980 and 1997. Numbers in the bottom row in italics indicate the number of those jobs held by immigrant women.

decline in the number of jobs held by women with a high school education only. This process is most evident in some high-skill industries that lost hundreds of thousands of jobs filled by such workers. For instance, banking, colleges and universities, and government lost even more jobs filled by high school graduates only than they have lost jobs filled by high school dropouts. In a repeat of the pattern taking place at the lowest level of education, immigrant women with a high school level education are increasingly replacing native-born women at this level of education as well.

Low-skill industries are continuing to increase the number of jobs filled by high school graduates, but in lower numbers than for college-educated labor. The textile and apparel industry suffered a loss in the number of jobs filled by high school graduates only.

Window on Specific Industries

Immigrant women are beginning to dominate the labor force of some industries. As we have seen, they already do so in states such as California, whereas in others they are increasingly replacing native-born women in low-skill occupations. In this section, we examine in greater details the role immigrant labor generally, and immigrant women in particular, play in specific industries. It has been suggested that immigrant labor has permitted some industries to continue to be profitable in the United States in the face of increasing competition from cheaper labor in other parts of the world (including the source countries of immigrants). Although our aggregate occupational and industrial analyses found no evidence to support the claim that immigrants are doing jobs that native-borns will not do, it may be that this proposition still holds in specific industries including the household services and the hotel and motel industries. It is suggested at the same time that immigrant labor provides the technological skills that are in short supply in the United States, helping some industries to develop here faster than they otherwise would.

To address these questions, we examine the role that immigrants have played in specific industries selected for their disproportionate dependence on immigrant labor, their employment of a large number of immigrants, or their importance to the economic base of the nation as technological development or exports leaders:

- High-immigrant-dependent industries: textile and apparel, perishable goods, agriculture, and household services

- High-technology industries: computer and office equipment and electronic

- Export industries: instruments and related products

- Service industries: motel and hotel, hospitals, and banking

For each of these industries we compare trends in growth, education, and racial/ethnic composition of the labor force; labor costs; and investments and productivity (for manufacturing industries). We compare these trends in these industries in California and in the nation. The large variations in dependence on immigrant labor between these two areas add to our understanding of how immigrant labor is integrated into various industries and with what effects on industry growth and the native workers within each specific industry. Recall that the share of female immigrant labor has increased from 10 percent in 1970 to 29 percent in 1997 in California. By contrast, this share has increased minimally in the rest of the nation from 6 percent in 1970 to 10 percent in 1997.

"Immigrant Dependent" Industries

As noted earlier, a number of service and manufacturing industries employ a disproportionate share of immigrant women including the textile and apparel, private households, services-to-buildings, and hotel and motel industries. On the average, one in every four female workers in these industries is foreign-born, more than twice the national average; in California, the majority of the female labor force in these industries is foreign-born.

In addition to their relatively high "dependence" on immigrant labor, these industries have a number of characteristics in common (table 6.5). They all have a predominantly female labor force ranging from 90 percent in the private household industry to 50 percent in the services-to-buildings industry. The dominance of women in the labor forces of these industries has remained generally constant over time in all but the services-to-buildings industry. This latter industry is rapidly being transformed from a male- to a female-dominated industry. Its share of women in the labor force increased significantly from 27 percent in 1970 to 51 percent in 1997. Although the overall education of their respective labor forces has increased, all four industries remain low-skill, with about one-third of their labor forces having fewer than 12 years of education in 1997—twice the national average—down from more than 50 percent in 1970. Overall, the labor forces of these industries continued to average fewer than 12 years of education in 1997.

Although the general labor-force characteristics of these industries are similar, their growth patterns over time have varied. At the national level, employment in the textile and apparel industry stagnated during the 1970s and then declined (by 18 percent) in the 1980s and again in the 1990s. Employment in the private household industry also declined in the 1980s but experienced renewed growth in the 1990s (42 percent). By contrast, employment growth in the services-to-buildings and in the hotel and motel industries has been vigorous since 1970 at three times or more the national average.

Table 6.5

Characteristics of Selected High-Immigrant Industries, Nation, 1970–1997

Indicators	Textile and Apparel 1970	Textile and Apparel 1997	Services to Buildings 1970	Services to Buildings 1997	Private Households 1970	Private Households 1997	Hotel and Motel 1970	Hotel and Motel 1997
Number of employers (thousands)	2,300	1,695	179	934	1,219	953	595	1,546
Employment growth in previous decade[a] (percent)	5	14	99	18	-38	42	61	18
Percent immigrants	11	28	10	24	7	30	11	27
Percent women	65	62	27	51	90	92	57	51
Labor-force characteristics								
Mean years of education	9.6	11.4	10.1	11.6	8.7	11.0	10.4	12.2
Percent with fewer than 12 years	64	33	58	31	77	41	54	26
Earnings ratio of immigrants divided by native-borns with fewer than 12 years of education	1.12	.77	1.09	1.07	1.54	1.09	1.31	1.19
Immigrant women								
Percent in female labor force	13	28	15	27	7	30	8	23
Growth in previous decade[a] (percent)	35	16	158	57	8	60	139	48
Education ratios of immigrants divided by native-borns:								
Mean years of education	.78	.77	.77	.83	.95	.85	.91	.87
Percent with fewer than 12 years	1.20	2.30	1.32	1.33	.94	1.54	1.04	1.54
Percent with 13 years or more	1.48	.67	.62	1.00	1.22	1.84	1.30	.84
Earnings ratio of immigrants divided by native-borns with fewer than 12 years of education	1.08	.78	1.38	1.07	1.51	1.16	1.25	1.20
Racial/ethnic composition								
Asian	1	7	1	4	1	2	2	9
Black	10	21	19	13	49	17	20	17
Hispanic	8	21	7	20	4	27	6	17
Non-Hispanic White	80	50	73	62	46	53	72	57

Sources: 1970 and 1990 PUMS and the 1997 Current Population Survey of the U.S. Bureau of the Census.

[a]Percent growth in the 1970 column represents the percent growth in employment from 1970 to 1980; in the 1997 column, it represents employment growth from 1990 to 1997.

Growth in these two industries has slowed considerably in the 1990s, however.

Regardless of whether these industries have grown or declined, immigrant women have been playing an increasing role in them. They filled 17 percent of the net new jobs created in the hotel and motel industry and 16 percent of the more than 600,000 new jobs created by the services-to-buildings industry. In the private household industry, immigrant women have increased in number by 187,000 at the same time that the industry lost 266,000 jobs. Similarly, in the textile and apparel industry none of the more than 400,000 jobs lost between 1970 to 1997 was lost to immigrant women.

As the share of immigrant women in these industries has increased, an increasing divergence has occurred in education and earnings between immigrant and native-born women in all four industries examined. Whereas in 1970, immigrant women were only slightly more likely to have fewer than 12 years of education, by 1997, they were 50 percent or more likely to be so.

Earnings of immigrant women relative to native-born women have also declined over time. In 1970, for instance, immigrant women with fewer than 12 years of education earned from 8 percent (in the textile and apparel industry) to 51 percent (in private households) *more* than native-born women with the same level of education. By 1997, this gap had narrowed considerably. By then, immigrant women in the textile and apparel industry earned 22 percent *less* than native-born women. In the three other industries, immigrant women still earned more than native-born women, but their relative earnings advantage was reduced from 38 to 7 percent in the services-to-buildings industry and from 51 to 16 percent in the private-household industry.

The earnings differential between immigrant and native-born women in these industries is fully accounted for by the first group working longer hours than the second. Indeed, hourly wages in all four high-immigrant industries were typically lower for immigrants than for native-born women at all levels of education (table 6.6). For instance, immigrant women with fewer than 12 years of education earned 16 percent less per hour in the hotel and motel industry than native-born women and 7 percent less in the private-household industry. All but the textile and apparel industry are service industries with irregular hours and often requiring evening and night work. Immigrant women may be more willing to be flexible than native-born women in this regard. By contrast, in the textile and apparel industry, the ratio of weekly earnings and hourly wages is similar.

As a result of the increasing role of immigrants in these industries, all have increased their share of Hispanics and Asians, with the first group having increased most rapidly. This increase has generally been primarily at the expense of non-Hispanic Whites. In the growing hotel and motel industry, Black women have seen their share decrease from 20 percent in 1970 to 17 percent in 1997. Perhaps more unexpected is the increase in the share of Black women in the textile and apparel industry, from 10 percent in 1970 to

Table 6.6

Ratio of Hourly Wages between Immigrant and Native-Born Women in Selected High-Immigrant Industries by Education, 1997

	Education (Years)			
Industry	<12	=12	13–15	16+
Hotel and motel	.84	.84	1.12	.91
Private households	.93	1.26	.70	—
Services to buildings	.98	.96	.97	1.10
Textile and apparel	.79	.84	.78	.78

Source: 1997 Current Population Survey of the U.S. Bureau of the Census.

21 percent in 1997. The private-household industry, however, experienced a reverse trend. In this rapidly declining industry, Black women have decreased their share from nearly half of its labor force in 1970 to 17 percent in 1997. Earnings in this industry have also been consistently the lowest of the 70 industries we have examined. Higher-paying opportunities in other sectors of the economy may be one reason for the decline in the share of Black women in this industry.

In the high-immigration state of California,[2] the trends described above have been singularly more pronounced with somewhat different effects on the characteristics of these industries' labor force and growth (table 6.7). In California, half or more of the labor force of these industries is foreign-born—a share that has doubled to tripled since 1970. This rapid increase in immigrant labor has led to four trends in these industries that differ markedly from national trends. First, the California labor force of these industries has become considerably less educated than their counterparts in the rest of the nation. Whereas the national trend has been a steady increase in the educational level of the labor force, the educational level of the California labor force has remained constant in three of the four industries and increased significantly less rapidly in the hotel and motel industry. The disproportionate increase in the share of immigrants in California is the main reason for this relative deterioration in education. The net result has been a disproportionate increase in educational disparities between immigrant and native-born labor in these California industries relative to the same industries in the rest of the nation. For instance, whereas immigrant women in the nation and in these industries were twice as likely as native-born women to have fewer than 12 years of education, in California, they were three to four times more likely to have this low level of education.

Second, the disparities in earnings between immigrants and natives in the textile and apparel and in the services-to-buildings industries have been consistently larger and have increased more rapidly in California than in the

Table 6.7

Characteristics of Selected High-Immigrant Industries, California, 1970–1990

Indicators	Textile and Apparel		Services to Buildings		Private Households		Hotel and Motel	
	1970	1990	1970	1990	1970	1990	1970	1990
Share of national employment (percent)	3.7	9.4	16.7	14.7	8.6	18.2	10.2	12.3
Employment growth (percent)	58	38	74	135	-14	36	65	63
Percent immigrants	41	75	13	46	17	59	21	44
Mean years of education: California divided by the nation	1.04	.88	1.07	.94	1.13	.91	1.04	.97
Earnings ratio of immigrants divided by native-borns with fewer than 12 years of education	1.07	.80	1.07	.80	1.24	1.14	1.14	1.22
Immigrant women								
Percent with fewer than 12 years of education: immigrants divided by native-borns	1.35	4.06	1.34	3.02	1.03	2.21	1.06	3.33
Earnings: immigrants divided by native-borns with fewer than 12 years of education	.90	.68	.95[a]	.98	1.21	1.16	1.22	1.48
Earnings of immigrants with fewer than 12 years of education: California divided by the nation	.96	.93	.98[a]	.96	.92	.94	1.09	1.01
Racial/ethnic composition								
Asian	12	21	1	4	3	6	2	12
Black	10	2	30	6	21	6	11	5
Hispanic	38	59	10	53	12	57	11	36
Non-Hispanic White	39	17	58	36	63	30	75	46
Value added per employee: California divided by the nation	1.08	1.07	NA	NA	NA	NA	NA	NA
New capital per employee: California divided by the nation	1.02	.89	NA	NA	NA	NA	NA	NA

Sources: 1970 and 1990 PUMS of the U.S. Bureau of the Census.
Note: NA means not applicable.
[a]This figure is for 1980. The number of observations in 1970 is too small for a reliable estimate.

rest of the nation. Earnings of immigrants with fewer than 12 years of education in the textile and apparel industry were 10 percent lower than those of
native-borns in 1970 but 32 percent lower in 1990. And whereas immigrants'
earnings in the services-to-buildings industry were 7 percent higher than
those of native-borns in 1970, they were 20 percent lower in 1990. In the
other two industries—private households and hotels and motels—immigrants' earnings have been consistently higher than those of natives, but the
gap has been consistently lower in California than in the rest of the nation.
The earnings of immigrant women in California have also been consistently
lower than those of immigrant women in the nation with the exception of
those in the hotel and motel industry. In this industry, the positive differential
has declined from 9 percent in 1970 to parity in 1990.

A third significant difference between trends in California and the nation
in these high-immigrant industries concerns changes in their racial/ethnic
composition, most specifically with regard to the share of Black women.
Whereas Black women have maintained and even increased their share in
high-immigrant industries at the national level, their share in the same industries in California has moved decidedly in the other direction. Nowhere is
this trend more evident than in the textile and apparel industry where the
share of Black women has declined from 10 percent in 1970 to a nominal 2
percent in 1990. Similarly large declines in the share of African Americans
have taken place in the other California high-immigrant industries, with the
highest decline occurring in the services-to-buildings industry, which saw this
share decline from 30 percent in 1970 to 6 percent in 1990. "Network hiring"
for low-skill jobs that have historically favored non-Hispanic Whites over
Blacks has increasingly been replaced today by an immigrant "hiring
network" that favors Hispanics over Blacks in areas where their numbers are
growing disproportionately.

Finally, with a labor force that is increasingly less educated in California
relative to the nation and with immigrant earnings increasingly lower than
those of native-borns, one would expect that productivity in California's industries might have declined relative to the nation. But such was not the case,
at least in the one high-immigrant manufacturing industry for which such a
measure is available, the textile and apparel industry. As shown in table 6.8,
value added per employee has remained higher in California than in the nation, suggesting that high immigration into California has not negatively affected the productivity of this California industry. Trends in capital expenditures per employee, however, lend mild support for the argument that high
dependency on lower-cost immigrants may delay capital investments. At least
in the textile and apparel industry, new capital per employee has been consistently lower in California than in the nation throughout the 1980s and in the
first half of the 1990s.[3]

Table 6.8

Value Added and Capital Investments in the Textile and Apparel Industry, 1967–1994

	1967	1972	1977	1982	1987	1992	1994
Value added per employee:							
California divided by the nation	1.07	1.10	1.19	1.10	1.04	1.10	1.04
New capital per employee:							
California divided by the nation	.95	1.10	.96	1.53	.84	.94	.80

Source: Census of Manufacturers of the U.S. Bureau of the Census.

High-Technology Industries

The role of immigrants in high-technology industries is of particular interest because these industries are major contributors to growth in the country's exports and to the national economy. Below we examine three such industries including computer and office equipment, instruments and related products, and electronic and other electric equipment machines. Employment in the first two industries grew from two to three times more rapidly than in the economy at large during the 1970–1997 time period, with most of that growth occurring during the 1970–1980 decade. All three industries experienced a significant slowdown in their employment growth during the 1990s (table 6.9).

All three industries have increased their dependence on immigrant labor at a rate exceeding that for the economy as a whole. The share of women in these industries, however, has grown at about the same rate as the share of women in the economy as a whole. These industries also have experienced a rapid upgrading in the education of their respective labor forces. The share of their college-educated labor has more than doubled in all three industries while their share of workers with fewer than 12 years of education has declined threefold or more. Indeed, all three industries have experienced not only a sizeable reduction (in excess of 50 percent) in the number of jobs filled by high school dropouts, they also have experienced a reduction in the number of jobs filled by workers with a high school education only.

The number of immigrant women working in these high-tech industries has increased more rapidly than their respective aggregate employment, most particularly during the 1990 decade. In these industries, as in low-skill industries, there has been a relative increase in the educational gap between immigrant and native-born women. At the lower end of the educational distribution, immigrant women were already more likely to have fewer than 12 years of education than native-born women in 1970, and this tendency has significantly increased over time. Conversely, at the high end of the educational distribution, immigrant women who were significantly more likely to be college educated have become less so over time.

In contrast to low-skill industries, the earnings of immigrant women in high-tech industries have typically been lower than those of native-born women regardless of the level of education. The earnings gap between immigrant and native-born women has been consistently larger for college graduates, ranging from 8 to 18 percent lower in 1990, than for high school dropouts where earnings ranged form 2 to 8 percent lower in 1990. This pattern changed in the 1990s for college-educated immigrant women (table 6.9). By 1997, immigrant women who had some college or who were college graduates were earning more than native-born women with an equivalent level of education. The cause for this reversal remains to be investigated. In contrast, immigrant women with 12 years of education or fewer—a plural majority in these industries—continued to command earnings significantly lower than their native-born counterparts.

Whereas in low-skill industries, Hispanic women increased their share of the labor force the most, in high-technology industries it is the generally better educated Asian women who increased their share the most. In 1970, few, if any, Asian women were working in these industries. By 1997, Asian women accounted for 11 to 13 percent of their female labor force. The share of Black women in these industries has also increased as has the share of Hispanics, although not to the same extent.

Trends in California in these industries have also been more pronounced than in the nation as a whole (table 6.10). The share of immigrants in these industries has tripled from 1970 to 1990 compared to a doubling in the rest of the nation. And the gap in level of education and earnings between immigrant and native women has grown more rapidly in California than in the nation as a whole. Whereas in the nation, immigrant college graduates earned on the average 18 percent less than native-born women in the electronic and other electric equipment industry in 1990, in California they earned 28 percent less. Generally the earnings gap at each level of education has increased in California while it has remained constant in the rest of the nation, at least during the 1970–1990 time period.[4]

In spite of the lower labor costs of immigrant women compared with native-born women in California and in the nation, productivity—value added per employee—in California's high-tech industries has increased relative to the nation while investments in new capital have remained roughly constant. For instance, in the electronic and other electric equipment industry, value added per employee, which was 2 percent higher in California than in the nation in 1970, became 12 percent higher in 1990, while at the same time investments declined from 15 percent higher in 1970 to 11 percent higher in 1990. Similar trends were experienced in the instrument and related products industry, although productivity as well as new capital investments in this industry have been consistently lower in California than in the nation. By contrast, California's computer industry experienced a major increase in productivity relative to the nation's industry, along with a significant increase in new

Table 6.9

Characteristics of Selected High-Tech Industries, Nation, 1970–1997

Indicators	Computer and Office Equipment		Electronic and Other Electric Equipment		Instruments and Related Products	
	1970	1997	1970	1997	1970	1997
Number of employees (thousands)	331	682	2,013	1,958	348	800
Employment growth (percent)[a]	66	12	15	-2	90	21
Percent immigrants	6	18	6	20	8	20
Percent women	28	36	40	37	37	36
Labor-force characteristics						
Mean years of education	12.7	14.5	11.7	13.6	11.8	13.8
Percent with fewer than 12 years of education	19	3	34	10	31	9
Percent with 13 to 15 years of education	19	28	13	27	15	28
Percent with 16+ years of education	21	49	11	29	12	34
Earnings: immigrants divided by native-borns with 13 to 15 years of education	1.03	1.30	.94	.95	1.08	1.11
Earnings: immigrants divided by native-borns with 16 or more years of education	1.00	1.04	.91	.95	.76	1.15
Immigrant women						
Percent in female labor force	7	21	6	18	7	20
Growth (percent)[a]	143	76	79	14	125	70
Education: immigrants divided by native-borns						
Mean years of education	.89	.92	.90	.93	.90	.94
Percent with fewer than 12 years of education	1.64	2.56	1.32	3.2	1.31	3.53
Percent with 13 to 15 years of education	.79	.60	1.27	.73	1.07	.63
Percent with 16 or more years of education	1.09	.69	2.29	1.19	2.42	1.48
Earnings: immigrants divided by native-borns with fewer than 12 years of education	.99	.93	.97	.80	1.00	1.07
13 to 15 years of education	1.00	1.20	.92	.98	.88	1.32
16 or more years of education	.88	1.10	.84	1.25	.78	1.32
Racial/ethnic composition						
Asian	1	11	0	11	0	13
Black	7	12	9	15	6	9
Hispanic	5	7	5	10	5	7
Non-Hispanic White	87	69	85	64	89	69

Sources: 1970 PUMS and the 1997 Current Population Survey of the U.S. Bureau of the Census.

[a] Percent growth in the 1970 column represents the percent growth in employment from 1970 to 1980; in the 1997 column, it represents employment growth from 1990 to 1997.

Table 6.10

Characteristics of Selected High-Tech Industries, California, 1970–1990

Indicators	Computer and Office Equipment		Electronic and Other Electric Equipment		Instruments and Related Products	
	1970	1990	1970	1990	1970	1990
Share of national employment (percent)	15.4	24.8	11.1	17.3	9.1	15.0
Employment growth (percent)	119	37	49	3	173	15
Percent immigrants	10	30	11	37	14	30
Mean years of education: California divided by the nation	1.03	1.01	1.06	1.01	1.02	1.02
Earnings ratio of immigrants divided by native-borns with 16 or more years of education	.94	.90	.85	.82	.73	.86
Immigrant women						
Percent with fewer than 12 years of education: immigrants divided by native-borns	1.04	4.54	1.06	2.81	1.28	3.12
Percent with 13–15 Years of Education: Immigrants Divided by Native-borns	.90	.71	1.11	.60	1.47	.64
Percent with 16+ years of education: immigrants divided by native-borns	1.34	.86	1.95	.82	0	.68
Earnings: immigrants divided by native-borns with fewer than 12 years of education	.88	.81	.90	.83	1.00	.71
Earnings: immigrants divided by native-borns with 16+ years of education	1.54	.91	.84	.72	—	.66
Racial/ethnic composition						
Asian[a]	2	21	2	23	1	16
Black	5	5	6	5	4	4
Hispanic	16	14	14	26	15	23
Non-Hispanic White	76	58	77	45	77	54
Value added per employee: California divided by the Nation	.92	1.39	1.02	1.12	.83	.97
New capital per employee: California divided by the nation	1.25	1.39	1.15	1.11	.87	.82

Source: 1970 and 1990 PUMS of the U.S. Bureau of the Census.

[a]This figure is for 1980. The number of observations in 1970 is too small for a reliable estimate.

capital investments. In brief, all high-tech industries in California experienced disproportionate gains in productivity at the same time as their share of immigrants increased disproportionately. These gains occurred with no relative increase in new capital investments in two of the three high-tech industries examined and with a major increase in capital investments in the other one.

Benefiting from both lower costs of immigrant labor and increases in productivity, high-tech industries have grown significantly more rapidly in California than in the nation as a whole and hence have increased their share of national employment more than in most other industries. In 1997, 27 percent of the nation's workers employed in the computer and office equipment industry resided in California, up from 15 percent in 1970. The California share of the nation's workers in the instruments and related products industry has tripled to 32 percent, while that for the electronic and other electric equipment has increased from 11 to 19 percent.

In California, as in the nation, Asian women have increased their share in high-tech industries, and at a much higher rate than in the nation as a whole. As in the nation, there were nearly no women of Asian origin working in these industries in 1970, but by 1990, 20 percent or more of their respective female labor forces were of Asian origin. And unlike in the nation, the share of Black women in the female labor force has remained constant or has declined slightly. By 1990, at least one of these industries—the electronic and other electric equipment—already had reached the status of a multiminorities industry, with no one racial/ethnic group constituting a majority of its female labor force.

Service Industries

Industries employing the largest number of immigrant women are mostly service industries. Below, we examine the characteristics of immigrant women in four such industries including hospitals—one of the largest employers of immigrant women—banking and credit, government, and communications. Although the latter is not a large employer of immigrant women, the increasing role of the communications industry in the economy also justifies our including it for closer scrutiny.

All of these industries have experienced positive growth in employment, in both the 1970 and the 1980 decades, although at significantly different rates (table 6.11). In general, hospitals and banking and credit have experienced more vigorous employment growth than communications and government. However, employment in all four industries stagnated or even declined in the 1990s, with the sharpest decline experienced in the government sector. Unlike in the low-skill and high-technology industries, employment growth in these industries has been similar in both the nation and in California.

Table 6.11

Characteristics of Selected Service Industries, Nation, 1970–1997

Indicators	Banking and Credit		Communications		Government		Hospitals	
	1970	1997	1970	1997	1970	1997	1970	1997
Number of employees (thousands)	1,317	2,797	1,098	1,690	3,607	5,200	2,750	5,306
Employment growth (percent)[a]	121	-4	52	1	57	-8	94	0
Percent immigrants	6	10	3	7	3	6	7	11
Percent women	61	70	49	43	33	49	77	76
Labor-force characteristics								
Mean years of education	12.6	14.0	12.3	14.2	12.2	14.3	12.1	14.4
Percent with fewer than 12 years of education	13	2	14	4	23	3	29	4
Percent with 13 to 15 years of education	22	36	19	35	18	37	20	35
Percent with 16+ years of education	13	32	7	36	15	34	14	35
Earnings ratio: immigrants divided by native-borns with 13 to 15 years of education	1.03	.91	1.07	.71	.97	.84	1.12	1.03
Earnings ratio: immigrants divided by native-borns with 16 or more years of education	.76	.93	.93	.99	1.03	.95	1.11	1.29
Immigrant women								
Percent in female labor force	6	9	3	7	3	6	6	10
Growth (percent)[a]	138	72	75	17	173	17	107	5
Education: immigrants divided by native-borns								
Mean years of education	.97	1.05	.96	1.09	1.00	1.03	1.00	1.00
Percent with fewer than 12 years of education	1.88	2.18	2.04	.52	1.34	2.59	1.09	2.77
Percent with 13 to 15 years of education	1.05	.97	.87	.28	1.00	.78	.77	.70
Percent with 16+ years of education	2.19	1.81	1.81	2.18	1.83	1.17	2.33	1.48
Earnings: immigrants divided by native-borns with								
fewer than 12 years of education	1.09	1.06	1.03	.84	.94	.81	1.19	1.13
13–15 years of education	1.11	.89	1.01	.71	1.04	.82	1.10	1.03
16 or more years of education	.76	.80	1.06	.84	.95	.90	1.13	1.40
Racial/ethnic composition								
Asian	1	3	0	4	2	4	1	4
Black	5	14	11	24	14	19	16	16
Hispanic	4	7	3	5	3	7	3	6
Non-Hispanic White	90	76	86	65	82	70	79	73

Sources: 1970 PUMS and the 1997 Current Population Survey of the U.S. Bureau of the Census.

[a] Percent growth in the 1970 column represents the percent growth in employment from 1970 to 1980; in the 1997 column, it represents employment growth from 1990 to 1997.

The share of immigrants in these industries was equal to or lower than the national average in 1970, and although it has increased over time, it remained disproportionately low in 1997. This result is particularly the case for government and communications.

There are more variations in the share of women among these industries than among low-skill high-immigrant and high-tech industries. Hospitals and banking and credit are female-dominated industries, while the labor force in the communications industry is roughly evenly distributed between men and women. Among service industries, government had the lowest share of women in its labor force in 1970, but this share has increased significantly since, from a low 33 percent in 1970 to 49 percent in 1997.

As in the economy as a whole, all four industries have experienced an increase in the average level of education of workers. Their respective shares of workers with some college or more have doubled from one-third in 1970 to more than two-thirds in 1997. The largest increase took place in the communications industry where the share of such workers increased from one-quarter to two-thirds.

The rate of growth in the number of immigrant women in these industries has consistently exceeded the growth in total employment. By and large, the female labor force—immigrant and native-born—in these industries shares the same average level of education. However, their distribution differs. Generally, immigrant women are both much more likely to be college graduates and much more likely to have fewer than 12 years of education than are native-born women. These tendencies have increased over time. In 1997, immigrant women were still from 1.5 to two times more likely to be college graduates in three of these service industries. In the government sector, however, the relative share of immigrant college graduates has declined.

The pattern of earnings of immigrant women relative to native-born women has changed significantly over time in all four of these service industries. In 1970 immigrant women earned generally more than native-born women, unlike in high-tech industries. This differential was reversed by 1997, with immigrant women earning significantly less than native-born women with similar levels of education. The one exception is in the hospital industry where the earnings of immigrant women continued to outpace those of native-born women. Like the personal-services, household, and services-to-buildings industries discussed earlier, the hospital industry requires night shifts and irregular hours. And as in these other industries, differences in the number of hours worked per week between immigrant and native-born women explain most of the noted differentials in weekly earnings. Indeed, the hourly wages of immigrant women with fewer than 12 years of education were 13 percent lower than those of native-born women in 1997, and those of immigrant women with some college education were 9 percent lower. However, hourly wages of college graduate immigrant women still exceeded those of native-born women, although by a lower margin than for weekly earnings.

The share of Asian and Hispanic women has modestly increased in all four industries. Notably their increased share has not been as large as the increase in the share of Black women in these industries. Black women have doubled their share of the female labor force in the communications industry from 11 percent in 1970 to 24 percent in 1997, while Hispanics increased their share from 3 to 5 percent. Black women also significantly increased their share of the female labor force in the banking industry. In the government sector, the share of Hispanics increased from 3 to 7 percent between 1970 and 1997, whereas the share of Blacks increased from 14 to 20 percent. Clearly, access to these service industries by immigrants and more generally Asian- and Hispanic-origin workers has been slower to increase than in the other industries examined in this chapter.

The hospital industry is an exception to this pattern for service industries. In this industry neither Asians, Hispanics, nor Black women have increased their share significantly: by 1, 2, and 1 percentage points respectively. Blacks, however, have maintained their relatively high share—1.5 times the national average—in this industry.

California trends in these industries have been generally similar to those in the nation (table 6.12). Although the share of immigrants in their respective labor force is larger than in the nation, that share is equal to the share of immigrants in the overall California economy for the banking and credit and the hospital industries and about half that share for communications and for government. In California, immigrant women have also experienced a growing gap in earnings relative to native-born women. Whereas college graduate immigrant women earned 15 percent less than native-born women in 1970, that differential grew to 29 percent by 1990. Similar trends were experienced by immigrants at all levels of education in communications and in government. The hospital industry, once again, is an exception. In that industry, immigrant women earned as much as or more than native-born women in 1970, and this differential had increased by 1990.

Changes in the racial/ethnic composition in the California industries differ from those in the nation. In California, both Asians and Hispanics have significantly increased their share in the labor forces of these service industries while Blacks have held their share constant or increased it only nominally. For instance, whereas in the nation, Black women in communications increased their share by 6 percentage points and Asians and Hispanics by 5 percentage points between 1970 and 1990, in California, Blacks increased their share by a lower 2 percentage points compared to 16 percentage points for Asians and Hispanics. And whereas in the hospital industry in the nation there was no major change in the share of either Asians, Hispanics, or Blacks in California, Asians increased their share threefold to 14 percent and Hispanics doubled their share to 16 percent. The share of Blacks remained unchanged at 12 percent.

Conclusions

Immigrant women have increased their share in all sectors and industries of the national economy. The increase in their share, however, has been larger in low-skill industries (e.g., durable manufacturing, personal services) than in high-skill industries (e.g., health, professional services). Also the share of immigrant women remains the lowest in the public sector, including in education and in government.

Although immigrant and native-born female laborers work side by side in all sectors of the economy, their respective roles differ across sectors. In low-skill sectors, immigrant women are more likely than native-born women to provide the low-educated labor force "in the back office" whereas higher-educated native-born women are more likely to be in the "front office." In high-skill industries, by contrast, there is no apparent differentiation between the roles of immigrant and of native-born workers.

As of 1997, no industry was dominated by immigrant female labor. Even in industries often cited in the press as having become "immigrant" industries—such as the textile and apparel, household-services, or services-to-buildings industries—immigrant female labor did not exceed a third of the female labor force. However, a glimpse at how some industries may come to be dominated by immigrant female labor can be seen in California, where immigrants are disproportionately concentrated. There, immigrant women provide nearly all of the female labor force (85 percent in 1997) in industries such as textile and apparel, services to buildings, and laundry and cleaning. They account for two-thirds of the labor force in household services.

Still, the largest number of immigrant women work in large relatively high-skill industries including hospitals, education, banking, and business services. In these industries, low-educated immigrant female labor are replacing native-born women in low-skill jobs at the same time as these industries are increasingly losing jobs that are filled by high school dropouts and even by high school graduates only. Even industries viewed as low-skill are not immune to this "creeping up" of the education of their labor forces including such industries as hotel and motels, and eat and drink places. Although these industries have grown sizably over the past two decades, their number of jobs filled by people with fewer than 12 years of education has remained stagnant.

In addition to the above, there are a few other notable trends that are common to nearly all industries.

One such trend is an increase in the disparities between the education of immigrant women and that of native-born women in the labor forces of most industries. This relative deterioration is particularly sharp in low-skill industries, but has also taken place in high-tech industries. The reverse trend, however, has taken place in high-skill service industries that require daily contacts with clients. In these industries, immigrant women are more educated

Table 6.12

Characteristics of Selected Service Industries, California, 1970–1990

Indicators	Banking and Credit		Communications		Government		Hospitals	
	1970	1990	1970	1990	1970	1990	1970	1990
Share of national employment (percent)	11.2	12.8	12.8	12.3	12.0	11.2	9.5	10.6
Employment growth (percent)	95	29	32	11	31	13	84	17
Percent immigrants	13	22	6	12	4	11	11	25
Mean years of education: California divided by the nation	1.02	1.00	1.02	1.01	1.05	1.01	1.04	1.01
Earnings ratio of immigrants divided by native-borns with 16 or more years of education	.65	.73	.83	.73	.93	.85	1.01	.97
Immigrant women								
Percent with fewer than 12 years of education: Immigrants divided by native-borns	1.36	1.79	2.34	2.45	1.50	2.78	1.11	2.55
Percent with 13 to 15 years of education: immigrants divided by native-borns	.99	.84	.77	.84	96	.74	.70	.66
Percent with 16 or more years of education: immigrants divided by native-borns	1.97	1.85	2.01	1.31	1.55	1.54	1.78	1.35
Earnings: immigrants divided by native-borns with fewer than 13 to 15 years of education	.97	.96	.92	.88	1.05	.87	1.05	1.23
Earnings: immigrants divided by native-borns with 16+ years of education	.85	.71	.99	.70	.82	.85	.99	1.06
Racial/ethnic composition								
Asian	4	13	1	7	3	9	4	14
Black	5	7	10	12	12	15	12	12
Hispanic	9	17	6	16	6	17	7	16
Non-Hispanic White	82	62	82	64	78	58	77	58

Sources: 1970 and 1990 PUMS of the U.S. Bureau of the Census.

than native-born women, the differential having most likely to do with command of the English language.

Second, earnings of immigrant women have typically been lower than those of native-born women, and that discrepancy has increased over time. But exceptions do exist, most notably in industries in which work hours may be irregular or at night, such as in the private-household, hospital, and hotel and motel industries. These industries provide services around the clock, and it may be that immigrant women are more willing to work more hours. Their hourly wages in these industries are typically lower than those of native-born women.

Another constant across most industries is the increasing diversity of the racial/ethnic composition of the labor force. Less-educated Hispanic women have dramatically increased their presence in low-skill industries, whereas the more-educated Asian women have seen their share increase tenfold or more in high-tech industries. The relatively high-skill service industries—including government—have experienced a lower dependence on immigrant labor than other industries, and their racial/ethnic composition has been changing at a much slower pace than that of other industries. This shift in the racial/ethnic composition in all industries has not led to a decline in the share of Black women. Indeed, their share has increased in some low-skill as well as in high-tech industries. However, they have enjoyed their largest share increase in the large high-skill service industries we have examined such as banking, communications, and hospitals.

Another observation is that the penetration of the labor force by immigrants as well as the racial/ethnic diversification of the labor force in the nation is taking place at a more rapid pace in the private than in the public sector. The share of immigrants in the public sector remains less than proportional to the share of immigrants in the economy as a whole. Similarly, there has been no major shift in the share of Asians and Hispanics in the nation's public sector. Blacks, however, have continued to make major gains in their share of public sector jobs at the national level.

Finally, a common thread across nearly all industries is that the trends noted above for the nation as a whole have generally been more pronounced in California, the state that has experienced the highest level of immigration in the nation. This is the case for the relative increase in the educational gap between immigrant and native-born women and for the lower earnings of immigrant-women as opposed to native-born women. Indeed, in nearly all California industries the gap in earnings between immigrant and native-born women has been larger than for the same industries in the nation as a whole. On the other hand, employment growth in most industries has been greater in California than in the rest of the nation, in part because of the relative lower costs of immigrant labor in California (McCarthy and Vernez, 1997).

California also stands out in relation to trends in the share of Blacks in the female labor forces of its industries. Generally, their share has declined in

California while it has increased or remained constant in the same industries in the rest of the nation. These trends are consistent with and lend further support to recent findings that high levels of immigration into California have had a disproportionate effect not only on long-term earnings of immigrants and low-skill workers, but also on the job opportunities of Blacks (McCarthy and Vernez, 1997; Waldinger, 1996).

One other notable characteristic of the California labor force is its rapidly increasing racial/ethnic diversity. It is notable because already by 1990, no one group constituted a majority of the labor force in many industries with few if any reported problems arising in the work place.

Notes

1. Although we focus on the 1980–1997 decades in table 6.4, the trends displayed began in the 1960s and have accelerated over time (McCarthy and Vernez, 1997).

2. Because of the relatively small sample of the Current Population Survey, state-specific data are not as reliable as national-level data. Hence, for California, we use the latest 1990 Census data instead of the 1997 Current Population Survey data.

3. McCarthy and Vernez (1997) show that productivity in California's manufacturing industry as a whole has exceeded that in the nation throughout the 1963–1994 time period, in spite of generally lower new capital investments, larger increases in the share of immigrants, and a decline in average schooling of this sector's labor force relative to that in the nation. Although productivity in California's manufacturing remained higher than in the nation in the mid-1990s, the California productivity advantage has been eroding steadily since the early 1980s (pp. 172–178).

4. Data from the 1997 Current Population Survey suggests that even highly educated immigrant women in California high-tech industries continued to command lower earnings than their native-born counterparts, unlike the patterns observed at the national level.

Chapter 7

Performance of Immigrant Women in the Labor Market[1]

Previous chapters have considered what immigrant women do, where they work, and what role they play in our changing national economy. In this chapter, we provide an overview of how immigrant women perform in the United States labor market and of how their performance has changed over time relative to that of native-born women.

The chapter begins with a comparison of the labor market outcomes between immigrant and native-born women as a whole over the 1970–1990 time period. Six major labor-market outcomes are considered: labor-force participation rate, unemployment rate, weeks worked per year, hours worked per week, earnings, and self-employment rate. The first two indicators measure the extent to which immigrant women engage in remunerated work and the extent to which they are successful in finding the work they seek. "Weeks worked per year" and "hours worked per week" measure the work effort immigrant women are willing to make. Weekly earnings are a measure of the level of compensation immigrant women receive for their labor. Finally, the self-employment rate measures the net effect of the enterpreneurship of immigrant women and their ability to otherwise access the labor market.

Having identified differences between immigrant and native-born women in labor-market outcomes over time, the second section of this chapter endeavors to identify the extent to which differences in age, education, family responsibilities, and English proficiency can explain these differences. The third section, in turn, examines in detail the differences in labor-market outcomes of immigrant women of different origins and identifies the factors that explain those differences.

First, it is important to explain the analytical approach used in this chapter. Unlike the previous three chapters, which focused on all women in the labor force regardless of age, this chapter focuses on women aged 25 to 60. We exclude from our analysis young women just leaving school or in the early years of their careers because of the higher turnover experienced by such workers. And we exclude older workers (aged 61 or more) because they have reached early retirement age and many are retiring.

With respect to our measures of labor-market outcomes, the reader should keep two things in mind. First, our measure of earnings is median weekly earnings rather than hourly wages. The latter measure is not available in the 1970 census. Second, all weekly earnings are expressed in real 1990 dollars. We have used the Consumer Price Index for urban consumers to adjust earnings over time.

Regression analysis is used to explain differences in labor-market outcomes between immigrant and native-born women and between immigrant women from different countries of origin. The outcomes analyzed in the regressions are labor-force participation, annual hours worked among those who worked, and weekly earnings among those who had positive weekly earnings. For each of these three outcomes in each of the three census years, four models were estimated. The first model (Model 1) includes a dummy indicator for whether the women were immigrants and it controls for age (in quadratic form). Model 2 then adds education (in quadratic form) to Model 1. Model 3 builds on Model 2 by including the number of children ever born. The final model, Model 4, controls for age, education, number of children ever born, and ability to speak English (with an indicator variable for each of four language-ability levels and the reference group being those people who speak only English at home). Model 4 cannot be estimated for 1970 because information on English language skills was not obtained in the 1970 census. The appendix contains the estimated coefficients for the four models.

Trends in Labor-Market Outcomes

In 1970, few differences were evidenced in labor-market outcomes between immigrant and native-born women. Both groups participated equally in the labor force, worked the same number of weeks a year, earned the same amount weekly, and had equally low levels of self-employment. The slightly higher unemployment rate of immigrant women was the only notable difference in labor market outcomes between these two groups. In the subsequent 20 years, however, a gap has developed in favor of native-born women, most particularly with respect to participation in the labor force, unemployment, and earnings.

Table 7.1 compares the changes in labor-market outcomes between immigrant and native-born women in 1970, 1980, and 1990. Both immigrant and native-born women have significantly increased their participation in the labor force, although at differing rates. Participation rates were fairly similar for native-born and immigrant women in 1970 and 1980, rising from 49 percent to 59 percent (i.e., 61 percent for native-born women and 59 percent for immigrant women) during that ten-year period. In 1990, the participation rates for native-borns continued to rise rapidly, to 73 percent. While immigrant women were also more likely to work in 1990 than in 1980, in 1990 they were not as likely to participate in the labor force as were native-born

Table 7.1

Labor-Market Outcomes for Working-Age Immigrant and Native-Born Women, 1970–1990

Outcomes	1970		1980		1990	
	Native-born	Immigrant	Native-born	Immigrant	Native-born	Immigrant
Share in labor force (%)	49.2	48.9	61.1	58.5	72.7	65.6
Unemployment rate (%)	4.2	5.5	5.1	6.8	4.8	7.9
Weeks per year[a]	40.3	40.7	42.2	41.8	44.1	43.1
Hours per week[a]	NA[b]	NA[b]	35.6	36.5	37.1	38.0
Weekly earnings[c]	$277	$280	$302	$290	$333	$291
Share self-employed (%)	3.0	3.3	3.7	3.7	5.8	6.1

Source: 1970, 1980, and 1990 PUMS of the U.S. Bureau of the Census.

[a]Hours and weeks are averages among people working in the year prior to census.

[b]NA=data not available.

[c]Weekly earnings are the median among working women, and they are expressed in 1990 dollars.

women, with a difference of 7 percentage points between the two groups. This pattern is distinct from the 1990 pattern for immigrant men, who were equally likely to participate in the labor force as native-born men.

For immigrant women, unemployment rates are higher—a disadvantage that increased between 1970 and 1990. In 1970 there was a gap of 1 percentage point in favor of native-borns. The gap increased to 3 percentage points in 1990, with 8 percent of immigrant women and 5 percent of native-born women unemployed. In contrast, 1990 unemployment rates for men were roughly equivalent for foreign-born and native-born men (6 percent).

As labor-force participation has risen, so too has the number of weeks worked during the year and the number of hours worked per week (conditional on working). For native-born women, the number of weeks worked increased from 40 to 44 between 1970 and 1990. The magnitude of change for immigrant women was similar. The number of hours worked per week increased by 1.5 hours between 1980 and 1990 for both immigrant and native-born women. Overall, when they work, both immigrant and native-born women have steadily worked roughly the same number of weeks per year and the same number of hours per week.[2]

Earnings between immigrant and native-born women have diverged. Both groups had similar median weekly earnings in 1970. But whereas the median real earnings of immigrant women have remained constant throughout the 20-year period considered (at about $290 weekly), those of native-born women have increased by 20 percent. The result has been an increasing gap in earnings between the two groups, from 4 percent in 1980 to 14 percent in 1990. This increased differential is not explained by relative changes in hours worked per week, because immigrant women have consistently worked about one hour more than native-born women.

Finally, both immigrant and native-born women have been consistently as likely to be self-employed as native-born women. Three percent of both groups were self-employed in 1970. Since then, both groups have doubled (from 3 to 6 percent) their respective propensities to be self-employed. This similarity in the rate of self-employment between immigrant and native-born women suggests that no difference exists between immigrant and native-born women in their respective entrepreneurship.

In brief, since 1970, immigrant women have consistently worked the same number of weeks and the same number of hours as native-born women and they have been no more likely to be self-employed than native-born women. However, they have become somewhat less likely to enter the labor market than native-born women. And when they do, they have become more likely to be unemployed and to command lower earnings than native-born women.

Factors Affecting Trends in Labor-Market Outcomes

Education is the main factor that explains the differentials between immigrant and native-born women noted above. Differentials in family responsibilities and in English proficiency also contribute to the differences in labor-market outcomes, but to a lesser extent.

Significant differences in education, family responsibilities, and English proficiency between immigrant and native-born women as a whole and between immigrant women of different origins are displayed in table 7.2 (see also chapter 3). Focusing first on the differences between immigrant and native-born women as a whole, the differential in years of schooling has increased from 1.1 years in 1970 to 1.5 years in 1990. The share of immigrants who do not speak English well has also increased. And whereas immigrant women had an average of 0.3 children fewer than native-born women in 1970, by 1990 they had an average of 0.2 children more.

The differential in education between immigrant women and native-born women explains about two thirds of the 1990 differential in labor-force participation between the two groups (figure 7.1). The remaining differential in labor-force participation is fully accounted for by differences in English proficiency. Differences in age and family responsibilities do not contribute significantly to the difference in labor-force participation, at least when comparing immigrant and native-born women as a whole.

Similarly, education is the most significant factor explaining the 13 percent difference in 1990 median weekly earnings between immigrant and native-born women (figure 7.2).

Table 7.2

**Demographic Characteristics of Working-Age Women by Country/Region
of Birth, 1970–1990**

Country/ Region of Birth	1970		1980			1990		
	Years of School	Children Ever Born[b]	Years of School	Children Ever Born	English Poorly Spoken[c]	Years of School	Children Ever Born	English Poorly Spoken
U.K., Canada	11.3	2.2	12.4	2.2	0.8	13.1	1.9	0.6
Europe	9.9	2.0	11.2	2.1	14.2	12.0	1.9	11.7
Japan, Korea, China	10.9	2.1	12.0	1.8	31.6	12.8	1.6	32.1
Indochina	a	a	9.4	3.0	49.8	8.9	2.8	50.1
Philippines	12.5	2.1	13.6	2.1	6.1	13.9	1.9	4.5
Mexico	6.1	3.7	7.0	3.4	59.6	7.6	3.0	54.7
Central America	10.3	2.0	10.1	2.2	35.9	9.6	2.3	44.6
Mid-East, Other Asia	11.5	2.1	12.6	1.9	17.0	13.2	1.9	14.4
Carib., Afr., Ocna., S. Am.	10.0	1.9	11.3	2.0	30.1	11.8	1.9	24.6
All immigrants	10.1	2.2	10.9	2.3	23.7	11.2	2.2	27.2
Native-born								
Non-Hispanic Whites	11.5	2.5	12.4	2.2	0.0	13.0	1.9	0.0
Non-Hispanic Blacks	9.8	3.2	11.3	2.8	0.0	12.3	2.4	0.0
Hispanics	8.5	3.3	9.9	2.9	14.7	11.5	2.4	7.7
Others	11.2	2.4	11.6	2.6	4.1	12.7	2.1	2.0
All Native-Born	11.2	2.5	12.2	2.3	0.7	12.9	2.0	0.7

Source: Schoeni, 1998a, table 6, p. 68.

[a]Too few observations for reliable estimation.

[b]The average number of children ever born.

[c]The share who speak English not well or not at all.

Indeed, if immigrant women had the same level of education as native-born women, our estimate suggests they would earn about 5 percent more than native-born women. Also note that English proficiency does not affect the earnings of immigrant women when considered as a whole.

Differences in Labor-Market Performance among Immigrant Women

Table 7.2 above also displays the large differences in educational, family responsibilities, and English proficiency among immigrant women of differ-

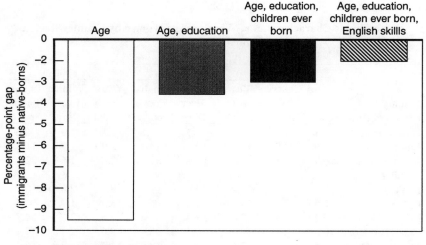

Source: Schoeni, 1998a.

**Figure 7.1—Gap in Labor-Force Participation with and without Adjusting
for Age, Education, Number of Children Ever Born,
and English Skills, Nation, 1990**

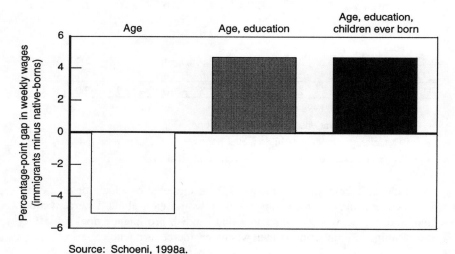

Source: Schoeni, 1998a.

**Figure 7.2—Immigrant Women's Advantage in Weekly Wages with
and without Controlling for Age, Education,
and English Skills, Nation, 1990**

ent origin. A few of these differences merit mention here. The first is that immigrant women from Mexico have been considerably and increasingly less educated, not only relative to native-born women but also relative to native-born Hispanic women. Their educational gap relative to Hispanic native-born women has increased from 2.4 years in 1970 to 3.9 years in 1990. Mexican immigrant women also continuously have had the highest number of children of any immigrant group, even though that number has declined over time from an average 3.7 children in 1970 to 3.0 in 1990. The average number of children born to native-born Hispanic women has declined even more rapidly, from 3.3 in 1970 to 2.4 in 1990.

A second notable observation is that the education of immigrant women from Central America has decreased since 1970 by 0.7 years, as has the education of immigrant women from Indochina. In contrast, immigrant women from all other regions of the world have increased their education between 1970 and 1990 by 1.5 to 2.0 years. These two groups of immigrants also have relatively low levels of education, second only to immigrant women from Mexico. Moreover, like Mexican immigrant women, they have a relatively high number of children and significantly lower proficiency in English than do other immigrant groups.

Immigrant women from all other parts of the world have educational and family responsibilities that are closer to those of native-born women than they are to those of Mexican, Central American, and Indochinese origin.

Given these considerable variations in the characteristics of immigrant women, we should expect broad variations in their labor-market outcomes, and indeed there are.

Tables 7.3, 7.4, and 7.5 show the labor-market outcomes of immigrant women by country/region of origin and over time. They also compare their labor-market outcomes to those of native-born women by racial/ethnic groupings. Below, we examine these differences in some detail.

Labor-Force Participation

Because of their lower level of education, Mexican women were the least likely to participate in the labor force (table 7.3). Immigrants from Indochina and Vietnam also have low levels of education and relatively low rates of participation. European immigrants were more likely to participate than Mexican immigrants, but in 1990 they were 7 percentage points less likely to participate than native-born white women. On the other hand, Filipinas have had a high attachment to the labor force, with 85 percent participating in 1990, which is consistent with findings reported by Duleep and Sanders (1993). The exceptionally high rate for Filipinas in the United States is somewhat surprising given that Filipinas in the Philippines do not have unusually high rates of participation. According to the International Labour Office (ILO), only 54 percent of women in the Philippines 25 to 65 years old

Table 7.3

**Employment Status of Working-Age Women by Country/Region of Birth,
1970–1990 (Percent)**

Country/Region of Birth	1970 Share in Labor Force	1970 Unemployment Rate	1980 Share in Labor Force	1980 Unemployment Rate	1990 Share in Labor Force	1990 Unemployment Rate
U.K., Canada, Europe	48.1	3.8	57.5	4.7	68.0	3.6
Europe	48.4	5.7	57.0	6.1	65.8	5.7
Japan, Korea, China	45.2	5.1	60.1	5.3	62.1	5.0
Indochina	a	a	51.6	12.9	56.9	7.8
Philippines	58.7	4.4	78.0	3.9	85.2	4.0
Mexico	36.0	7.6	46.8	11.4	54.8	14.7
Central America	61.8	6.0	67.2	7.8	71.2	12.7
Mid-East, Other Asia	42.6	6.9	51.6	7.4	59.0	6.9
Native-born						
Non-Hispanic Whites	48.1	3.8	60.1	4.5	73.2	3.9
Non-Hispanic Blacks	58.5	6.1	66.2	8.3	73.2	9.8
Hispanics	39.7	6.6	51.7	7.8	65.8	8.0
Others	50.3	4.6	63.3	6.2	71.0	7.4
All Native-born	49.2	4.2	61.1	5.1	72.7	4.8

Source: Schoeni, 1998a, table 4, p. 65.

[a]Too few observations for reliable estimation.

were economically active in 1989, which is roughly 30 percentage points lower than the labor-force participation rate among Filipinas in the United States. This finding may be explained by the fact that Filipinas in the United States have several years more education than Filipinas in the Philippines and more-educated women are more likely to work than less-educated women. According to the 1993 Demographic and Health Survey of the Philippines, the average years of completed schooling among Filipinas 25 to 49 years old (average of 35) was 8.9, while in our sample of Filipinas in the United States in 1990, the average years of schooling was 13.9.

The labor-force participation rate for women 25 to 60 years old in Mexico was 39 percent in 1988, which is lower than the participation rate of 55 percent for Mexican women in the United States in 1990. However, the labor-force participation rates for Japanese, Korean, Canadian, and British women in their home countries (61 percent, 54 percent, 68 percent, and 71 percent, respectively) were relatively similar to the participation rates of their counterparts living in the United States.[3]

Despite the large rise in immigration from Mexico and the low participation rate of Mexicans, the change in country of origin mix between 1970 and 1990 does not explain the rise in the gap in participation between immigrants

and native-borns. If the distribution of immigrants by origin in 1990 had remained the same as it was in 1970, the total participation rate for immigrant
women would have been 66.5, only 1 percentage point higher than the actual
rate of 65.6 and still 6.2 percentage points below the rate for native-borns
(table 7.1). The reason for the gap is that while the share of immigrants born
in Mexico rose, so too did the share of immigrants born in the Philippines,
Central America, the Caribbean, Africa, Oceania, and South America, and
these immigrants had relatively high rates of participation in 1990.

Education plays an important role in determining the differences in labor-force participation among immigrant groups. Adjusting for differences in
number of years of schooling, the gap between Mexican and native-born
White women is nearly completely eliminated in 1990 (figure 7.3). Similarly,
the gap between Mexicans and native-born Hispanics is completely eliminated after education is adjusted. And, after adjusting for education of Central
Americans in 1990, these immigrants are actually 9 percentage points more
likely to be in the labor force than native-born White women.

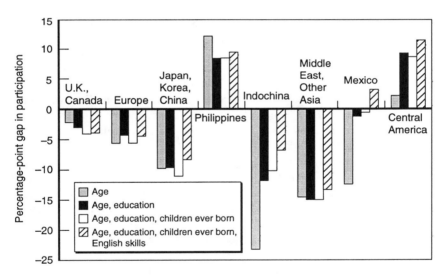

Source: Computations by RAND based on 1970, 1980, and 1990 PUMS of
the U.S. Bureau of the Census.

**Figure 7.3—Difference in Labor-Force Participation (Immigrants Minus
Native-Borns) with and without Controlling for Age, Education,
Number of Children Ever Born, and English Skills,
Nation, 1990**

Because Filipinas are more educated than native-borns, adjusting for years of schooling narrows the gap between these two groups but does not eliminate it.

Although education and English skills explain a substantial share of the differences among some immigrants, differences remain of as much as 15 percentage points among some groups even after adjusting for these characteristics. In particular, these factors do not explain why immigrant women from Europe; Canada; Japan, Korea, and China; and the Middle East have lower labor-force participation rates than non-Hispanic White native-born women. Other factors such as differences in school quality and in attitude toward women working may be important. We come back to this question in the next chapter.

Among the Mexican and Central American women who do participate in the labor force, a higher share, 14.7 percent and 12.7 percent, respectively, in 1990 were unemployed relative to other women (table 7.3). Other immigrant groups had rates of 5 to 7 percent—close to the unemployment rate of 4.8 percent for native-born women. Differences in unemployment are similar for men, with Mexican immigrant men more likely to be unemployed than native-born men, and most Asian and non-Hispanic White immigrant men no more likely to be unemployed than native-born men (Frey, 1995).

The lower English proficiency and greater family responsibilities of Mexican, Central American, and Indochinese women also contribute to their lower participation in the labor force. For instance, controlling for family responsibilities reduces the gap between Indochinese and non-Hispanic White native-born women by 1.6 percentage points, and further controlling for English proficiency reduces the gap by an additional 3.6 percent. After controlling for these factors in addition to education, Mexican immigrant women are more likely to participate in the labor force than non-Hispanic White women. Among immigrant women who work, the differences in the number of weeks or hours worked are fairly small (table 7.4). An exception is that Mexican women worked 39 weeks on average in 1990, while most other groups worked 42 to 45 weeks. However, during the weeks they did work, Mexicans worked just as many hours as most other groups.

Again, the differences between native-borns and Mexican immigrants in the amount of time they work, as measured by total hours worked in the year, is largely explained by education (figure 7.4). In general, after controlling for education, the differences in annual hours worked in 1990 among immigrant groups are fairly modest, with the exception that Filipinas worked substantially more hours than other women (122 hours more than native-born White women), as did Indochinese women.

Family responsibilities and English proficiency also contribute to the fewer hours worked by Mexican immigrant women and also to the lower hours worked by Central American and Indochinese women. These factors had no effects on other immigrant women.

Table 7.4

**Mean Weeks per Year and Hours per Week Worked for Working Women
by Country/Region of Birth, 1970 to 1990**

	1970		1980		1990	
Country/Region of Birth	Weeks Per Year[a]	Hours Per Week[a]	Weeks Per Year[a]	Hours Per Week[a]	Weeks Per Year[a]	Hours Per Week[a]
U.K., Canada, Europe	40.8	NA[b]	41.7	34.7	43.5	36.6
Europe	41.4	NA	42.6	35.6	44.5	36.7
Japan, Korea, China	39.8	NA	41.5	37.4	42.9	39.1
Indochina	—[c]	NA	38.1	37.7	44.7	39.9
Philippines	39.8	NA	44.0	38.6	45.8	39.5
Mexico	40.2	NA	38.2	37.3	38.9	38.1
Central America	41.9	NA	41.7	37.3	42.6	38.2
Mid-East, Other Asia	37.9	NA	41.2	36.7	42.7	37.5
Caribbean, Africa, Oceania, and South						
America	41.6	NA	42.8	37.1	43.9	38.2
Native-Born						
Non-Hispanic Whites	40.2	NA	42.1	35.5	44.2	36.9
Non-Hispanic Blacks	40.8	NA	43.0	36.4	43.8	38.2
Hispanics	38.9	NA	40.8	36.1	42.7	37.6
Others	40.4	NA	41.8	36.7	42.6	38.3
All Native-Born	40.3	NA	42.2	35.6	44.1	37.1

Source: Schoeni, 1998a, table 7, p. 68.

[a]Hours and weeks are averages among women working during the year prior to census.

[b]NA=data not available.

[c]Too few observations for reliable estimation.

Earnings

Immigrants born in different countries have very different labor market earnings (table 7.5). In 1990, immigrant women from the Philippines; Japan, Korea and China; Europe; the U.K. and Canada; and the Middle East and other Asian countries earned just as much as or more, on average, than native-born women. At the same time, Mexican and Central American women earned only 67 and 64 percent of the earnings of native-born women, respectively. This finding represents a substantial drop in relative earnings between 1970 and 1990, especially for Central Americans, who in 1970 earned about the same weekly earnings as native-born women. Virtually all of the decline in the weekly earnings of Mexican relative to native-born women occurred in the 1980s, a drop from 79 to 67 percent. The earnings of Mexican men relative to native-born men has followed an identical path,

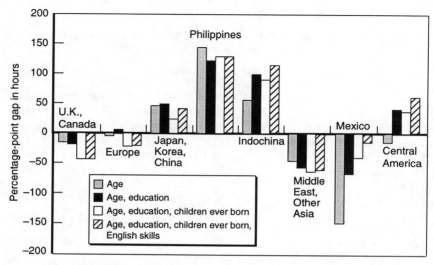

Source: Computations by RAND based on 1970, 1980, and 1990 PUMS of the U.S. Bureau of the Census.

Figure 7.4—Difference in Annual Hours (Immigrant Minus Native-Born Women) with and without Controlling for Age, Education, Number of Children Ever Born, and English Skills, Nation, 1990

Table 7.5

Ratio of Median Weekly Earnings of Immigrant Women Relative to Native-Born Working Women by Country/Region of Birth, 1970–1990

Country/Region of Birth	1970	1980	1990
U.K./Canada	110	106	115
Europe	109	99	102
Japan, Korea, China	91	98	104
Indochina	a	94	94
Philippines	111	119	118
Mexico	80	79	67
Central America	99	78	64
Middle East, Other Asia	111	103	104
Caribbean, Africa, Oceania, S. America	96	98	95

Source: Schoeni, 1998a, table 8, p. 69.

[a]Too few observations to obtain reliable estimates.

remaining fairly steady through the 1970s and then declining substantially in the 1980s (Borjas, 1997).

The relative drop in weekly earnings of Mexican and Central American immigrants is not explained by differences in hours worked during the week. Mexican and Central American immigrants who were employed worked a slightly greater number of hours than native-born women, and the change in hours between 1980 and 1990 (the two years for which hours data are available) was roughly the same for these groups. The drop in relative earnings is in part because of the fact that the gap in education between native-born and Central American women increased substantially. In fact, despite the improvement in education between 1970 and 1990 of 1.5 to 2 years for all other groups, the education of Central American women in the United States declined by 0.7 years. After adjusting for education, the gap drops significantly (figure 7.5).

Disparities in education also explain the low earnings of Mexican immigrant women. Without adjusting for education, the gap between Mexican and native-born White women was 29 percent in 1990. Adjusting for education, this gap is reduced to 4 percent and is eliminated after controlling, in addition, for English skills.

At the same time, Filipinas earned 14 percent higher wages than native-born White women in 1990, which is expected given their high levels of education. After adjusting for difference in education, the gap in favor of Filipinas is basically eliminated, dropping to 1 percent.

In general, completed years of schooling explains most of the disparities in earning among women born in different countries. Despite the fact that other differences in earnings without controls (other than age) are as large as 43 percent (between British/Canadian and Mexican immigrant women), no difference greater than 15 percent was found between the groups of women after adjusting for education, and most differences ranged between 0 and 10 percent.

Lower English proficiency also lead to lower earnings for most immigrant women. If immigrant women were as proficient in English as non-Hispanic White women, the increase in earnings was a low 1 percentage point for women from Europe, Canada, Japan, Korea, China, and the Philippines and an increase of 6 to 8 percentage points for women from Central America and Mexico, respectively.

Self-Employment

Although there is little difference in self-employment rates between immigrant and native-born women, substantial differences are seen among immigrants and, for that matter, among native-borns of different origins (table 7.6). Europeans and Japanese, Korean, and Chinese immigrant women are the most likely to be self-employed, with a rate of 10 and 11 percent in 1990, re-

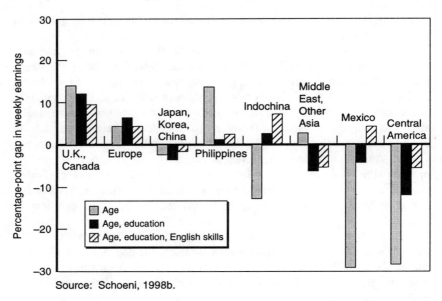

Source: Schoeni, 1998b.

**Figure 7.5—Immigrant Women's Weekly Wages Relative to Native-Born
Women's with and without Controlling for Age, Education,
and English Skills, Nation, 1990**

spectively. Filipinas and Mexican woman are the least likely to be self-employed (4 percent each). The same pattern holds for native-born women from
these various origins, with one exception. Native-born women of European
and Japanese, Korean, and Chinese origin are less likely than their immigrant
counterparts to be self-employed.

There is also little difference in self-employment rates between immigrant and native-born men, but their rates in 1990 were twice as large as those
of women: 11 percent in 1990 for both immigrant and native-born men. This
rate has remained constant since 1970, unlike that of women,which has doubled. Filipino (5 percent) and Mexican men (6 percent) also have the lowest
self-employment rates, while European and Japanese, Korean, and Chinese
men have the highest, 18 and 17 percent respectively.

Conclusions

In 1970, immigrant and native-born women performed similarly in the United
States labor market. Since 1970, however, immigrant women have become
less likely than native-born women to participate in the labor force, more
likely to be unemployed, and more likely to command lower earnings than
native-born women. By 1990, the gap in labor-force participation had grown

Table 7.6

Percentage Self-Employed by Immigration Status, Gender, and Country/Region of Origin, 1970–1990

Country/Region of Origin	Immigrant			Native-born		
	1970	1980	1990	1970	1980	1990
Female						
Canada/U.K./Europe	5	6	10	4	6	7
Japan/Korea/China	6	7	11	1	5	6
Philippines	1	3	4	NA	4	3
Indochina	NA	4	7	NA	0	6
Other Asia	NA	4	7	NA	4	4
Mexico	2	2	5	2	2	4
Other Latin American	2	3	7	3	2	5
Others	2	3	5	3	2	4
All	4	5	7	3	4	6
Male						
Canada/U.K./Europe	14	15	18	12	12	12
Japan/Korea/china	13	15	17	13	13	10
Philippines	4	6	5	2	3	5
Indochina	NA	4	8	NA	3	7
Other Asia	NA	9	11	NA	6	6
Mexico	5	4	6	5	5	6
Other Latin American	7	10	10	7	6	8
Others	4	9	7	7	7	6
All	12	11	11	11	11	11

Source: 1970, 1980, and 1990 PUMS of the U.S. Bureau of the Census

Note: This table includes persons aged 18 to 64. NA means not available.

to 7 percentage points and the gap in weekly earnings to 13 percent. Otherwise, immigrant women have consistently worked the same number of weeks in the year and the same number of hours a week as native-born women. They also have been consistently just as likely to be self-employed as native-born women. Although both groups have doubled their self-employment rate, their rate remains relatively low, 6 percent in 1990.

An increase over time in the educational gap between immigrant and native-born women is the main factor that explains the relative increase in the gap in labor-force participation and in earnings between immigrant and native-born women. Differences in English proficiency also contribute to the difference in labor-force participation and to the gap in earnings, most particularly among low-educated immigrants. Differences in family responsibilities do not significantly contribute to these differentials.

Looking beyond the aggregate groupings by immigration status, there are large differences in labor-market outcomes between immigrant women from different countries of origin. Again, a substantial amount, but not all, of these differentials are explained by differences in education, English proficiency, and to a much lesser extent, differences in family responsibilities.

Because of their lower education, lower proficiency in English, and greater family responsibilities, immigrant women from Mexico are the least likely to participate in the labor force, and when they do, they are also the most likely to be unemployed, to work fewer hours during the week, and to command low earnings. They also are among the least likely to be self-employed. The gap in labor market outcomes between them and other immigrant women has increased over time in large measure because the gap between their education and that of other immigrant women and native-born women has increased the most. For instance, Mexican women were earning 20 percent less than native-born women in 1970, but by 1990, they were earning 37 percent less.

Immigrant women from Central America and Indochina have sociodemographic characteristics generally comparable to those of Mexican immigrant women and, hence, have similar labor-market outcomes, with a couple of exceptions. Women from Central America have one of the highest labor-force participation rates. And Indochinese women's earnings have been almost at par with those of native-born women.

Filipinas are at the other extreme of labor-market performance. They are the most likely to participate in the labor market of any immigrant women and 15 percentage points more likely than native-born women. They also are the least likely to be unemployed and to work the longest number of hours during the week. Their earnings, as well, have been consistently higher than those of other immigrants and native-born women. These positive differentials are in large measure explained by the higher level of education of Filipinas.

Other immigrant women—from Europe and Asia, including Japan, Korea, and China—have labor-market outcomes generally similar to those of native-born women, with a significant exception. All have labor-force participation rates that have remained lower than those of native-born women, and these differentials cannot be explained by differentials in education. Their participation rates remain similar to those of women in their home countries, in contrast to immigrant women from Mexico, Central America, and the Philippines who have much higher labor-force participation rates in the United States than they have at home. The reasons for these differences in behavior by women from different countries of origin remain to be identified.

Finally, our analyses suggest that the image of the entrepreneurial immigrant does not extend to all immigrants. Certainly, immigrant women from Europe, Canada, China, Korea, and Japan fit this image. They are about twice as likely as native-born women and immigrant women from other countries to be self-employed. But immigrant women from other parts of the world are no more likely than native-born women to be self-employed.

Notes

1. This chapter is based on analyses performed for this project by RAND colleague Robert Schoeni. See also Robert Schoeni, "Labor Market Outcomes of Immigrant Women in the United States: 1970 to 1990," *International Migration Review* 32 (1), Spring 1998.

2. As noted in chapter 6, however, exceptions exist in service industries requiring night work and /or irregular work hours.

3. The rate for each of these four countries is based on women 25 to 60 years old, except for Canada, where the estimates are for women 25 to 65. For Japan, Korea, and Canada, the estimates are for 1989, and for the U.K., they are for 1990.

Chapter 8

Integration of Immigrant Women[1]

The process of the integration of male immigrants over their lifetimes into the labor market has been the focus of many past and recent studies and is by now fairly well understood (e.g., Borjas, 1985, 1987, 1995, Chiswick, 1980; Long, 1980; McCarthy and Vernez, 1997; Schoeni, McCarthy, and Vernez, 1996; . By and large, male immigrants are as likely to enter the labor market as native-born men. At entry, they initially earn less than their native-born counterparts, and the extent to which they experience relative earnings growth varies significantly depending on the human capital (e.g., education, experience, and skills) they bring with them.

Education obtained in the home country prior to entering the United States is a prime determinant of the economic progress a male immigrant will experience in his lifetime in the U.S. labor market. Today's college-educated male immigrants—originating primarily from Asia, some parts of the Middle East, and South America—assimilate and progress quickly in the U.S. labor market. On the other hand, today's male immigrants with 12 or fewer years of education—originating primarily from Mexico, Central America, and South-east Asia—command relatively low wages at entry and typically do so throughout their working lives in the United States.

The importance of education as a determinant of the relative success of male immigrants in the U.S. labor market is further underlined by the fact that immigrants who come to the United States as children and obtain most, if not all, of their education in the United States significantly narrow their earnings gap relative to their native-born counterparts. By the second or third generation, the level of education obtained in the United States becomes the primary, although not the sole, determinant of earnings in the U.S. labor market.

Finally, some evidence indicates that the rate of economic progress of low-educated immigrants is slower today than it was 20 or so years ago. This is particularly the case for immigrants from Mexico (Schoeni et al., 1996).

In contrast to males, the integration of female immigrants into the labor market has not been submitted to the same degree of inquiry; thus, anecdotes taint the perceptions immigration analysts and policymakers have about the integration of female immigrants in the labor market. As documented in chapter 1, female immigrants are perceived as facing greater obstacles to entry in the labor market because of family responsibilities as well as certain cultural mores they bring with them. Once they enter the labor market, they are primarily perceived as working in household services and in other low-skill dead-end jobs, as well as being discriminated against, if not exploited. In the three previous chapters, we have presented evidence that dispels the worst of these perceptions and that presents a generally more balanced view of immigrant women in the U.S. labor market.

In this chapter, we continue to pursue this line of inquiry, focusing on the economic progress that immigrant women make within their lifetimes in the U.S. labor market. In the first section, we begin by examining the path that women immigrants follow when entering the labor market and then examine the extent to which family responsibilities, age, and education influence the decision to enter the labor market over time. For those who have entered the labor market, we then examine their earnings path over their lifetimes. In the third section we compare the lifetime earnings profiles of immigrant women to those of immigrant men. And in the fourth section, we take a brief look at the educational, language, economic, and social integration of the children of immigrants. But first, a brief methodological note.

Methodological Note

Ideally, to determine the degree to which immigrants' labor-market outcomes change following their entry into the United States, we would want to have labor-market data obtained from periodic interviews with the same immigrants (and natives). With this information, earnings and employment outcomes could be traced over an individual immigrant's working life and compared with the pattern for natives. However, such data do not currently exist.[2] Therefore, we employ the "cohort method" (Baker and Benjamin, 1994; Borjas, 1985, 1993, 1995; Friedberg, 1991; LaLonde and Topel, 1992)—using the information on age and date of entry into the United States contained in the 1970, 1980, and 1990 censuses—to investigate changes in immigrants' labor-market outcomes. That is, we follow a given age-specific immigration-year entry group from 1970 to 1980 to 1990. For example, we can compare the earnings, reported in the 1970 census, of 25- to 34-year-olds who immigrated between 1965 and 1969 with immigrants who were 35 to 44 years old in the 1980 census and who also reported that they immigrated between 1965 and 1969. This same *arrival cohort* can then be followed through the 1980s by examining the earnings of 45- to 54-year-olds as reported in the 1990 census. The earnings of these immigrants can be compared with the earnings of native-born workers of comparable age to determine whether there is any improvement in the relative earnings of immigrants.

To determine the role of education and to separate out the effects of experience, education, and assimilation, we also conduct multivariate analyses, which are a regression-extension of the cohort method; details of the multivariate methods are described in the appendix. Based on these regression analyses, we present participation and earnings profiles of each immigrant group. These profiles represent the path of employment earnings of an immigrant who entered the United States at age 25 and who has the characteristics of the typical immigrant born in a particular country. As the immigrant ages, her employment probability and earnings change as a result of the effect of age and the effect of assimilation. The lifetime profiles of employment and wages displayed below are based on analyses for immigrants in the nation as a whole.

Economic Progress: Entering the Labor Market

We begin our analysis by presenting the participation rate in the labor market of immigrants who were aged 25 to 34 in 1970 and who entered at various periods between 1950 and 1980. Table 8.1 shows a steady increase in the labor-force participation of immigrant women in the labor market. For instance, 45 percent of female immigrants aged 25 to 34 who entered the country between 1965 and 1969 were in the labor force in 1970. Their rate increased to 64 percent in 1980 and to 71 percent by 1990. A similar increasing pattern is observed for immigrant women who entered at earlier and later time periods.

As the participation rate of immigrant women increases with age, so does the participation rate of native-born women, so that the ratio between the two has remained generally constant (table 8.1, bottom panel). This pattern, relative to native-born women, is observed for immigrants who arrived in the United States at different times, although the participation rate for immigrant women in some years increased faster relative to comparably aged native-born women. For instance, the labor-force participation rate ratio between women immigrants aged 35 to 44 who arrived between 1975 and 1979 and native-born women of the same age was 84 percent in 1980, but ten years later it had increased to 95 percent for the same women.

Using the method described in the preceding section, we also developed lifetime employment rate profiles for immigrants from different countries of origin. The results are displayed in figure 8.1, which compares the lifetime changes in employment rates of immigrant women by origin group, with those of native-born women. The latter's employment rate is already fairly high in the mid-to-late 20-year-olds, hovering around 68 percent. The employment rate increases slightly when native-born women are in their 30s and 40s, peaking at about age 46. It then begins to decline.

In general, immigrant women of all origins display a similar, but more pronounced, inverted U-shaped life-cycle pattern of working. However, the level of employment, the age at which employment peaks, and the degree of disparities between ages differ dramatically between immigrant groups.

Table 8.1

**Percent Immigrant Women Working Relative to Native-born Women,
by Arrival Cohort, Nation, 1970–1990**

	Year of Arrival					
Year: Age in Year	Before 1950	1950–1959	1960–1964	1965–1969	1970–1974	1975–1979
Labor-Force Participation of Immigrants						
1970: 25–34	43	41	43	45		
1980: 35–44	62	63	64	64	66	54
1990: 45–54	71	70	69	71	72	68
Relative Labor-Force Participation[a]						
1970: 25–34	94	90	94	99		
1980: 35–44	95	96	98	99	102	84
1990: 45–54	98	97	96	99	100	95

Source: 1970, 1980, and 1990 PUMS of the U.S. Bureau of the Census.

[a]Ratio of labor-force participation rates of immigrant women and native-born women.

Female immigrants from Europe, Canada, and the United Kingdom display the pattern closest to that of native-born women. They, however, start out at a somewhat lower level of employment than native-born women and although their employment rate increases in similar fashion, they generally remain about 10 percent below that of native-born women.

In contrast to all other immigrant groups, the employment pattern of Philippine women is unique. They have the highest level of employment (about 72 percent) at entry, even higher than that of native-born women, and their employment rate increases sharply over the next 10 years exceeding 80 percent throughout their prime working ages. At the other extreme are women immigrants from Mexico and from the Middle East. They start at a level of employment that is nearly half that of native-born women, and although their employment rate increases over the next 20 years as they get older, their peak employment rate at around age 40 does not exceed 55 percent.

Women from Japan, Korea, and China behave somewhat in between these two extremes. Their employment rates start relatively low at about 50 percent but increase steadily over the next 20 years and beyond, reaching parity with native-born women by approximately age 40. Thereafter, their remaining lifetime working profile matches that of native-born women.

Finally, and in contrast to Mexican women, women from Central America have a relatively high employment rate at entry, similar to that of European women. Also, their rate of employment increases the most rapidly of any group, peaking within ten years at about 70 percent; however, their em-

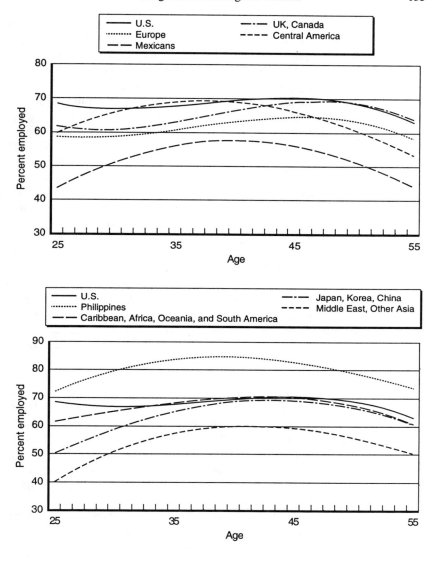

Figure 8.1—Age Profile of Female Employment by Country of Origin

ployment rates decline thereafter more rapidly than for other immigrant groups.

Two reasons for these differences in patterns of employment are differentials in level of education and differentials in family responsibilities between immigrant women from different origins. Figure 8.2 displays the lifetime employment rate if each immigrant group had a level of education and a number of children equal to that of native-born women. It shows that controlling for education in this manner closes the employment-rate gap between Mexican-origin and native-born women by nearly one-third and that the larger number of children born to Mexican women closes another one-third to one-half of the remaining gap.

These two factors, however, contribute little to understanding why other female immigrants have typically lower participation rates than native-born women. In particular, European and Canadian female immigrants have similar levels of education and family responsibilities as native-borns, yet they remain less likely to work throughout their lifetime.

The labor market behavior of Asian women, including Filipinas, contrasts with that of other groups. If they behaved as do native-born women with similar education and family responsibilities, we would expect them to have employment rates that are lower than their actual rates as shown in figure 8.2. Finally, differences in education and family responsibilities have relatively no effect in the gap between women immigrants from Central America or from the Middle East.

Given these unexplained variances in labor-market participation among female immigrant groups, we can only speculate about other factors that may contribute to these differences. One possible factor may be cultural, that is, the long-held attitudes immigrants bring with them regarding the appropriate respective roles of men and women relative to family responsibilities versus remunerated work. It is well documented that the labor-force participation of women in most countries is lower than in the United States. Today, it is still about 10 to 15 percentage points lower in western European countries, 20 percentage points lower in Mexico, and 10 percentage points lower in Japan. Our findings suggest that these cultural mores (if indeed they affect immigrant women's decisions about whether or not to enter the labor market) are weakened but not completely overcome within an immigrant's lifetime. Our findings also suggest that Asian women assimilate into the U.S. female labor market somewhat more rapidly than immigrant women from other parts of the world.

One should be careful not to carry this "cultural" explanation too far, however. Differentials in employment rates among women of different origins may also be associated with the reasons why these immigrant women came here in the first place. As has been documented in chapter 2, the flow of immigrant women from some countries was actually initiated by active recruitment of women by would-be employers in the United States. Such was the case, for instance, for women from Central America who were sought after as household maids and child-care workers (most particularly on the East Coast) and for women from the Philippines who were recruited for nursing and other health occupations. These patterns of initial self-selectivity of women coming to the United States to work (rather than to merely reunite with a spouse), once started, may well endure over time as suggested by the

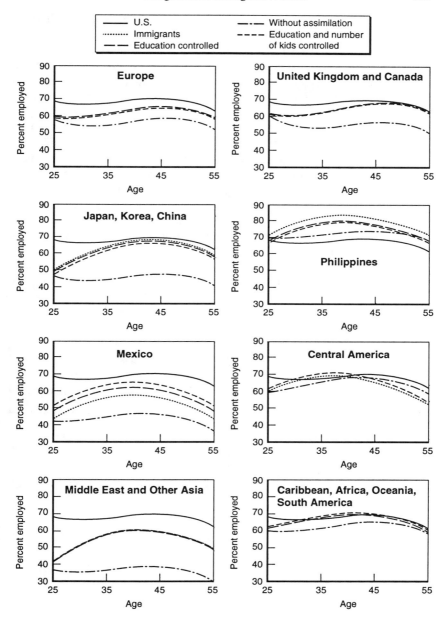

Figure 8.2—Age Profile of Female Employment, with and without Various Controls, by Country of Origin

continuing relatively high employment rates of immigrant women from these two culturally different regions of the world.

Whether an immigrant woman has entered the country as a child, and hence has been fully or partially educated in the United States, or has entered as an adult, also affects her eventual employment rate. Figure 8.3 contrasts the lifetime employment rate of women who arrived as children with those who came in as adults, for immigrants from Mexico and from Japan, Korea, and China. In both instances, the employment rates of immigrants who have been educated in the United States are higher than for their immigrant adult counterparts. Mexican women educated in the United States are about 50 percent more likely to participate in the labor force than Mexican women who came here as adults. Still, this finding is not enough to entirely close the employment-rate gap between them and native-born women. Part of the reason for this continuing disparity is that Mexican women who are educated here continue to trail native-born women in educational attainment (see last section in this chapter).

In contrast to Mexican women educated here, Asian immigrants educated in the United States not only significantly outperform their immigrant adult counterparts with respect to their employment rates, they also outperform native-born women throughout their lifetime. Consistent with our ob-

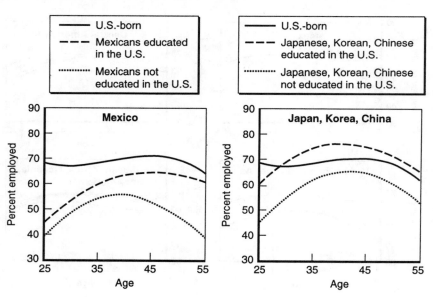

Figure 8.3—Age Profile of Female Employment by whether Educated in the United States, by Country of Origin

servations above, these Asian immigrants assimilate fully in their attitudes toward working.

Economic Progress: Earnings

So far, we have seen that immigrant women increase their involvement in the labor market over their lifetimes in pretty much the same way that native-born women do. However, and even though they assimilate relative to native-born women, their employment rates remain typically lower than those of native-born women, with the exception of Filipinas.

Once an immigrant woman has entered the labor market in the United States, the next question that arises is how her earnings change over the course of her working life and whether that change matches or differs from that of native-born women in the labor force.

As we have done previously, we begin by following the pattern of weekly earnings for cohorts of immigrant women who were ages 25 to 34 in 1970 and who had entered the country at different times over the past 30 years (table 8.2). As for employment, immigrant women's real earnings increase with the length of time spent in the United States. For instance, immigrant women who arrived between 1965 and 1969 and were ages 25 to 34 years old in 1970 had median weekly wages of $270 in 1970, $311 ten years later, and by 1990, when they were 45 to 55 years old, $346. But then, the wages of native-born women increased with their longer time in the labor market, so that the ratio of immigrant women's earnings to those of native-born women does not improve substantially over time. For the 1965–1969 cohort, relative earnings increased from 94 percent to 100 percent over the 20 year time period, 1970–1990. And most other cohorts experienced little or no gain in relative real earnings.

Significantly, however, for almost all cohorts of female immigrants, their earnings have been roughly equal to the earnings of native-borns even shortly after they have arrived in the United States with one exception. Immigrant women aged 25 to 44 who arrived in the late 1970s had earnings that were 14 percent lower than those of their native-born counterparts, and that gap remained unchanged ten years later.

As we did for employment, we constructed lifetime earnings profiles for native-born women and for immigrant women from different origins (figure 8.4). The lifetime earnings profile of immigrant women can be divided into three groups.

The first group consists of immigrant women from Europe, Canada, and the United Kingdom. Their earnings at entry are similar to those of native-

Table 8.2

Median Weekly Earnings of Immigrants Relative to Native-Born Women by Arrival Cohort and Origin, Nation, 1970–1990

Year: Age in Year	Year of Arrival					
	Before 1950	1950–1959	1960–1964	1965–1969	1970–1974	1975–1979
Median Earnings of Immigrants						
1970: 25–34	324	307	307	270		
1980: 35–44	325	301	295	311	290	256
1990: 45–54	384	358	349	346	317	288
Relative Median Earnings[a]						
1970: 25–34	113	107	107	94		
1980: 35–44	109	101	100	105	98	86
1990: 45–54	111	103	101	100	92	83

Sources: 1970, 1980, and 1990 PUMS of the U.S. Bureau of the Census.

Note: Earnings are expressed in 1990 dollars.

[a]Ratio of median earnings of immigrant women and native-born women.

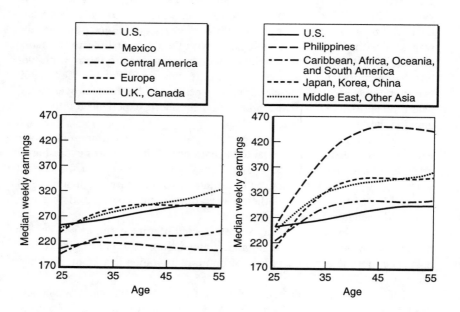

Figure 8.4—Age Profile of Women's Weekly Wages by Country of Origin

born women and their lifetime earnings path is similar to that of native-born women.

The second group consists of immigrant women from Asia and the Middle East. Like the first group, their earnings at entry are similar to those of native-born women. Their earnings, however, increase rapidly peaking after 15 to 20 years in the country at a level that is significantly higher than that of native-born women. Among Asians and certainly among immigrant women, Filipinas stand out: their lifetime growth in real earnings outperforms all other groups.

Immigrant women from Mexico and Central America constitute the last group. These women command significantly lower earnings than native-borns at entry, and the gap between them and native-born women not only remains negative over their lifetime, it increases, most particularly for female immigrants of Mexican origin. In other words, unlike other immigrant women, these women enjoy no upward economic mobility over their lifetimes, and their earnings remain relatively low.

Again, education is a main factor in explaining the differences in the lifetime earnings path (figure 8.5). Mexico's immigrant women have an average of three years of education compared to 12.2 for native-borns. If Mexican and Central American women had the same level of education as native-born women, the gap between their earnings and those of native-born women would be reduced by 50 to 75 percent. It would not, however, be fully eliminated. A potential reason for this remaining differential may be associated with differences in quality of education between Mexico and the United States and remaining differences in English proficiency within the first generation of Mexican immigrants. As noted in chapter 3, a majority of Mexican and Central Americans continue to have difficulties with the language over their lifetimes.

Education is also a major reason why Filipinas earn more than native-born women. It explains some 50 percent of the gap between the two groups. Differences in levels of education explain only part of the differential between other Asian and Middle Eastern immigrant women and native-born women. Further analyses are needed to identify the factors that contribute to this differential in real earnings. Filipinas and Asian women do not work significantly longer hours (at most, an average of two hours more) than native-born women, so other factors must have more significance. Differences in occupational distribution between Asian and native-born women with similar levels of education offer a more likely explanation for this gap. By and large, Asian women are more likely to be employed in high-wage technical and health-related occupations and less likely to be working in lower-wage occupations such as teachers.

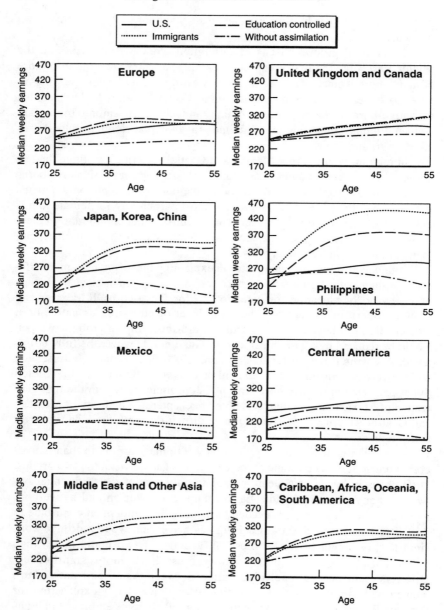

Figure 8.5—Age Profile of Women's Weekly Wages with and without Various Controls by Country of Origin (1990 Dollars)

So far, we have shown that immigrant women have experienced an upward economic mobility that has exceeded that of native-born women, with the exceptions of low-educated immigrant women from Mexico and Central America. The latter, however, are a significant (37 percent) portion of all immigrant women in the national labor force. And they are half of immigrant women in the labor force who have settled in the state of California.

Immigrant women who have come to the United States as children and have been educated in this country do even better than their parents who entered as adults regardless of origin. Figure 8.6 shows that Mexican immigrants educated in the United States have higher earnings than immigrant women who have been educated in Mexico. Their earnings, however, remain somewhat lower than those of native-born women. A major reason for this pattern is, of course, the higher level of education these young Mexican immigrants acquire in the United States than they acquire in Mexico. Their level of education, however, remains lower than that of native-born women. Similarly, the earnings of Japanese, Korean, and Chinese immigrant women educated in the United States are higher than those of their counterparts educated in their country of origin. And in contrast to women of Mexican origin, their lifetime earnings are much higher than those of native-born women.

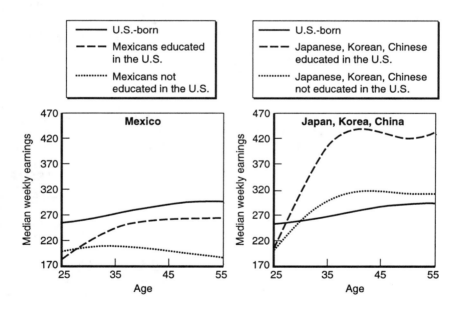

Figure 8.6—Age Profile of Weekly Wages by whether Educated in the United States, by Country of Origin

Changes in the Rate of Economic Progress

As increasingly larger numbers of immigrant women continuously enter the United States, the question arises as to whether their economic mobility is affected over time—that is, is the economic progress of the larger cohorts of recent immigrants slower than that of the smaller cohorts of immigrants who came earlier? Over the years, as documented in chapter 6, immigrants are increasingly dominating the labor forces of some industries, and the continuous arrival of new immigrants may generate increased competition for jobs in these industries. At the same time, returns to education have increased for immigrants and native-borns with some college or more. As a result, low-educated immigrants may find it increasingly more difficult to command greater relative earnings.

Our analyses provide evidence that the rate of economic progress of Mexican, Central American, and European immigrant women has declined since the 1965–1969 time period (table 8.3). For instance, women immigrants from Mexico who arrived between 1975–1979 were earning 13 percent less than those who entered in the earlier period. And those who entered in 1985–1989 were earning 33 percent less than those who entered in 1965–1969.

The rate of economic progress, however, has remained relatively constant over the years for all other immigrants including those from Asia (including the Philippines) and those from the Middle East. This pattern is consistent with increased competition among low-educated workers, combined with increasing demand for more-educated workers.

Table 8.3

Estimated Percent Change in Rate of Earnings across Female-Immigrant Cohorts That Arrived at Different Times, by Selected Country of Origin (Relative to the 1965–1969 Cohort)

Period of Entry	Mexico	Central America	Japan, Korea, China	Philippines	Europe	U.K., Canada
1965–1969	–0.0	0.0	0.0	0.0	0.0	0.0
1970–1974	–3.3	0.0	2.9	4.7	–3.0	–3.2
1975–1979	–12.8	–9.5	4.8	1.0	–4.8	2.6
1980–1984	–23.2	–15.3	0.0	1.7	–6.5	9.6
1985–1990	–32.7	–22.9	–2.0	–2.3	–11.5	4.7

Note: The figures in this table are estimates of the difference in weekly earnings of the specified cohort relative to the weekly earnings of the 1965–1969 cohorts after controlling for age and education.

Comparison with Immigrant Men

At first glance, the lifetime-earnings profiles of immigrant women from specific areas of origin appear to be similar to those of their immigrant men counterparts (figure 8.7). Both earn less than their native counterparts at the beginning of their working careers in the United States, but their earnings increase over time and typically reach parity after a few years in the United States. Both immigrant men and women from Mexico and Central America are significant exceptions to this pattern. Their earnings gap relative to their native counterparts increases rather than decreases over their lifetimes (Schoeni et al., 1996; McCarthy and Vernez, 1997).

Notable differences in the lifetime-earnings profiles also exist between immigrant men and women from specific countries of origin. The earnings differential between Mexican immigrant and native-born women at entry (82 percent) is lower than it is between Mexican immigrant and native-born men (72 percent). After entry, however, the real earnings of Mexican immigrant men increase over time, even though the earnings relative to native-born men decrease (down to 64 percent). By contrast, Mexican immigrant women experience an absolute decline in real earnings, in spite of a slight increase in the early years of their working careers in the United States. By age 50, their earnings gap relative to native-born women has increased (down to 69 percent).

The largest difference in lifetime-earnings profiles between men and women from the same country of origin is between immigrants from the Philippines. As noted earlier, although Filipinas earn less at entry than native-born women—just as Filipinos do relative to native men—the earnings of the first reach parity with native-born women within three to four years, and then continuously and sharply exceed those of their native-born counterparts. The lifetime earnings profile for Filipinos follows a reverse pattern. After briefly increasing after entry, their earnings growth slows down and then increasingly lags behind the growth in earnings of native-born men.

Immigrant women and men from Japan, Korea, and China, and from the Middle East, show differentials in their lifetime-earnings profiles similar to those of immigrants from the Philippines, but their differentials are not as large. Immigrant women reach earnings parity with native-born women more rapidly than men do relative to native-born men, and their earnings relative to native-born women grow at a faster rate than the earnings of immigrant men relative to native-born men.

In brief, immigrant women who enter the labor force typically enjoy a rate of economic growth that exceeds that of native-born men and also exceeds the economic progress of immigrant men relative to native-born men. Once again, immigrants from Mexico, and to a lesser degree immigrants from Central America, are a notable exception to these lifetime earnings profiles.

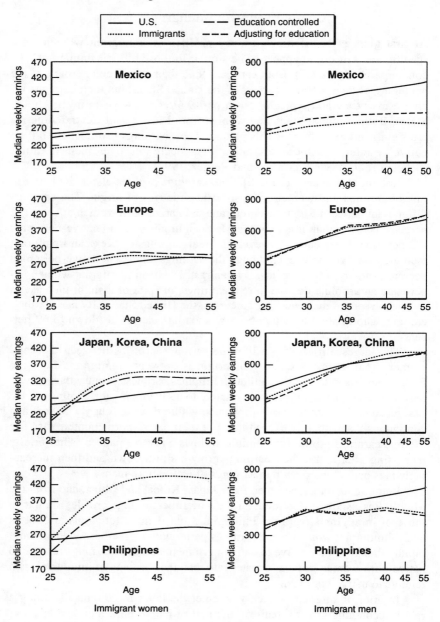

Figure 8.7—Comparison of Lifetime Earnings between Immigrant Men and Women

Intergenerational Integration of Immigrant Women

In chapter 3, we documented significant differences in socioeconomic characteristics among immigrant women of different countries or regional origins as well as significant differences between immigrants and native-borns as a whole. And in the preceding sections, we have also shown how immigrant women with different human capital endowments and from different areas of origin progress economically at different rates within their lifetime in the United States.

In this section, we briefly examine the extent to which the socioeconomic characteristics of subsequent generations of immigrant women differ from those of their immigrant parents. Table 8.4 provides a 1990 snapshot of differences and similarities with respect to fertility, household arrangements, marriage rates, education, and English proficiency. These comparisons reflect the dynamic intergenerational process of assimilation. The reader should keep in mind that because the peak time of arrival of different groups of immigrant women differs (see chapter 2), the share of their descendants in each subsequent generation will differ at any point in time. For instance, the native-born descendants of European origin consist of many generations; they were the first to settle in the country, but although new immigrants from Europe have continued to come, they have done so in decreasing numbers for several decades now. At the other extreme, the native-born descendants of Vietnamese immigrants consist primarily of the first generation of children of this newest wave of immigrants, many of whom have not yet reached adulthood as implied by the significantly lower mean age of the native-borns of Vietnamese origin (27 years old) compared with the mean age of immigrants of Vietnamese origin (35 years old).

Table 8.4 shows that, regardless of country/region of origin, the native-born descendants of immigrants have lower marriage and fertility rates, live in smaller households, have higher levels of education, and achieve higher English proficiency than their immigrant parents or forebearers. The relative magnitude of the change appears to depend on two primary factors: (1) how large is the difference on a given characteristic between the immigrant women from a specific country of origin and the native-born population; and (2) how many successive generations of children have been born by 1990. By and large, the greater the "distance" between immigrants and native-borns and the more recent the immigrant flow, the lesser the relative "assimilation" of their descendants. The outcome of this intergenerational process is best illustrated by initially comparing the characteristics of the oldest and of the newest immigrants to the United States: the European and the Indochinese immigrant women. Current European immigrant women have fertility, family arrangements, and educational characteristics that are similar to those of native-borns as a whole and similar to the characteristics of native-borns of

Table 8.4

Selected Characteristics of Immigrant Women and Their Descendants, Ages 18 to 64, 1990

Country/Region of Origin	Mean Age		Number of Persons per Household		Fertility of Married Women Aged 40–44		Education Mean Years		Education Percent <12 Years		Percent >16 Years		Percent Who Speak English Poorly		Percent Married		Mean Number of Children	
	I	N	I	N	I	N	I	N	I	N	I	N	I	N	I	N	I	N
Europe	43.4	38.5	3.1	3.0	2.207	2.142	12.4	13.0	18	11	21	22	9	0	72	64	1.9	1.7
Black[a]	36.3	36.7	3.8	3.6	2.606	2.533	12.3	12.2	17	22	17	13	6	0	46	34	1.8	2.1
American Indians	37.2	36.3	3.5	3.7	3.407	2.731	11.7	11.8	26	26	13	10	6	1	52	52	2.1	2.3
Asia																		
China/Japan/Korea	38.1	36.4	3.6	3.1	1.980	1.865	12.6	14.1	18	3	33	42	30	2	71	52	1.5	1.1
Philippines	38.5	31.2	4.3	3.9	2.158	2.300	13.8	13.2	11	9	50	27	4	2	67	46	1.8	1.3
Indochina	34.8	26.8	5.2	5.1	3.504	.799	8.9	11.5	47	25	9	7	42	15	61	27	2.3	.8
Other Asia	36.2	30.0	4.0	3.9	2.170	2.596	13.3	12.8	16	16	46	26	12	4	76	40	1.7	1.3
Latin America																		
Mexico	34.5	34.6	5.4	4.0	3.798	2.831	7.6	11.3	69	31	3	8	53	5	65	55	2.6	2.1
Central America	34.7	29.6	4.8	3.8	2.895	2.942	9.4	12.8	49	13	7	26	48	8	52	36	2.0	1.1
Cuba	43.3	29.2	3.4	3.2	2.067	1.693	11.4	13.2	29	10	16	26	34	1	64	40	1.7	.9
Other Hispanics	38.5	38.4	3.9	3.1	2.419	2.334	11.2	12.1	30	25	15	15	31	5	57	48	1.8	1.8
Other	36.1	35.8	4.0	3.8	2.589	2.733	10.6	12.2	39	18	14	12	25	1	56	52	1.8	2.0
All	38.5	38.1	4.1	3.2	2.544	2.196	11.1	12.8	31	14	20	20	27	1	65	59	2.0	1.8

Source: 1990 PUMS of the U.S. Bureau of the Census.

Note: I means immigrants; N means native-borns.

[a]Includes Blacks from Africa, the Caribbean, and Latin America.

European origins. The one exception is a significantly higher marriage rate among European immigrants than among native-borns of European origin.

Indochinese immigrants, by contrast, are significantly different from native-borns of Indochinese origin. They have higher fertility rates, have lower education, and, naturally, lower English proficiency than native-borns as a whole. The first generation of these most recent immigrants displays characteristics that move toward those of native-borns in general, but there remain significant differences. For instance, the share of women of Indochinese origin with fewer than 12 years of education was cut from 36 percent for foreign-borns to 25 percent for native-borns of the first generation. The latter, however, remain twice that of native-borns as a whole. And there is no change in the relatively large size of households in which immigrant and native-born women of Indochinese origin live, possibly reflecting the maintenance of social and family norms at least through early adulthood of the first native-born generation of Indochinese in the United States.

Between these two extremes fall the immigrant and the native-born women of Mexican origin and those of Chinese, Japanese, and Korean origin. Immigrants from these countries have already produced at least two sizable generations of native-borns, if not more, although not as many generations of significant size as among European immigrants.[3] But the characteristics of these immigrants differ significantly from each other and from native-borns as a whole and so do the 1990 characteristics of their native-born counterparts.

Mexican immigrants are entering this country with characteristics that are the most different from those of native-borns of any group of immigrants. Although their native-born counterparts show significant convergence toward the fertility, household arrangements, educational attainment, and marriage rates of native-borns as a whole, significant differences subsist. For instance, we observe a significant decline between immigrants from Mexico and their descendants in fertility rate (from 3.8 to 2.8 for women aged 40 to 44) and in average size of households (from 5.4 to 4.0), but these rates remain 25 percent higher than those of native-borns as a whole. A similar convergence has taken place with respect to education in which the high 69 percent share of Mexican immigrants with fewer than 12 years of education is reduced to 31 percent among their descendants. The latter's share, however, is still more than twice as large as it is for native-borns as a whole. Similarly, and although the share of college graduates of native-borns of Mexican origin is twice as large as that of Mexican immigrants—8 percent versus 3 percent—it remains much below that of native-borns in general (20 percent).

Noteworthy, however, is the rapid convergence to English proficiency of the descendants of Mexican immigrants. More than half of Mexican immigrants spoke English poorly or not at all in 1990, but only 5 percent of their native-born counterparts do so. This intergenerational pattern suggests that concerns that the English language might be eventually supplanted by Spanish among subsequent generations of Hispanic native-borns are unfounded. A similar rapid convergence to English proficiency within one generation is apparent among the descendants of other Hispanic immigrants.

Immigrants from China, Japan, and Korea differ from native-borns mainly with respect to their higher share of college graduates and higher marriage rates than native-borns as a whole. They otherwise have similar fertility rates and they live in households that are only slightly larger in size. Their native-born counterparts acquire even more education than the foreign-borns have, so that they increasingly diverge from all other groups in their educational attainment. By 1990, 42 percent of native-born women from Western Asia were college graduates, more than twice the share for other native-borns. Their average years of 14.1 years of education is nearly 1.2 years higher than that of any other group. At the same time, their marriage rate is one of the lowest among native-borns.

The process of convergence by U.S. native-borns from various countries of origin toward the prevailing pattern for all native-borns holds for the descendants of immigrants from all the countries/regions of origin examined, with one significant exception. Female immigrants from the Philippines have the highest level of education among immigrants, with 50 percent having graduated from college. They also have one of the lowest fertility rates. In contrast to the descendants from other immigrant groups, however, the educational level of the descendants of Filipina immigrants declined from an average 13.8 to 13.2 years. The share of college graduates among the descendants of Philippine immigrants is nearly one-half lower than that of their parent immigrants.

This brief comparison of the characteristics of immigrants and native-borns from the same country/region of origin demonstrates the powerful process of intergenerational assimilation that continues to be at work for the native-born descendants of even the most recent waves of immigrants. The process is most powerful and rapid with respect to acquisition of the English language but is at work in all areas examined here from education to marriage and family formation.

Conclusions

Immigrant women from different parts of the world arrive in the United States with different educational endowments and family responsibilities and, hence, their lifetime experience in the U.S. labor market defies easy generalizations.

Surely, all immigrant women increase their participation in the labor market over their lifetime in pretty much the same way that native-born women do. However, their employment rates remain typically lower than that of native-born women throughout their lifetimes. This is as far as we can generalize. Beyond that, immigrant women from different origins enter the labor market at significantly different rates upon arrival and increase those rates at equally significantly different rates. Moreover, once in the labor market, their lifetime earnings also differ significantly.

Most employed in the United States labor market are immigrant women from the Philippines. Upon arrival, their employment rate not only exceeds that of native-born women, it also increases throughout their lifetimes, exceeding 80 percent during their prime working ages. Similarly, their lifetime earnings exceed those of all other immigrant groups as well as those of native-born women.

At the other extreme, immigrant women from Mexico are least employed in the United States labor market. Their employment rate at entry is the lowest of any immigrant group and is about half that of native-born women. Their employment rate increases with age but remains about 15 percentage points lower than that of native-born women and lower than that of any other immigrant group. They also command the lowest earnings of any immigrant groups at entry, and the earnings gap between them and native-born and other immigrant women increases rather than decreases over time. A sizeable portion (about 20 percent) of immigrant women in today's labor market is from Mexico.

Immigrant women from other parts of the world have lifetime labor-force attachment and lifetime-earnings patterns that fall in between these two extremes. Immigrant women from Central America have lifetime-earnings patterns similar to those of immigrant women from Mexico, but they have higher employment rates at entry and throughout their lifetimes. Immigrant women from Asia have low rates of employment at entry but increase that rate the most rapidly of any group reaching parity with native-born women within ten years or so. And their earnings exceed those of native-born women throughout most of their lifetimes. Immigrant women from Europe also have a lower rate of employment than native-born women at entry, but in contrast to Asian women they do not close the gap over their lifetimes. And also in contrast to Asian immigrant women, their lifetime earnings remain generally similar to those of native-born women.

Differences in education go a long way to explain the lifetime employment and earnings patterns described above. For instance, education explains about one-third of the lower employment and more than 50 percent of the lifetime-earnings differentials between Mexican immigrant women and native-born women. Responsibilities for more children explain another one-third of the employment differentials between Mexican immigrant women and native-born women. Education is also a major reason why Filipinas are more likely to be employed and command higher earnings than native-born women.

But variations in these factors are not the whole story. For instance, European immigrant women and native-born women have similar education and family responsibilities, yet the first remain about 10 percent less likely to be working than native-born women. Inversely, given the relatively low differential in education and family responsibilities between Asian immigrant women (including Filipinas) and native-born women, we would expect lower differences in their respective lifetime-employment and lifetime-earnings patterns. At this juncture, we can only speculate about other factors that may contribute to these differences. Maintenance of cultural mores may explain some of these differences whereas selectivity resulting from active recruitment for specific occupations may explain others. Also, differentials in choice of occupational patterns may help explain variations in lifetime-earnings patterns that are not accounted for by differentials in levels of education.

In this chapter, we also briefly examined the extent of assimilation of the subsequent generations of immigrants. Generally, and in keeping with previous studies, we found considerable convergence across subsequent generations of immigrants from different origins and with different characteristics at entry with regard to educational attainment and family responsibilities (marriage rates and number of children). This convergence is all the greater the smaller the difference is between immigrants at entry and native-borns on a given socioeconomic characteristic and, of course, the more generations have been born to a given immigrant group. This multigenerational assimilation process is at work even for the most recent waves of immigrants and is most powerful and rapid with respect to acquisition of the English language, which typically is completed in one generation. Assimilation with respect to educational attainment, however, may take longer—most particularly for immigrant groups whose educational attainment at entry is significantly lower than that of native-borns.

Notes

1. I thank my colleague Robert F. Schoeni who performed the analyses whose results are presented in this chapter. For a more detailed discussion see Robert F. Schoeni and Georges Vernez (1997), *The Economic Progress of Immigrant Women*, Santa Monica, Calif.: RAND, DRU-1705-AMF, 1997; and Robert F. Schoeni (1998a), "Labor Market Assimilation of Immigrant Women," *Industrial and Labor Relations Review* 51 (3): 483–504.

2. Chiswick (1980) examines the National Longitudinal Survey, which follows respondents over time; however, that survey interviewed only 98 immigrants.

3. Clearly, many generations of descendants of Mexican and Asian immigrants have been residing in the country since the eighteenth and, most particularly, the nineteenth century. Their numbers, however, are small relative to the first- and second-generation descendants of the post-World War II larger immigration flows from these countries.

Chapter 9

Use of Public Services by Immigrant Women

Previous chapters have documented that a sizable portion of recent female immigrants arrive with a relatively low level of education and eventually work in low-skilled occupations and industries that pay relatively low wages. In this chapter we examine the extent to which these immigrants upgrade their education or make use of available training programs. We also examine their reliance on available safety net programs.

The chapter begins with a brief review of past and recent changes in federal policies governing the eligibility for, and access of, immigrants to federal and state public programs and services. Prior to 1996, legal permanent immigrants enjoyed the same access to public services as citizens. Now they are barred from access to most safety net programs until they have been naturalized or have worked in the United States for ten years.

It will be several years before we know what effects, if any, these legislative changes will have on patterns of new immigration, on immigrants already here, and on the use of public services. To provide a baseline to eventually measure the effects of the new legislation, the remainder of this section examines how immigrants have used federal and state services under the previous regime of "equal access." It documents how immigrant women have used education and training programs to upgrade their skills and to otherwise compete in the U.S. labor market. Having found that immigrant women use these programs typically less than native-born women, we then examine the extent to which immigrant women have made use of safety net public programs to support themselves and their families.

Changes in Access to Services

Until Congress recently enacted, and the president signed into federal law the Personal Responsibility and Work Opportunity Reconciliation Act of 1996 (PRWORA), legal permanent immigrants enjoyed the same access to federal, state, and local entitlement programs and other public services as native-borns and other U.S. citizens. This "equal treatment" policy assured immigrants access to federal and state welfare, health, social service, and scholarship programs if they qualified on the basis of needs (see table 9.1). In addition, refugees were provided—and continue to be provided—with special resettlement assistance that includes cash assistance, instruction in the English language, and assistance in finding housing and jobs. However, immigrants here on Temporary Protective Status (TPS), asylum seekers, and illegal immigrants were not eligible for certain cash assistance and nonemergency medical services. They were eligible, though, to receive primary and secondary education, federal housing, and selected nutritional programs including WIC (Women, Infants, and Children) and the school lunch and breakfast programs for their children. In addition, antidiscrimination and other laws governing the functioning of the labor and housing markets protect all immigrants.

Although the PRWORA involves significant changes in the treatment of legal immigrants, it does not affect other immigrants. It reasserts the exclusion of illegal immigrants from access to welfare and nonemergency federal health services, although it does not extend this exclusion to child nutrition programs, immunization or treatment of communicable diseases, and K–12 public education. Refugees and asylees continue to be treated differently, as before: they continue to be eligible for all federal services as well as for special refugee assistance through the Federal Office of Refugee Resettlement.

Under the PRWORA, legal immigrants are barred from access to the Supplemental Security Income (SSI) program, to the safety net federal program for the Disabled, Blind, and the Aged, and to the Food Stamps program until they become naturalized or work in the United States for ten years. In addition, legal immigrants who arrived after January 1997 are barred from access for five years to most federal means-tested programs, including the Aid to Families with Dependent Children (AFDC) and the Temporary Assistance to Needy Families (TANF) programs, Medicaid, housing, and social services programs. Exemptions are provided for emergency medical assistance, child nutrition, immunizations, foster care and adoption assistance, higher education, Headstart, and the Job Training and Partnership Act (JTPA).

Under PRWORA, each state will decide how new legal immigrants will be treated after the five-year ban, as well as how legal immigrants who arrived prior to January 1997 and are not yet naturalized will be treated. Depending on the state, these immigrants may be covered for all, some, or none of the means-tested federal programs. And if a state extends eligibility to immigrants for some or all federal programs, it will also have to deem the income and resources of any person who executed an affidavit in support of the immigrant as being available to the immigrant applying for a program's benefits. States have the option of waiving the deeming provision provided they use their own funds to cover the federal share. Finally, states may provide public services to illegal immigrants only by enacting a state law so specifying and using their own funds. This delegation of federal authority in formulating policies toward immigrants opens the possibility that immigrants may be treated differently in different states.

Congressional approval of PRWORA followed several years of debate about the growing costs of immigration, most particularly illegal immigration, being imposed on federal, state, and local governments (Clark et al. 1994; Huddle, 1994; McCarthy and Vernez 1997; National Research Council, 1997; Romero et al., 1994; Rothman and Espenshade, 1992; U.S. General Accounting Office, 1995; Vernez and McCarthy, 1996;). In the early 1990s, concerns about the public costs of providing services to immigrants were heightened by a slowdown of the nation's economic growth and two decades of slow growth in the real wages of a majority of American workers (McCarthy and Vernez, 1997; Mishel and Bernstein, 1994). Nowhere was this public concern greater than in California, which was experiencing both the longest and deepest recession and the highest level of immigration, both legal and illegal, it had ever known (McCarthy and Vernez, 1997). A popular initiative, known as Proposition 187, seeking to deny education, health, and other public services to illegal immigrants, was placed on the 1995 California ballot. Eventually, supported by the governor, this proposition was overwhelmingly approved by California voters. Although the major provisions of Proposition 187 were eventually ruled to be unconstitutional by a federal court—on the ground that it usurped the prerogative of the federal government to formulate immigration policy—the intensity of concerns about the public costs of immigration and the concomitant public backlash against illegal immigration prompted Congress and the administration to not only enact PRWORA,[1] but also to enact new legislation, the Illegal Immigration Reform and Immigrant Responsibility Act of 1996 (IIRIRA), designed to crack down anew on illegal immigration. The latter legislation makes it easier to deport illegal immigrants and authorizes more resources for enforcement of immigration laws, most particularly enforcement along the 2,200-mile border with Mexico.

The IIRIRA also tightened the deeming provisions enacted under PRWORA. It provides that all family-sponsored immigrants file an affidavit of support. It requires that the sponsor must be able to support the immigrant and his/her family at a minimum of 125 percent of the federal poverty guideline. The affidavit is enforceable by the federal government or any state or local government.

Methodological Note

The estimates of public-service use by immigrant and native-born women presented in the remainder of this section are based on data from the 1990 and 1991 national Survey of Income and Program Participation (SIPP) of the U.S. Bureau of the Census, Department of Commerce. This sample survey

Table 9.1

Overview of Immigrant Eligibility for Federal Programs Prior to the Personal Responsibility and Work Opportunities Reconciliation Act of 1996 (PRWORA)

Program/ Immigrant Status	AFDC/ TANF	SSI	Unemployment Insurance	Refugee Assistance	Medicaid
Legal permanent resident	Yes/*No*[a]	Yes/*No*[b]	Yes/*No*[a]	Yes, if Amerasian, former refugee, or asylee	Yes/*No*[a,c]
Family unity	Same as amnesty alien	Yes	Yes	No/*No*	Same as amnesty alien
Refugee/asylee	Yes	Yes/*Yes*	Yes/*Yes*	Yes/*Yes*	Yes/*Yes*
Parolee, Cuban/Haitian entrant	Yes	Yes	Yes	Yes, if paroled as refugee or asylee, or if national of Cuba or Haiti	Yes
Temporary protective status	No	No	Yes	No/*No*	Emergency Services
Deferred enforced departure	Arguably, yes as PRUCOL*	Yes/*Yes*	Yes/*Yes*	No/*No*	Yes/*Yes*
Asylum applicant	No**	Arguably, yes as PRUCOL*	Yes (if work authorized)	No, unless national of Cuba or Haiti	Emergency Services**
Undocumented	No/*No*	No/*No*	No/*No*	No, unless national of Cuba or Haiti/*No*	Emergency Services

Source: National Immigration Law Center, 1993, and Personal Responsibility and Work Opportunity Reconciliation Act of 1996 (PRWORA).

Note: Italicized yes/no answers are current as of the passage of PRWORA.

*Permanently residing in the United States under color of law.

**Some states such as Florida and Massachusetts recognize PRUCOL.

[a]New legal immigrants are ineligible for federal means-tested services. Coverage of current immigrants (i.e., arrived prior to January 1997) is at states' discretion.

[b]Ineligible until citizenship has been obtained or work record is ten years or 40 quarters.

[c]Except emergency medical assistance.

[d]Current recipients may continue to receive certain housing benefits.

Table 9.1—continued

Food Stamps	WIC	School Breakfast and Lunch	Headstart, K–6, K–12	Title IV Federal Loans	JTPA	Federal Housing
Yes/No[b]	Yes/Yes	Yes/Yes	Yes/Yes	Yes/No[a]	Yes/Yes	Yes/No[a]
Yes	Yes	Yes/Yes	Yes/Yes	Yes	Yes (if work authorized)	Yes
Yes/Yes	Yes/Yes	Yes/Yes	Yes/Yes	Yes/Yes	Yes/Yes	Yes/Yes
Yes	Yes/Yes	Yes/Yes	Yes/Yes	Yes	Yes	Yes/Yes
No	Yes	Yes/Yes	Yes/Yes	Arguably, yes	Yes (if work authorized)	Yes
No/Yes	Yes/Yes	Yes/Yes	Yes/Yes	Arguably, yes	Yes/Yes (if work authorized)	Yes/Yes
No	Yes	Yes	Yes/Yes	Arguably, yes	Yes (if work authorized)	Yes
No/No	Yes/Yes	Yes/Yes	Yes	No/No	No/No	Yes/No[d]

contains information on the participation of more than 100,000 native- and foreign-born individuals in a broad range of public service programs. It also contains socioeconomic information on the families and households of which these individuals are a part. The participation rate in a specific program is defined as the probability that a person of any one age has benefited from that program in an average month during the 1990–1993 time period.

Since children under age 15 were not asked where they were born, we attribute to them the nativity of their respective head of family. In other words, and for this analysis, a child is categorized as an "immigrant" if he/she lives in a family in which the head of the family is foreign-born, regardless of whether that child was actually born in the United States or abroad. The rationale for this choice is that regardless of where they were born, these children have immigrant parents and hence would not use public services in the

United States had their parents not immigrated in the first place. This choice is expected to result in slightly higher participation rates for immigrants than would otherwise be the case.

We also chose to report participation rates on an individual basis rather than on a family or household basis as other studies typically have done (Borjas and Hilton, 1995). The latter two measures are sensitive to variations in family or household composition and to the clustering of program participants in a few households or families tending to bias program participation of immigrants upward. For instance, Bean et al. (1996) show that the welfare participation rates of immigrants relative to native-borns differ depending on the choice of unit of observation. They show that when computed on a household basis, the welfare participation rate of "immigrant" households is higher than that of "native-born" households. However, when that rate is computed on an individual basis, native-born individuals have a higher welfare participation rate than immigrants. Part of the reason is that not all members in a household are immigrants and not all of them may participate in a specific public program.

Finally, the reader should keep in mind that the 1990–1993 period of observation included a recessionary period. Hence, we should expect that the participation rates in most of the assistance programs discussed in this section would be somewhat higher than during periods of time characterized by steady economic growth.

Education of Immigrant Women in the United States

As noted earlier, a significant proportion of adult immigrant women come to the United States with less than a college education and even less than a high school education. This section examines the extent to which they pursue additional education after arriving here.

Few Adult Immigrants Pursue an Education in the United States

Whereas nearly all immigrant children aged 15 years or less and U.S.-born children of immigrants complete or receive all their education in American schools and colleges, only a small proportion of immigrant women or men who come to the United States as adults (aged 18 or older) receive any education in American educational institutions. Figure 9.1 shows that less than 9 percent of immigrant women aged 18 or older received any education in the United States compared to 7 percent for immigrant men.

Table 9.2 shows that this pattern is consistent across countries of origin and for both refugees and other immigrants. For instance, Asian immigrant women who came to the United States at age 18 or older were no more likely than their Mexican or other Hispanic immigrant female counterparts to pursue an education in the United States. And immigrant women were no less

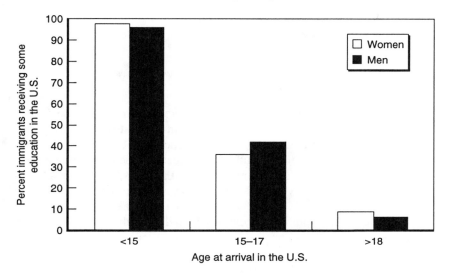

Source: Survey of Income and Program Participation, 1990–1993.
Note: Universe is immigrants aged 18 to 64 at time of survey.

**Figure 9.1—Percent Immigrants Receiving Some Education in the
United States by Age at Arrival, 1990–1993**

Table 9.2

**Percent of Immigrants Aged 18–64 Who Received Some Education in the
United States by Age at Arrival and Country of Origin, 1990–1993**

Country of Origin	Age at Time of Arrival			
	< 15		> 18	
	Women	Men	Women	Men
Canada/U.K.	100.0	100.0	7.6	7.3
Other Europe	98.9	99.2	10.3	6.0
China, Japan, Korea, and the Philippines	99.2	100.0	4.5	4.9
Vietnam	100.0	100.0	4.5	10.4
Mexico	94.8	90.9	4.6	5.4
Cuba	100.0	100.0	5.5	0.0
Central America	98.8	94.3	10.7	5.7
South America	100.0	100.0	9.4	9.2
Total	97.5	96.2	8.9	6.6

Source: Survey of Income and Progress Participation of the Bureau of the Census,1990–1993.

likely to pursue an education in the United States than immigrant men. Both men and women do so at low rates.

Many Immigrant Youths Fail to Complete Their Education in the United States

Between these two extremes are immigrant youths who enter the United States between the ages of 15 and 17. Because in the United States we generally expect native-born youths to remain in school until completion of high school, we would expect these youths also to continue their education at least through high school. But such is not typically the case. As many as 60 percent of these immigrant youths do not receive any education in the United States (figure 9.1). This finding supports previous research findings that a significant number of immigrant youths who fail to graduate from U.S. high schools do not actually drop out. Rather, they never enter the U.S. school system in the first place (Vernez and Abrahamse, 1996).

Enrollment in American schools of immigrant youths arriving in the United States between the ages of 15 and 17 is particularly low for youths of Mexican origin. More than eight out of ten Mexican youths ages 15 to 17 do not pursue an education in the United States (table 9.3). We suspect that the low enrollment of these Mexican immigrant youths in American schools reflects, at least in part, the fact that in Mexico school was mandated until recently only through sixth grade, that is, until the age of 12. In 1993, Mexico increased mandatory schooling through junior high school, that is, ninth grade or 15 years of age. But it will be many years before this change is widely implemented, especially in rural areas. In 1990, Mexicans older than 15 years of age had completed an average 4.7 years of schooling. In rural areas, where a significant portion of immigrants from Mexico come to the United states, 75 percent of school-age children do not finish the first six years of primary school. Hence, by the age of 14 or 15 years or older, the majority of Mexican youths have been out of school for two or more years. It is not surprising, hence, that a substantial share of Mexican youths simply do not enroll in an American school either by choice or because of inability

Table 9.3

Percent of Immigrants Aged 15 to 17 at Arrival Who Received Some Education in the United States, 1990–1993

Country of Origin	Men	Women	All
Mexico	11.9	19.4	13.0
All	36.1	42.0	38.2
All minus Mexico	65.9	56.5	61.0

Source: Survey of Income and Program Participation of the Bureau of the Census,1990–1993.

to catch up with na-tive-borns and other immigrants who have benefited from uninterrupted schooling in their home countries. The need to support themselves and their families economically may also be an important factor associated with this phenomenon.

U.S. Education Benefits Immigrants Who Are Already Better Educated

Table 9.4 indicates that fewer than one in 20 immigrants who entered the country when they were 18 or older, and who had 12 or fewer years of education, received any additional education in the United States. By contrast, a much larger proportion of immigrants with some college or a college degree have received at least some of their education in this country. This is particularly the case for immigrant women, one-third of whom received some of their postsecondary education in this country. By and large, immigrant women are more likely than men to pursue some additional education in the United States, possibly because women are more likely to engage in vocational training.

Table 9.4 also suggests that the extent to which immigrant women or men continue their education in the United States is independent of family income. The lack of a relationship between income and the pursuit of education in the United States may simply reflect the fact that so few at any level of income continue their education.

Who Pays for the Education of Immigrants?

Immigrant women aged 18 or older at time of entry who continued their education in the United States were nearly as likely as native-born women to

Table 9.4

Percent of Immigrants Aged 18 or Older at Arrival Who Received Some Education in the United States, by Current Educational Attainment and by Current Family Income, 1990–1993

Items	Women	Men
Current Educational Attainment (Years)		
< 12	3.0	4.0
= 12	8.3	2.3
13–15	36.8	20.6
16 or more	27.2	19.9
Current Family Income		
< $16,000	9.6	5.7
$16,000–24,999	5.0	9.4

Source: Survey of Income and Program Participation of the Bureau of the Census, 1990–1993.

receive some form of government or other assistance—42 versus 47 percent (table 9.5).[2] The sources of that assistance are similar for both groups: fellowships or scholarships are the most frequent form of assistance and both groups are equally likely to receive loans. Immigrant women, however, are less likely than native-born women to have employers support their education.

In contrast to immigrant women, immigrant men are about half as likely as native-born men to receive financial assistance in pursuit of further education in the United States—23 versus 48 percent. Table 9.4 suggests that the main reason for this discrepancy is that few, if any, receive assistance in the form of fellowships/scholarships or loans. The reason for this pattern, which is in striking contrast with that of immigrant women, remains to be researched. However, immigrant men are nearly as likely as native-born men and more likely than immigrant women to receive assistance from employers in pursuit of an education in the United States.

Immigrant Women's Training in the United States

The federal government and many states provide workers, most particularly disadvantaged workers, with a broad set of work-related services ranging from job search assistance to classroom or other forms of training. In addition, employers often provide specific on-the-job training to their workers. This subsection examines the extent to which female immigrants are using these programs and compares their utilization patterns with those of native-born women and with men. As newcomers to the United States with

Table 9.5

Percent of Immigrants and Native-Borns[a] Receiving Financial Assistance, by Source of Funding and by Gender

	Immigrants			Native-Borns			
Sources of funding	Women	Men	All	Women	Men	All	All
Fellowships/Scholarships	24.4	1.4	15.5	23.6	17.2	20.6	20.6
Loans	14.9	3.1	10.3	15.9	14.2	15.1	15.1
Employers	2.9	12.8	26.7	14.5	19.3	16.7	16.6
Others	15.5	12.4	14.3	14.6	15.7	15.1	15.1
Total[b]	42.0	23.3	34.8	46.8	48.3	47.5	47.4

Source: Survey of Income and Program Participation of the Bureau of the Census, 1990–1993.

[a]Includes nonrefugee immigrants aged 18 or older at entry who received some education in the United States and native-borns aged 18 to 64.

[b]Column totals may be lower than the sums of individual items because individuals may receive aid from more than one source.

little knowledge of the functioning of the U.S. labor market and of the institutions governing it, immigrants might be expected to need such assistance at least as much as, if not more than, the native-born population.

Few Immigrants Receive Formal Training in the United States

Immigrant women and men who arrive here as adults (aged 18 or older) are about half as likely as their native-born counterparts to receive any form of formal training in the United States (16 versus 26 percent). Table 9.6 shows that this differential is particularly large for Hispanic immigrants. For instance, Mexican immigrant women were nearly three times less likely to have received training in the United States than native-born women of the same origin. By contrast, European and Asian immigrants were just as likely as their native-born counterparts to have received formal training in the United States.

The More Educated Also Receive More Training

A reason for the pattern noted above for Hispanics is that they are generally less educated at arrival than other immigrants and the native-borns. Table 9.6

Table 9.6

Percent of Adults Ages 18 to 64 Who Received Job Training, by Immigration Status and Gender, 1990–1993

	Immigrants[a]		Native-Borns[a]	
	Women	Men	Women	Men
Origin				
Europe/Canada	23.0	25.0	25.7	28.3
Asia	18.0	18.1	17.8	19.3
Mexico	8.8	9.6	22.4	18.4
Cuba	10.2	20.8	22.0	0.0
Other Hispanics	15.1	6.8	23.7	12.2
Non-Hispanic Blacks	27.8	25.4	26.1	22.4
Education (years)				
< 12	8.7	9.0	13.9	17.4
= 12	14.2	17.1	29.0	30.9
13–15	25.9	20.4	27.7	25.9
16 or more	25.5	20.6	24.1	25.1
Total	16.6	16.3	25.5	27.1

Source: Survey of Income and Program Participation of the Bureau of the Census, 1990–1993.

[a]Includes nonrefugee immigrants aged 18 to 64 at time of interview and who were 18 or older at time of entry. Native-borns include all persons aged 18 to 64.

shows that the portion of immigrants receiving training increases from 9 percent for immigrants with fewer than 12 years of education to up to 25 percent for those with some college or more. Native-borns with fewer than 12 years of education are also less likely to receive training than high school graduates and those with some college or more.

Immigrants with some college or more are no less likely to receive training than their native-born counterparts. All of the gap in training between immigrants and native-borns is accounted for by differences among the least educated. Differences in English proficiency, occupational structure, and/or perceived transiency between the two groups may motivate employers to provide fewer training opportunities to low-educated immigrants than to low-educated native-borns.

Type of Training Received

Generally, immigrants receiving some training in the United States received it from the same programs, at the same location, and in the same form as native-borns (table 9.7). Nearly half of both groups received their training in schools or colleges. Both immigrant and native-born women are more likely to receive training in this setting than men. The reverse is the case for on-the-job training, the second most frequent form and location of training received by both immigrants and native-borns. About one-third of immigrant women who received training received on-the-job training compared to nearly half of the immigrant men.

Only a small share (2 percent) of immigrant women have ever received training for job searching, a share that is similar to native-born women. This finding is consistent with the well-known tendency for most people to rely on word of mouth and networking in their job search activities, most particularly for low-skill jobs (Waldinger, 1996).

Overall, federal government programs play a small role in the actual provision of training, in part because most of these programs are targeted to disadvantaged groups and toward the lower end of the labor market. Overall, about 7 percent of immigrant women and men who received any training reported receiving it through a federal government program, compared to a somewhat higher 13 percent for native-born women and 11 percent for native-born men. Typically, immigrants have been lower users of federal training programs than native-borns. Indeed, the only federal program in which immigrants have participated is the JTPA program. This program is the largest of the federal programs, is broadly targeted, and generally is community/private-sector based.

Table 9.7

Sponsorship and Type of Training Received by Women Who Received Training, by Immigration Status, 1990–1993

	Immigrant		Native-Born	
	Women	Men	Women	Men
Job Training Program				
JTPA	5.2	4.5	8.3	4.8
CETA	.5	.9	2.3	1.3
WIN	0	0	0	0
Trade adjustment	.7	1.0	.3	4.3
Veterans training	.7	1.0	.3	4.3
Other programs	92.8	92.6	89.5	89.2
Where Received				
Apprenticeship	2.1	1.0	1.7	6.9
School or college	51.8	40.1	47.8	36.2
High school	4.5	1.3	6.1	4.7
On-the-job training	35.3	40.6	33.7	37.9
Other	18.2	20.8	25.0	33.1
Type of Training				
Classroom	71.2	57.9	71.1	67.2
On-the-job training	37.3	48.9	36.1	42.6
Job search assistance	2.2	.5	1.8	4.6
Work experience	8.3	7.5	8.7	12.2
Other	8.8	9.5	9.2	11.5

Source: Survey of Income and Program Participation of the Bureau of the Census, 1990–1993.

Note: Column totals may exceed 100 percent because of individuals who benefit from more than one program or type of training.

Participation of immigrants in training programs targeted to welfare recipients (Work Incentive, or WIN program), to displaced workers (Trade Adjustments), and to veterans has been extremely low, as would be expected, most particularly for the latter program. Although immigrants are eligible to serve in the all-voluntary armed forces (and were required to serve under the previous draft system), their participation rates have been much lower than for native-borns. Their similarly low participation in the CETA (Comprehensive Employment and Training Act) programs is in part explained by the fact that this program was operational primarily in the 1970s and was folded into the JTPA program in the 1980s. Hence, it was operational at a time when the bulk of the new immigrants to the United States had not yet arrived.

Safety Net Programs

The relative economic success of immigrant women in the U.S. labor market has been mixed (chapters 5 and 6). And as documented above, their participation in education and training programs—both public and private—that might have made them more competitive in the U.S. labor market, has been lower than for native-borns. To what extent, then, have they relied on the broad network of federal and other safety net and entitlement programs—including welfare, nutrition, health, and housing—that were enacted or expanded during the 1960s at the outset of the new wave of immigration (chapter 1). Have they benefited from these services to a smaller or greater extent than native-born women similarly situated? This question is examined below.

Differences by Country of Origin

Just are differences exist in levels of education, family income, and other individual and family characteristics among immigrant women (chapter 3), wide variations exist in the extent to which immigrant women rely on the nation's safety net programs. Table 9.8 shows the average monthly participation rates of immigrant women in a broad range of cash assistance, nutrition, health, housing, and social insurance programs by region of origin. Several key observations can be made from this table, first for nonelderly immigrants and then for elderly immigrants.

Nonelderly Immigrants. Female refugees used public services at much higher rates than immigrants who entered the country for family reunification or economic reasons. About one-third of female refugees—primarily those from Indochina and secondarily from the former Soviet Union—depend on government cash and nutritional assistance and health care. This pattern of high use of safety net programs by refugees reflects, in part, their low level of education and command of the English language and, hence, the difficulties they encounter in the U.S. labor market. It may also reflect, in part, that refugees, unlike other immigrants, are eligible upon arrival for cash assistance and other special programs through federally funded Refugee Resettlement agencies. Indeed, some have raised concerns that this policy provides an incentive for refugees to "settle" into dependency on governmental programs.

Refugees are also more likely than other immigrants to benefit from public housing and low-rent assistance, reflecting the priority given to housing refugees in various parts of the country.

Participation in safety net programs by other female immigrants varies depending on their socioeconomic characteristics. Hence, immigrant women from Central America have the highest rates of participation in safety net programs, reflecting their relatively low levels of education and income and

Table 9.8

Participation Rates[a] in Selected Safety Net Programs of Immigrant Women by Country of Origin, 1990–1993 (Percentage)

| Program | Age Group | Nonrefugees | | | | | | | | | Refugees[b] |
| | | U.K./Canada | Europe | Asia | Latin America | | | | Africa | Middle East | |
					Mexico	Cuba	Central America	South America			
Cash											
AFDC	0–64	.9	2.4	.2	8.0	3.1	12.4	4.5	1.0	8.2	29.0
General assistance	0–64	.3	.3	.3	.7	0	.9	.5	0	8.7	1.7
SSI	0–64	1.4	1.4	.8	.7	8.2	2.3	.9	.7	1.7	5.1
	65 or older	1.3	4.2	28.1	43.8	32.1	66.9	16.8	—	22.7	45.1
Nutrition											
Food stamps	All	2.3	3.7	.9	16.5	14.3	18.8	7.2	2.5	16.0	34.3
WIC	0–44	1.2	.3	.1	4.0	0	2.6	1.4	0	.6	3.7
School lunch	0–17	14.3	18.4	23.1	64.0	22.7	62.1	33.8	15.6	34.2	51.7
School breakfast	0–17	4.4	8.9	8.7	33.6	6.9	26.8	7.8	3.8	17.4	29.4
Health											
Medicaid	0–64	5.6	4.4	1.8	20.0	12.1	24.1	8.3	4.9	24.1	39.9
	65 or older	1.8	6.0	41.1	43.3	45.0	72.4	20.0	0	43.7	64.0
Medicare	0–64	2.7	4.1	1.0	.9	5.3	.3	.4	.2	.4	1.2
	65 or older	99.2	98.3	72.5	84.4	93.1	76.8	76.5	—	73.7	62.2
Housing											
Public housing	All	.3	.5	.6	3.6	.5	2.7	1.8	.1	0	4.9
Rent assistance	All	1.0	.7	1.0	3.3	5.6	6.6	1.9	.4	.1	4.5
Energy assistance	All	.6	1.1	.1	1.3	.2	2.3	.5	0	1.4	3.2
Other											
Unemployment	16–64	1.3	1.9	1.3	3.5	1.4	.7	1.8	1.8	.7	2.3
Social Security	0–64	8.0	8.2	1.9	2.8	10.1	2.7	1.5	0	.4	1.1
	65 or older	92.7	93.7	65.2	64.0	68.1	56.5	66.6	—	63.2	41.6

Source: Survey of Income and Program Participation of the Bureau of the Census, 1990–1993.
Note: "——" means not available.
[a]The participation rate is a monthly average participation rate over the time period extending from 1990 to 1993.
[b]Includes immigrants from Vietnam and the former Soviet Union.

their larger families. Their participation rates range from 24 percent in the Medicaid program to 19 percent in the food stamp program to 12 percent in the AFDC program. They are also more likely to benefit from public housing and low-rent assistance than immigrants from other countries. Also a majority, two-thirds, of the children of these immigrants benefit from the school lunch program.

Immigrant women from Mexico have socioeconomic characteristics similar to those of women from Central America, but they have somewhat lower rates of participation in safety net programs. For instance, 20 percent of Mexican immigrant women rely on Medicaid for their health care compared to 25 percent for Central American, and 8 percent receive AFDC benefits, compared to 12 percent for Central Americans. This pattern, in part, reflects the fact that immigrant women from Mexico are more likely to be illegal, and hence ineligible, for these services in the first place.

Other Hispanic immigrants from the Caribbean (Cuba) and from South America have much lower participation rates in safety net programs than their Mexican and Central American counterparts. For instance, Cubans and South Americans are about half as likely to participate in the Medicaid program as Mexicans and Central Americans and two to three times less likely to participate in the AFDC program. There are a few exceptions to this pattern, however. Immigrant women aged 64 or younger from Cuba are significantly more likely to participate in the SSI Disabled program than immigrant women from any other country. They also have as high a participation rate in the food stamp program as immigrant women from Mexico and Central America. In brief, Hispanic immigrants cannot be stereotyped into one set of descriptors anymore than Asians, Europeans, and native-borns can.

By comparison to other nonelderly immigrant women, Asians and Europeans who are not refugees are, by and large, relatively low users of safety net programs. Their participation rates range from a high 5 percent in the Medicaid program to 1 percent or lower in most other programs, including cash assistance programs.

Elderly Immigrants. The pattern of public-service use by elderly immigrant women—that is, those aged 65 or older—highlights the trade-off occurring between benefits received from social insurance programs, such as Social Security and Medicare, and those received from their corresponding safety net programs, SSI and Medicaid. For the more recently settled immigrant women from Asia, Latin America, and the Middle East, participation in Social Security and Medicare is significantly lower than that of their European counterparts while their participation in SSI and Medicaid is much higher. For instance, the most recently arrived elderly immigrant women from Central America have a low 56 percent participation rate in Social Security compared to an excess of 90 percent for European-origin immigrant women. Conversely, the first have a much higher participation—

67 percent—in the SSI program compared to a low 4 percent or less for the second group.

The relative pattern of participation by elderly female immigrants in Medicare and Medicaid mirrors that observed for Social Security and SSI. For instance, elderly Asian immigrant women have a relatively low (72 percent) participation rate in the Medicare program compared to 99 percent for European elderlies. But Asian elderly immigrant women are more likely to participate in the Medicaid program—46 percent—than their European counterparts—6 percent or less. The pattern is similar for elderly immigrant women from all parts of Latin America, although it is less pronounced for Cubans and South American immigrants whose flows peaked earlier in time than the more recently arrived Mexican and Central Americans.

Although the reasons for the above differences in patterns of use of social insurance versus safety net programs have not been explored, we suspect that two factors play a significant role. The first is the increasing number of older immigrants who are coming through the family reunification provisions of the immigration law, that is, the parent(s) of younger immigrants who preceded them here. The share of immigrants aged 65 or more at arrival in legal immigration flows has doubled since 1970 (chapter 2). The second is that today's older immigrants are less likely than native-borns to have accumulated enough years in the U.S. labor market—if they have participated in it at all—to qualify for Social Security and Medicare benefits: eligibility for benefits under these programs depend on having made contributions to them for a number of years. Alternatively, they may have contributed too little over their lifetime here to draw adequate Social Security benefits to sustain them.

In brief, there are not only wide variations in program use among immigrant women from different countries of origin, there are also different patterns of use between programs by immigrants from the same country of origin. Two important implications follow from these differentiated patterns of public-service use. The first is that state and local governments will be affected differentially depending on the origin composition of their immigrants, even when holding the share of immigrants constant. Hence, California, which has a higher concentration of relatively high users of safety net services—refugees, and Central American and Mexican immigrants—will be proportionately more affected than Florida, which has a high concentration of Cuban immigrants who are relatively low users of public service, and New York, which has a higher concentration of European and Caribbean immigrants.

A second implication is that states and local governments will be more affected fiscally than the federal government by the pattern of service use of more recent elderly immigrants. The reason is that social insurance programs, of which elderly immigrants are relatively low users, are financed entirely by the federal government through payroll tax deductions from workers and employers, whereas the safety net programs—Medicaid and SSI—of which elderly immigrants are relatively high users, are in part financed by state and local general tax revenues. We can expect that future demand for the latter safety net programs by elderly immigrants will increase as the newer and increasingly larger immigrant groups from Latin America age.

Differences between Immigrant and Native-Born Women

As a group—and in spite of sharp differences in reliance on "social safety net" programs among immigrants from different countries of origin—immigrant women are no more likely to rely on federal safety net programs than native-born women (table 9.9), unless they are refugees or elderly. For instance, 4.9 percent of immigrant women who are not refugees received benefits from the AFDC program in an average month compared to 5.6 percent for native-born women. Differences between "all" nonrefugee immigrants and "all" native-borns are equally small and statistically not significant for the food stamp program—9.1 versus 8.8 percent—and the Medicaid program—11.7 versus 10.2 percent. There are a few exceptions among elderlies and among children to this generally undifferentiated pattern of service use between immigrants and native-borns.

Elderly immigrant women, however, are significantly more likely than native-born women to use safety net programs, but are significantly less likely to benefit from social insurance programs either because they have not been here long enough to qualify for the latter or because their social benefits are low and need to be supplemented, as already noted above. Elderly immigrant women are more than twice as likely to receive benefits from SSI as elderly native-born women (18.1 versus 8 percent) although they are less likely to receive benefits from Social Security (81 versus 94 percent). Immigrants are similarly more likely to rely on Medicaid for their health care while native-borns are more likely to qualify and be covered by Medicare.

Another exception concerns the children of immigrants, either foreign- or native-born. Children of immigrant parents are about twice as likely as children of native-born parents to benefit from the school lunch and breakfast programs. This pattern reflects the overall lower incomes of immigrant families and their larger family sizes.

The Effect of Income on Service Utilization

The aggregate similarities documented above in the use of safety net programs between immigrant and native-born women glance over differences in socioeconomic characteristics and, hence, mask significant differences in program "dependency" when these differences are taken into account. Eligibility for safety net programs typically depends on a number of

Table 9.9

**Recent Participation Rates of Women in Selected Safety Net Programs by
Immigration Status, 1990–1993**

			Immigrants		
Program	Age Group	Native-Borns	All Immigrants	Refugees[a]	Non-refugees
Cash					
AFDC	0–64	5.6	6.8	29.0	4.9
General assistance	0–64	.6	.8	1.7	.7
SSI	0–64	1.6	1.3	5.1	1.3
	65 or older	7.7	17.5	45.1	17.5
Nutrition					
Food stamps	ALL	8.8	11.0	34.3	9.1
WIC	0–44	1.8	2.1	3.7	1.9
School lunch	0–17	24.4	44.2	51.7	43.4
School breakfast	0–17	12.0	21.0	29.4	20.3
Health					
Medicaid	0–64	10.2	13.9	39.9	11.7
	65 or older	10.3	24.6	64.0	22.3
Medicare	0–64	2.7	1.5	1.2	1.5
	65 or older	98.2	91.4	62.2	91.4
Housing					
Public	All	1.3	1.8	4.9	1.6
Rent assistance	All	2.1	2.5	4.5	2.3
Energy assistance	All	1.1	1.1	3.2	.9
Other					
Unemployment	16–64	1.5	1.9	2.3	1.8
Social Security	0–64	6.0	3.6	1.1	3.6
	65 or older	94.3	81.2	41.6	81.2

Source: Survey of Income and Program Participation of the Bureau of the Census, 1990–1993.

[a]Includes immigrants from Vietnam and the former Soviet Union.

sociodemographic characteristics, no one of which is more important than family income. All safety net social programs are income-tested, with the exception of social security and Medicare eligibility, which are based on past earnings rather than on economic need. This means that consistent with their redistributive intent, eligibility for federal programs is typically limited to families with incomes below a specified level. The family income threshold above which a family is no longer eligible varies depending on the size of the family, the program, and in some instances the state. For instance, the (adjusted) income threshold for the food stamp program is generally the federal poverty income level which in 1993 was $9,430 for a family of two and $14,350 for a family of four. The income threshold for the school lunch and breakfast programs is generally the same. The income threshold for the

AFDC program is set by the states and hence varies across states. Some programs impose additional requirements for eligibility. For instance, the AFDC (but not the food stamp) program requires that one or both parents be absent from the home, be incapacitated, or be unemployed. SSI requires the applicant to be 65 or older, blind, or disabled .

Table 9.10 compares the average monthly participation rates to various programs of immigrant and native-born women at various levels of family income. As expected, the participation rates in means-tested programs drops sharply as family income increases. For instance, participation of immigrant women in the AFDC program drops from 18 percent for women in families

Table 9.10

Monthly Participation Data for Selected Safety Net Programs of Immigrant[a] and Native-Born Women by Family Income, 1990–1993

		Annual Income (dollars)					
		<15,999		16–24,000		>25,000	
Program	Age Group	I	N	I	N	I	N
Cash							
AFDC	0–64	17.6	25.0	4.7	3.6	.3	.8
General assistance	0–64	2.1	2.9	1.1	.3	.1	.1
SSI	0–64	3.5	6.4	.5	1.4	.7	.4
	65 or older	20.7	13.9	4.7	3.0	18.4	2.1
Nutrition							
Food stamps	ALL	27.9	32.8	8.3	6.4	1.0	1.0
WIC	0–44	5.4	5.6	2.5	3.7	.4	.4
School lunch	0–17	68.3	65.2	67.1	46.1	22.7	9.0
School breakfast	0–17	40.2	33.9	25.7	18.7	9.3	4.1
Health							
Medicaid	0–64	36.5	41.2	11.6	9.1	2.6	2.0
	65 or older	25.2	18.2	7.0	4.0	24.8	3.3
Medicare	0–64	2.0	6.1	1.5	3.3	1.3	1.6
	65 or older	16.6	98.6	96.2	98.0	82.2	98.1
Housing							
Public	All	3.2	4.5	2.8	1.1	.4	.2
Rent assistance	All	6.1	7.7	2.7	1.3	.5	.3
Energy assistance	All	2.7	3.8	.7	.8	.1	.1
Other							
Unemployment	16–64	2.8	1.9	2.2	2.1	1.5	1.3
Social Security	0–64	5.2	11.5	4.3	9.2	2.8	3.8
	65 or older	86.7	93.9	88.1	94.8	70.6	94.7

Source: Survey of Income and Program Participation of the Bureau of the Census, 1990–1993.

Note: I means immigrant, and N means native-born.

[a]Excludes refugees.

with $16,000 or less annually, to nearly zero for immigrant women in families with incomes exceeding $25,000. The same pattern is observed for native-born women, where participation in AFDC declines from 25 percent to less than 1 percent. The pattern of decline in participation rates as family income rises is even more pronounced in the Medicaid program, where participation declines from a high 40 percent for individuals in low-income families to 2 percent or so at higher incomes, regardless of immigration status. Although somewhat less pronounced, this pattern of decline in participation rates with increase in family income also holds for the general relief, SSI, food stamps, WIC, school lunch and breakfast, public housing, low-income rental assistance, and energy assistance programs.

As noted above, participation in social insurance programs is not means-tested and, as expected, there are few variations in participation rates in these programs across incomes. Participation in the Medicare and Social Security programs is nearly universal for native-born elderlies regardless of family income. That of elderly immigrants is lower than for native-borns and there is some decline as income increases. One potential explanation for this pattern is that immigrants with higher incomes are more likely than others to sponsor their parents through the family reunification provisions of U.S. immigration laws. These elderly parents, in turn, are less likely to be eligible for Social Security or Medicare than other immigrants who came here when they were younger and aged while residing and working in the United States.

Eligibility for unemployment insurance also depends on having been in the labor force. The slight decline in the monthly participation rates of women as family income increases reflects in part the greater job instability at the lower end of the labor market.

All Else Equal, Immigrant Women Have Relied Less on Safety Net Programs than Native-Born Women

Table 9.10 also indicates that at *low-income levels,* that is, less than $16,000 annually, immigrant women are less likely than native-born women to participate in safety net programs. For instance, 18 percent of immigrant women in families with incomes less than $16,000 participated in the AFDC program compared to 25 percent for native-born women. Similarly, 37 percent of nonelderly immigrant women relied on Medicaid for their health care compared to 41 percent for native-born women. This pattern is generally consistent across all programs including general relief, food stamps, public housing, low-rent assistance, and energy assistance.

Three exceptions to this pattern are familiar by now. First, elderly immigrant women in low-income families are more likely than native-born women to depend on SSI and Medicaid. Conversely, the first group is also less likely to benefit from Social Security and to be covered by Medicare.

The second exception concerns the school breakfast program in which children of immigrant parents in low-income families are more likely to participate than the children of native-born parents. Finally, immigrant mothers are
just as likely as native-born mothers to participate in the WIC program, which
provides supplemental food, nutrition counseling, and referrals to health care
for pregnant women, new mothers, infants, and children below the age of
five.

At *medium family income levels,* that is, between $16,000 and $25,000,
the relationship between immigrants and native-born women is reversed. At
those levels of family income, immigrant women are more likely than native-
born women to benefit from safety net programs of all kinds. The differentials, however, are not large, generally not exceeding two percentage points,
with the exception of the school lunch and breakfast programs where the differentials are considerably larger. One reason for this reverse pattern is the
presence of a larger number of children, especially children below the age of
six, in immigrant rather than in native-born families.

At *higher levels of income*—above $25,000 anually—participation in
safety net programs is equally low for both immigrant and native-born
women. At that income level, dependency of nonelderly women on cash and
housing assistance programs is typically less than one percent. But the same
two exceptions noted above apply to elderly women and children. Elderly
immigrant women are nearly ten times more likely to depend on SSI and
Medicaid than native-born women. Although these immigrant women live in
families with relatively high incomes, the resources of younger members of
the family, such as sons and daughters, cannot be fully counted as available to
the elderly member of the family under most states' laws of relative
responsibility. The higher participation of immigrant children in these
relatively high-income families is once again a result of larger family size.
The pattern of participation of immigrants in public services relative to that of
native-borns varies depending on which group of immigrants is compared to
which group of native-borns. Table 9.11 compares the participation rates of
immigrant and native-born women by major racial/ancestry groupings. A first
observation is that service use varies just as broadly among native-borns of
different ancestry as it does among immigrants from various
countries/regions of origin. The participation rate of nonelderly native-born
women in the Medicaid program ranges from 28 percent for African
Americans and 26 percent for Hispanic Americans from Central America
down to 5 and 6 percent for Hispanic Americans from Cuba and non-
Hispanic White Americans, respectively. The same varied patterns hold for
the participation of native-borns in the AFDC, school lunch and breakfast,
housing assistance, and even the SSI program. Participation of native-born
elderly women in the latter program ranges from a high 36 percent for
Hispanic Americans from Mexico to a low 3 percent for Asian Americans.
Generally, African Americans and Hispanic Americans from Mexico and

Central America are more dependent on safety net programs than Asian Americans, non-Hispanic White Americans, and Hispanic Americans from Cuba.

Within specific racial/ethnic groups, nonelderly, nonrefugee immigrant women are always *less* likely to rely on safety net programs than their native-born counterparts. For instance, nonelderly Asian immigrants are three times less likely than Asian Americans to participate in the Medicaid program—2 versus 7 percent—and many times less likely to participate in the AFDC and food stamp programs. The children of both groups, however, are equally likely to participate in the school lunch and breakfast programs. And elderly Asian immigrants are more than six times more likely than their Asian-American counterparts to participate in the SSI program—28 versus 2 percent—and the Medicaid program—41 versus 7 percent.

The pattern is generally similar between Mexican immigrants and Mexican Americans and between immigrants from Central America and Hispanic Americans from that region, with one major exception. Mexican immigrants and Mexican Americans are equally likely to participate in the Medicaid program, and the first group is more likely to draw unemployment benefits and benefit from public housing than the second. By contrast, Cuban immigrants are typically more likely to rely on safety net services than Cuban Americans. Finally, both non-Hispanic White and Black immigrants are also less likely than their native-born counterparts to use public services. The differential is particularly large between non-Hispanic Black immigrants and African Americans.

In addition, as noted earlier, elderly immigrants are always less likely than native-borns to benefit from Medicare and Social Security regardless of the racial/ethnic grouping. The differentials are larger among Asians, Hispanics, and non-Hispanic Blacks than among non-Hispanic Whites. For instance, only about two-thirds of the first group received benefits from Social Security compared to 90 percent or more for their native-born counterparts. Among non-Hispanic Whites, more than 90 percent of both immigrants and native-borns received social security benefits.

The reasons for these differences across racial/ethnic groups remains to be fully explored. Certainly differentials in income are likely to play a significant role. Another potential reason is that Asian and Hispanic immigrants, with the exception of Cubans, are recent immigrants—more than half have entered the country since 1980—and hence may be less likely to either know about their eligibility for certain services—most come from countries where such services are not available—or to be inclined to participate.

Table 9.11

Use of Safety Net Programs by Racial/Ethnic Groups and Immigration Status, 1990–1993 (Monthly Participation Rates[a])

Program	Age	Non-Hispanic Whites		Non-Hispanic Blacks	
		I	N	I	N
Cash					
AFDC	0–64	1.4	2.9	7.0	18.2
General assistance	0–64	.3	.4	.8	1.9
SSI	0–64	1.3	1.1	1.6	4.3
	65 or older	3.3	5.0	28.9	28.3
Nutrition					
Food stamps	All	2.9	5.1	11.8	26.5
WIC	0–44	.6	1.5	2.7	2.1
School lunch	0–17	16.4	15.0	38.0	55.9
School breakfast	0–17	6.4	5.6	17.5	37.8
Health					
Medicaid	0–64	4.4	6.2	12.3	27.9
	65 or older	5.1	7.2	28.9	34.4
Medicare	0–64	3.7	2.8	.9	3.1
	65 or older	98.6	98.5	93.9	95.8
Housing					
Public	All	.5	.7	.7	4.6
Rent assistance	All	.8	1.4	3.2	5.3
Energy assistance	All	.9	.8	.3	2.3
Other					
Unemployment	16–64	1.7	1.4	1.4	1.8
Social Security	0–64	8.3	5.9	2.1	7.0
	65 or older	93.3	95.1	69.9	87.2

Source: Survey of Income and Program Participation of the Bureau of the Census, 1990–1993.

Note: I means immigrants and N means native-born.; "—" means not available.

[a]The participation rate is a monthly average participation rate over the time period extending from 1990 to1993.

Immigrants Increase Use of Safety Net Services over Time

Reliance on safety net programs increases with the length of time immigrants remain in the country, at least for some programs. Figure 9.2 shows that generally, immigrant women who have been here for fewer than five

Table 9.11—continued

Asians		Hispanics					
		Mexican		Central/South American		Cuban	
I	N	I	N	I	N	I	N
.2	5.9	8.0	11.7	9.2	14.6	3.1	0.0
.3	0.0	.7	.5	.7	1.2	0.0	1.1
.8	.5	.7	1.3	1.7	5.4	8.2	0.0
28.1	2.9	43.8	35.5	40.8	—	32.0	—
.9	6.5	16.5	20.6	14.1	23.1	14.3	.2
0.1	.1	4.0	3.1	2.1	4.4	0.0	0.0
23.1	23.3	64.0	51.5	51.9	34.7	22.7	3.0
8.7	9.8	33.6	27.4	20.0	20.0	6.9	2.4
1.8	7.5	20.0	19.8	17.8	26.3	12.1	4.6
41.1	7.1	48.3	37.3	45.1	24.0	45.0	—
1.0	.9	.9	1.1	.3	3.4	5.3	0.0
72.5	94.9	84.4	97.6	76.7	—	93.1	—
.6	.3	3.6	1.2	2.3	5.4	.5	0.0
1.0	.2	3.3	3.4	4.7	8.6	5.6	.3
.1	.2	1.3	2.1	1.5	1.7	.2	0.0
1.3	.9	3.5	1.6	1.2	4.0	1.4	0.0
1.9	3.5	2.8	3.5	2.2	9.4	10.1	4.1
65.2	92.5	64.0	93.9	61.8	—	68.1	—

years have lower participation rates than those who have been here from six to ten years. Increases in participation rates of immigrant women are shown for the AFDC, food stamp, school breakfast, and public housing programs. Exceptions include the school lunch and the larger Medicaid program. Several reasons may explain why participation rates in the latter two programs remain stable or even decline over time. In the case of Medicaid, the need for prenatal and pediatric care is relatively high among immigrants, given their higher fertility rates, and this care is less likely to be postponed than the fulfillment of other needs. As for school lunches, this pattern may be "supply" driven because lunch programs are more likely to be available at the primary and middle school level than the high school level.

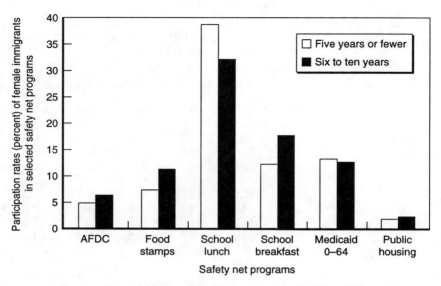

Source: Survey of Income and Program Participation of the Bureau of the
Census, 1990–1993.

**Figure 9.2—Monthly Participation Rates of Immigrants in Selected Safety Net
Programs, by Length of Stay in the United States, 1990–1993**

Conclusions and Implications

Few female immigrants acquire additional education or training after their
arrival in the United States. Typically, whatever human capital adult
immigrants come in with is the human capital with which they enter and remain in the U.S. labor market. Female immigrants are half as likely as their
native counterparts to acquire any formal training in the United States.

In a pattern similar to that of natives, however, the more highly educated
an immigrant woman is the more likely she is to acquire additional education
or to receive formal training in the United States. For instance, immigrant
women who are college graduates are three times more likely to benefit from
formal training than immigrant women with fewer than 12 years of education.
Indeed, college-educated immigrant women are just as likely as college-educated native women to benefit from formal training.

Immigrant women receiving some training in the United States received
it from the same programs, at the same locations, and in the same forms as
native women. About half receive their training in schools or colleges and
about one-third "on-the-job." Only a few members (about 2 percent) of either

group have ever received assistance in searching for a job, confirming the importance of networks for both groups. And, overall, federal programs play a small role in the actual provision of training. By and large, immigrant women (7 percent) are less likely than native women (13 percent) to receive their training from public sources. JTPA is the most frequent provider of training services to immigrants and native-born women alike.

The few immigrant women continuing their education in the United States were as likely as native-born women to have received some form of government or other assistance (42 versus 47 percent). Fellowships or scholarships are the most frequent form of assistance for both groups.

Consistent with previous findings (Vernez and Abrahamse, 1996), we found that only about one-third of immigrant youths who enter the United States between the ages of 15 and 18 go to school after arrival in the United States. Many immigrant youths in this age group come to the United States after they have already been out of school for several years in their own country. This is most particularly the case for immigrant women (as well as men) from Mexico. By the time they arrive in the United States, these youths have been out of school for an average two to three years.

Generalizations concerning the use of safety net programs by immigrant women cannot readily be made. We found that use of these programs varies broadly depending on immigration status (refugees vs. others), age (adults of working age vs. elderly and children), and income. Hence, the answer to the question of whether female immigrants are more or less dependent on safety net programs than native women will similarly depend on what comparison is made between which groups and within which programs.

Female refugees—primarily those from Indochina and the former Soviet Union—are exceptionally high users of safety net programs including cash, nutrition, health, housing, and other assistance programs. For instance, refugees are more than three times more likely than other immigrants to rely on AFDC for their subsistence and more than two times, to rely on Medicaid for their health care. This pattern is in part because they have low levels of education and have low participation rates in the labor force (chapter 4). Having often been forced to leave their home countries without any resources, refugees are also treated differently from voluntary immigrants. They are eligible for public services upon arrival and receive special assistance.

Significant variations also exist between immigrant women originating from different countries. Immigrant women from Mexico, Central America, and the Middle East have significantly higher participation rates in public services than nonrefugee immigrants from Asia and Europe. Whereas more than 20 percent of immigrants from the first group rely on Medicaid for health care, less than 5 percent of immigrants from the second group do so. These disparities by country or area of origin cut across all major safety net programs, including AFDC, WIC, food stamp, and housing programs.

These differentials in use of safety net by immigrants from different origin are primarily due to differences in income and in family size, most particularly the presence of young children. These are the main factors that determine eligibility for means-tested safety net programs, such as the ones considered here.

The preponderance of income in determining reliance on safety net programs also prevails when comparing participation rates between immigrant and native-born women. Participation rates for both groups decline rapidly with income. At low levels of income, the participation rate of immigrant women is actually lower than that of native-born women. For instance, 37 percent of immigrant women in families with less than $16,000 a year participated in the Medicaid program compared to 41 percent for native-born women. At medium family income levels—between $16,000 and $25,000—participation rates were significantly lower for both groups, but immigrant women have slightly higher participation rates than native women. One reason for this reverse pattern is the presence of a larger number of children. Finally, there is no difference in the use of safety net programs between immigrant and native women in high-income families.

Reliance on safety net programs varies just as broadly among native-born women from different ancestry as it does among immigrants from different countries of origin. Just like immigrant women, native-born women of Mexican and Central American origin are more dependent on safety net programs than Asian Americans and non-Hispanic Whites. And within specific racial/ethnic groups, nonelderly, nonrefugee women are always less likely to rely on safety net programs than their native counterparts.

Like refugees, elderly immigrants are consistently and significantly higher users of safety net programs—primarily SSI for subsistence and Medicaid for health care—regardless of country of origin and at all levels of income. Overall, elderly female immigrants are more than two times more likely to participate in the SSI and Medicaid programs than native-born women. And elderly immigrant women from Asia are just as likely to participate in these programs as immigrant women from Mexico and Central America. The reason for this pattern is that elderly immigrant women are much less likely to be eligible for Social Security and Medicare for one of two reasons. Some have come as elderly parents to be reunited with an adult child or children who preceded them to the United States. Having not worked in the United States, these elderly parents do not qualify to receive Medicare and Social Security benefits. Other immigrants retiring from jobs in the United States have contributed too little to these social insurance programs to receive any or adequate benefits.

Being cognizant of these variations, trade-offs, and complexities in the use of services by immigrants is not merely academic. Aggregate comparisons of service use between immigrants and native-borns have led to the conclusion that immigrants are higher users of services than native-borns and have contributed to barring the access to key safety net services of all immigrants, a blunt uninformed policy, indeed. Would Congress have acquiesced to the same policy if it had been fully aware that the relatively high service utilization of immigrants as a whole is attributable primarily to (1) refugees, a more vulnerable group admitted into the country not for economic, voluntary reasons but for humanitarian, nonvoluntary reasons and (2) elderly immigrants, many of whom have entered the country at an already advanced age to join their sons or daughters in the United States? For nonelderly immigrants, reliance on safety net programs is lower than for native-borns similarly situated with respect to income and other needs.

The pattern-of-service use described in this chapter prevailed when legal immigrants had the same access to services as native-borns, subject only to some limited restrictions. It remains to be seen how changes in service eligibility contained in the Personal Responsibility and Work Opportunity Reconciliation Act of 1996 will alter this pattern. Some groups of immigrants remain unaffected, including refugees—who continue to be treated differently from native-borns and other immigrants—and immigrants who had resided in the United States for five years or more as of 1997. The latter, a majority of immigrants currently in the United States, are eligible for naturalization. And, indeed the number of immigrants naturalizing has been rapidly increasing from a low 240,000 a year in 1992 to nearly 1 million in 1996 (INS, 1997).

The new federal legislation leaves a great deal of flexibility to states in determining the eligibility for safety net programs of those immigrants who have been residing for fewer than five years in the United States and for newcomers. Hence, eligibility and the eventual pattern-of-service use by these immigrants may change as well as differ across states.

Notes

1. PRWORA allows implementation of most of Proposition 187's provisions, except the denial of primary and secondary education to illegal immigrant children.

2. The 47 percent overall SIPP estimate of persons receiving financial assistance in pursuit of education beyond age 18 is higher than the 41 percent reported by the National Center for Education Statistics (1995, table 312) for the 1992 academic year. The higher SIPP estimate may be due to the fact that it includes proprietary vocational educational institutions that are not included in the NCES statistics; differences in time period; differences in the source of the data; differences in respondents, that is, individuals for the SIPP and postsecondary institutions for NCES; and/or differences in the population surveyed—all adults aged 18 to 64 in the SIPP and all persons attending postsecondary institutions in 1992, either full time or part time. Both estimates, however, are of the same order of magnitude.

10

Conclusions and Policy Implications

Immigrant women are playing an increasingly important role in the U.S. labor force and most particularly in the labor markets of states in which they are concentrated, including California, Florida, Illinois, New York, New Jersey, and Texas. Their numbers in the labor force have more than doubled since 1970, and today they are filling one of every five net new jobs filled by a women.

In contrast to the large amount of information available about the experiences of male immigrants in the U.S. labor market, little is known about that of immigrant women. Ignorance has raised concerns about their performance in the U.S. labor market. Immigrant women are perceived to face more cultural and social barriers than men and to be more vulnerable to exploitation. In the absence of proactive public policies facilitating their access to job search, training, and other labor-market services, a concern exists that their access to these services is disproportionately limited.

This study is the first to provide systematic information on the characteristics of immigrant women over time, the role they play in the various sectors of the economy, their performance, and their use of labor-market-related public services. Our main findings are summarized below. We then discuss the implications of our findings for public policy.

Key Findings

Our review of the role and performance of immigrant women in the U.S. labor market paints a complex and nuanced story that resists ready generalizations. Some immigrant women succeed above all expectations. Others struggle all through their lives in the United States. Education, family responsibilities, and the speed with which immigrant women learn English are three primary factors that determine whether an immigrant woman will join the labor force and what her economic mobility will be over her lifetime in the United States. Still, these factors do not tell the whole story. Long-term changes in the structure of the U.S. economy—which preceded, but have been accelerated by the globalization of the world economy since the early 1990s—are reducing the number of jobs and earnings opportunities among the least educated of both immigrant and native-born women. Moreover, cultural factors that define the respective roles of men and women appear to be more enduring for some groups of immigrant women (e.g., European and Mexican women) than for others (e.g., Asian and Central American women). Here we have touched only on the surface of this latter issue, which we hope others will eventually pursue.

Trends in Female Immigration

U.S. immigration policy plays a major role in determining the share of women in yearly immigrant flows. Female immigrants were a minority—about one-third—in the immigration flows during the unrestricted, primarily economically motivated, immigration of the past century and the beginning of the twentieth century. In the 1920s, family reunification became the cornerstone of the nation's immigration policy, and female immigrants have dominated immigration flows ever since. This pattern has remained unaffected even though the primary origin of immigrants has shifted from Europe to Asia and Latin America and the number of immigrants entering the country has more than tripled since 1970 to its current peak of more than 800,000 new immigrants a year.

The motivation for emigrating in the first place also affects the gender composition of immigration flows from a specific country of origin. Refugee flows are generally gender-balanced or female-dominated, whereas primarily economically motivated immigration—including illegal immigration—is male-dominated, at least initially. Over time, however, family reunification balances the share between genders.

Labor-Market Performance

Trends in education levels and family responsibilities, two key predictors of struggle or success in the workforce, have been diverging between immigrant and native-born women. Immigrant women have become two times more likely than native-born women to have fewer than 12 years of education. They remain, however, just as likely to have graduated from college. On the other hand, the fertility rate of immigrant women, 15 percent lower than that of native-born women in 1970, is now 16 percent higher. This trend guarantees that the already large gap in family responsibilities between the two groups will continue to increase, at least for the foreseeable future.

This divergence in relative education between immigrant and native-born women has led the first group to become increasingly less likely to participate in the labor force and more likely to be unemployed and to earn lower wages than the second group. Otherwise, immigrant women have consistently worked the same number of weeks and the same number of hours a week as native-born women. They also have been consistently just as likely to be self-employed as native-born women.

Wide variations exist, however, in the labor-market performance of immigrant women from different countries of origin, and these variations overlap with differences in education, family responsibilities, and proficiency in English. Because of their lower level of education, greater family responsibilities, and lower proficiency in English, Mexican women—about 25 percent of all immigrant women—are the least likely to participate in the labor force. When they do participate, they are also the most likely to become unemployed, to work fewer hours during the week, and to earn lower wages. Moreover, the gap in earnings between them and native-born and other immigrant women will increase over time. Immigrant women from Central America and Indochina—about 12 percent of immigrant women in the United States—have characteristics similar to those of Mexican women; hence, they perform similarly in the labor market, but with two exceptions: the labor-force participation of Central American women exceeds that of native-born women whereas the earnings of Indochinese women exceed those of native-born women.

The labor-market performance of all other immigrant women is equal to or exceeds that of native-born women. Immigrant women from Europe—about 19 percent of immigrant woman—have lifetime earnings similar to those of native-born women, but their employment rates remain about 10 percent lower than those of native-borns throughout their lifetimes. Asian women—about 25 percent of immigrant women—have lower rates of employment at entry, but they reach parity with native-born women within ten years or so and their earnings exceed those of native-born women throughout their lifetimes. Among Asians, Filipinas, the most educated women immigrating to the United States, have a labor-force participation rate that is 10 percent higher than that of native-born women. Filipinas' earnings also exceed those of native-born women throughout their lifetimes.

Not all the variations noted above, however—most specifically that of participation in the labor force—are explained by variation in education, family responsibilities, and proficiency in English. Cultural and other factors that are country-specific may also contribute. Cultural mores relative to women working outside the home may be more enduring in some groups than in others. The lower labor-force participation rate of European women in the United States, for example, remains equivalent to that of women in Europe throughout their lifetimes. And, Asian women have higher participation rates in the United States than at home—a rate that is increasing rapidly over time. Selectivity caused by labor recruitment may play a role in yet other groups, such as Filipinas and women from Central America, both of which have labor-force participation rates that far outpace those that would be expected judging by their education and other characteristics.

The entrepreneurial spirit of immigrants in starting new businesses in the United States is legendary. This image, however, does not fit all immigrant groups. Immigrant women from Europe and some Asian countries—primarily China, Korea, and Japan—have higher self-employment rates than native-born women. However, immigrant women from Mexico, Central America, and Indochina are either less likely or no more likely than native-born women to be self-employed. Overall, immigrant women are no more likely than native-born women to be self-employed. And although both groups have doubled their self-employment rates in the past 30 years, their rates remain equally low at 6 percent, or about half that of native-born and immigrant men.

Today's immigrants enter an economy that has changed significantly over the past 30 years. Today the majority of net new jobs are filled by workers with some college. This change is negatively affecting the performance of immigrant women relative to native-born women as the latter are lagging behind the first in educational improvements. As late as 1970, immigrant and native-born women had the same rate of employment and commanded the same earnings. By 1990, however, the employment rate of immigrant women trailed that of native-born women by 10 percentage points (68 vs. 58 percent) and their earnings were behind by 13 percent.

Role of Immigrant Women in the Labor Market

Seemingly operating within an integrated labor market, the occupational and industrial distribution of immigrant women is mediated by the divergence in their levels of education and proficiency in English relative to native-born women. Over time, immigrant women have become increasingly more likely to be employed in low-skill occupations—such as machine operators, farm laborers, workers in private households, and janitors—than native-born women. They are also more likely to work in low-skill sectors—including agriculture, construction, nondurable manufacturing, and personal services.

As the number of jobs filled by low-educated workers declined (by more than four million jobs between 1970 and 1997), immigrant women have increasingly replaced native-born women at the lower end of the labor market. They are taking the place of older native-born women who retire, while increasingly better-educated, younger native-born women fill the increasing number of jobs that require a high level of education.

After accounting for differences in education, however, few differences remain in the occupational distribution of immigrant and native-born women. To the extent that one group is more concentrated in a given occupation, this reflects differences in English proficiency or the need for certification in certain occupations. Hence, at lower levels of education, immigrant women are twice as likely to work as machine/equipment operators (occupations that do not require proficiency in English) and half as likely to work in clerical or sales occupations (where frequent interactions with coworkers and clients require proficiency in English). Similarly, among the college educated, immigrant women are more likely than native-born women to work in engineering and health-related occupations, whose requirements are generally universally shared, than to work as teachers, lawyers, and social workers—occupations that tend to be idiosyncratic to the culture of a particular country.

It does not appear that the certification requirement for many professions is a major barrier to immigrant women to practice the profession for which they have obtained their credentials in another country. By and large, college-educated immigrant women are just as likely as college-educated native-born women to work in the various professions. However, the relatively low portion of immigrant women who are teachers may reflect either a strong initial selectivity among immigrant women away from this profession or, indeed, difficulties in meeting the certification requirements to pursue this vocation in the United States.

Accordingly, no single industry in the nation has a labor force that is dominated by immigrant labor, including, perhaps somewhat surprisingly, the textile, apparel, and household-help industries. Indeed, the greatest number of immigrant women are working in such large industries as hospitals, banks, and business services. In the low-skill sectors of the job market, immigrant women are more likely than native-born women to make up "back office" labor, whereas college-educated, native-born women are more likely to find jobs in the "front office." In high-skill industries, however, no such sharp differentiation of roles exists.

The increasing number of immigrants and descendants in the U.S. labor force is leading to a diversification of the labor force in all industries, with Hispanic women disproportionately increasing their presence in low-skill industries, and Asian women increasing in high-skill industries. Overall, the increase in the share of minorities has been more rapid in the private than in the public sector. Indeed, the share of Hispanics and Asians in the nation's public sector has not changed in 27 years.

Immigrant women have consistently been paid lower wages than native-born women—regardless of their level of education or of the industry in which they work. The differential ranges from a few percentage points to as high as 22 percentage points in the textile and apparel industry. These wage discrepancies have been increasing over time, except in high-tech industries—computers, electronics, instruments—for college-educated immigrant women.

Even though the hourly wages of immigrant women are typically lower than those of native-born women, the first group commands higher weekly earnings than native-born women in industries such as household services, hospitals, and hotels and motels. These industries have irregular hours that often require evening and night work, and immigrant women in these industries are working longer hours than native-born women.

Finally, immigrant women, especially those with low levels of education, are less likely to acquire additional education or to receive formal training than their native-born counterparts. At the same time, with the exception of refugees and the elderly, they are no more likely to use safety net welfare and health services than native-born women.

Access to Public Services

One of the reasons that low-educated immigrant women who come to the United States as adults make little economic progress over their lifetimes here is that they acquire little additional education or training after they arrive. By and large, the human capital immigrant adults arrive with is the human capital they take into the U.S. labor market. Female immigrants are half as likely as their native-born counterparts to acquire any formal training in the United States.

Similarly, only one-third of immigrant women who enter the country as adolescents, that is, between the ages of 15 and 18, continue their education in the United States. Adolescents from developing countries with low educational requirements, such as Mexico, Laos, Vietnam, and some Central American countries, are the least likely to acquire additional education in the United States.

In the rare event that immigrant women receive additional education or training in the United States, they receive it from the same programs, at the same locations, and in the same forms as native-born women. And, like native-born women, more-educated immigrant women are more likely to acquire additional education or to receive training from employers than less-educated immigrant women.

Overall, only a small share (2 percent) of both immigrant and native-born women receive formal assistance in searching for a job. Similarly, federal programs play a small role in the actual provision of training. Most of the training that is received by immigrant women is employer-based, just as it is for native-born women.

By and large, immigrant women who encounter difficulties working or earning an adequate income in the U.S. labor market are no more likely, and in some cases are less likely, than native-born women to rely on safety net programs such as AFDC, food stamps , and health services (Medicaid). There are, however, two significant exceptions. Refugee women—primarily those from Indochina and the former Soviet Union—are three times more likely than other immigrants to rely on AFDC for their subsistence and more than two times as likely to rely on Medicaid for their health care. This pattern is in part becuse of their relatively low level of education and low participation rate in the labor market and in part because of their eligibility for such programs upon arrival.

The second exception is elderly immigrant women, who are more than twice as likely to participate in the SSI and Medicaid programs (the safety net programs) as elderly native-born women, because immigrant women are less likely than native-born women to be eligible for Social Security and Medicare. Some elderly women have come primarily to reunite with their adult children; they have not worked in the United States and are thus ineligible for Social Security. Others have contributed too little to Social Security during their lives in the United States and need to complement their Social Security benefits with SSI benefits.

Looking Forward

As the research for this book examined the experiences of immigrant women in the U.S. labor market over the past 30 years, a picture emerged of immigrant women who are being integrated into the nation's labor market fairly rapidly and who can perform in that market at the same levels as native-born women. However, a sizable minority of relatively low-educated immigrant women—mostly from Mexico, Central America, and Indochina—do not fare equally well. Their labor-force participation is relatively low, as are their earnings, which do not increase over their lifetimes. The growing size of this group raises several major long-term issues that require public-policy attention.

The first issue is whether current immigration policy encourages a balance between low-educated and college-educated workers that is consistent with the changing demand of the national economy. The economy has been steadily shedding jobs that are filled by workers with fewer than 12 years of education and adding fewer and fewer net new jobs filled by workers with a high school education only. Increasingly, pressures at the lower end of the labor market are negatively affecting both the job opportunities and the earnings of low-educated immigrant and native-born women alike. Consequently, if high levels of low-educated immigrants continue to enter the country, the creation of a new and growing underclass of Hispanics and Asians seems likely.

A second and related issue concerns the speed of upward mobility of this group of immigrants and their children. Left to its own pace, the education, and hence economic integration of recent waves of low-educated immigrants is likely to take time—perhaps several generations. The second generation of these immigrants is more likely than its parents to graduate from high school, but their college-going rates continue to significantly lag behind those of native-borns and children of other immigrants. Because most new jobs created by the economy are filled by workers with at least some formal postsecondary education, there is concern that this process is moving much too slowly to ensure that an increasing share of today's children will be provided with the tools they need to meet U.S. labor needs, let alone to successfully compete in today's economy. If we are to avoid an increase in educational and economic disparities between ethnic/racial groups, individual states and even the federal government need to get involved. Only they can see to it that many more second-generation immigrants have the opportunity for a college education.

This issue is all the more important, because a renewal in the number of births is in large measure driven by the higher fertility rates of immigrant women. These trends are placing increasing demand pressures on educational institutions in the states where immigrants are concentrated at the same time as the electorate is pressing for restraint in public expenditures.

One group of immigrant youths, albeit small in relative terms, is particularly vulnerable. These youths immigrate when they are between the ages of 15 and 17 with the majority of them not completing their schooling after arriving in the United States. Strategies to encourage these youths to continue their education in the United States need to be developed. Failure to do so means that these youths—over time these will number in the hundreds of thousands—will have little prospects for economic mobility and may turn to gangs, crime, or other illegal activities to sustain themselves.

A third issue concerns the majority of immigrants who arrive as adults who do not acquire additional education in the United States and are not likely to receive any type of formal training, especially if they have a low level of education at entry. It may not be realistic to expect adult immigrants who have been out of school for several years and who have family responsibilities to acquire additional education in the United States. Indeed, the resources needed to make a high school graduate of an adult immigrant with eight years of schooling in her home country, for instance, would likely be prohibitive. Still, the integration process of adult immigrants, as well as their economic prospects, could be enhanced by promoting the rapid acquisition of the English language. Providing support to help immigrants, most particularly the less educated, improve their verbal and written English-language skills is one way that the public and private sectors can accelerate the integration of immigrants. Expanding access to training in both the public and the private sectors, at least at par to the access provided to native-born workers, is another way.

Finally, the public sector has been lagging in its racial/ethnic diversification, in part because this sector has the most highly educated labor force. However, we believe that in the near future, pressure will be brought to bear on this sector and that as a result, diversification will indeed increase. Specifically, one area that has been slower than others in utilizing immigrant labor is the field of education. Given the expected large increase in demand for teachers in the years to come, this group should definitely be explored as an untapped supply.

Appendix

Effects of Immigrant Women's Characteristics on Labor-Market Outcomes

The analyses presented in chapters 7 and 8 are based on the 1970, 1980, and 1990 Public Use Micro Samples of the U.S. Census. In all descriptive analyses, the sample weights are used to produce unbiased population estimates.[1] The key variables examined include country of birth, year arrived in the United States (or arrival year), employment status, earnings, and education. An *immigrant* is defined as someone who was born in a foreign country; women who were born abroad of American parents (e.g., women whose parents were in the U.S. military and stationed abroad at the time they were born) are considered native-born women.

To abstract from school leaving and retirement, all analyses are restricted to women 25 to 60 years old. Immigrants from certain countries are grouped together on the basis of several criteria:

- Each origin group must constitute a significant share of the immigrant population.

- Most groupings include countries that are geographically close to one another.

- Women from the countries that are grouped together must have common backgrounds and experiences (e.g., language) that would lead them to have similar experiences in the U.S. labor market.

These criteria resulted in the nine country groupings listed in table A.1; the first seven groups are ranked in order of the share they represented among the immigrant population in the nation in 1990. These groups are narrowly defined. The last two groups are heterogeneous. As a result, we do not place as much emphasis on the results for women in those broader categories.

Table A.1

Percent of Immigrant Women by Country of Birth, Nation, 1970 and 1990

Country/region of birth	1970	1990
1. Mexico	8.9	19.7
2. Europe	41.4	16.8
3. Japan, Korea, and China	5.4	11.5
4. United Kingdom and Canada	23.5	8.1
5. Central America	1.7	6.3
6. Philippines	2.1	6.3
7. Indochina	0.2	4.1
8. Middle East and all other Asian countries not listed in the table	2.6	7.2
9. Caribbean, Africa, Oceania, and South America	13.9	20.2
Total	100	100

We examine several indicators of labor-market outcomes: labor-force participation, weekly wages, weeks and hours worked, unemployment, and self-employment. *Labor-force participation* is based on the individual's reported activity in the week prior to the census, and it includes women who were currently working or unemployed. For most analyses, the earnings are average *weekly wages* in the year prior to the census year, which include self-employment and wage and salary income. Women with negative earnings from a loss in business income were excluded from the analyses of weekly wages.[2] Wages are expressed in 1990 dollars, using the Consumer Price Index for urban consumers. *Hours worked*, which is only available in 1980 and 1990, is the number of hours worked in a typical week in the previous year. Both hours and *weeks worked* are reported for women who did in fact work in the year prior to the census. *Self-employment* is determined by the status of the worker (as indicated by the "class" of the worker) in the week prior to the census.

For most analyses, we group workers into various education categories, paralleling the census categories.[3] We also distinguish among immigrants with various levels of English language skills. Individuals who speak a language other than English in their home are asked to report their ability to speak English (i.e., very well, well, poorly, not at all); this information was collected in 1980 and 1990.

The outcomes analyzed in the regressions are labor-force participation, annual hours worked among those who worked, and log of weekly earnings among those who had positive weekly earnings.

For each of these three outcomes in each of the three census years, four models (three in 1970) are estimated, and the results are reported in table A.2. The first model (Model 1) includes a dummy indicator for whether the

Table A.2

Coefficient on Immigrant Indicator Variable in Models of Participation, Annual Hours, and Weekly Earnings with Various Controls, 1970, 1980, and 1990

Year/Dependent Variable	Model 1	Model 2	Model 3	Model 4
1970				
Participation (N=468095,	−0.003	0.017	0.001	NA[c]
Mean=0.493)[a]	(0.82)[b]	(5.32)[b]	(0.20)[b]	
Annual hours	NA[c]	NA[c]	NA[c]	NA[c]
Log weekly earnings[d] (N=255299,	0.062	0.121	0.090	NA[c]
Mean =5.48)[a]	(8.32)	(12.93)	(12.71)	
1980				
Participation (N=723772,	−0.037	0.004	-0.001	−0.002
Mean=0.614)[a]	(19.82)	(2.23)	(0.21)	(0.75)
Annual hours[d] (N=474830,	1.1	27.9	14.9	12.8
Mean=1549)[a]	(0.29)	(7.35)	(3.94)	(2.68)
Log weekly earnings[d] (N=468387,	−0.004	0.057	0.045	0.033
Mean =5.62)	(1.04)	(14.33)	(11.48)	(6.55)
1990				
Participation (N=882475,	−0.085	−0.026	−0.024	−0.007
Mean=0.713)[a]	(62.4)	(13.7)	(17.5)	(3.45)
Annual hours[d] (N=661976,	−16.2	22.4	22.4	20.3
Mean=1671)	(5.80)	(7.67)	(7.72)	(5.19)
Log weekly earnings[d] (N=655914,	−0.051	0.047	0.047	0.047
Mean =5.71)[a]	(16.68)	(15.41)	(15.55)	(11.51)
Control Variables				
Quartic in age?	Yes	Yes	Yes	Yes
Quadratic in years of schooling?	No	Yes	Yes	Yes
Number of children ever born?	No	No	Yes	Yes
Indicators for ability to speak English?	No	No	No	Yes

[a]N and Mean are for the unweighted data.

[b]Absolute value of t-statistic in parentheses.

[c]NA=data not available.

[d]The number of observations for weekly wages is fewer than the number of observations for annual hours because women with nonpositive earnings resulting from business losses are excluded from models of weekly wages, and because the number of missing values varies across items.

women were immigrants and controls for age (in quartic form). Model 2 then adds education (in quadratic form) to Model 1. Model 3 builds on Model 2 by including the number of children ever born. The final model, Model 4, controls for age, education, number of children ever born, and ability to speak English (with an indicator variable for each of the four language-ability levels, with the reference group being those people who speak only English at home). Model 4 cannot be estimated for 1970 because information on English

Table A.3

Coefficient on Country/Region of Birth Indicator Variables in Linear Probability Models of Labor-Force Participation with Various Controls, 1970, 1980, and 1990

Country of Birth/Race	1970[a]			1980	
	(1)	(2)	(3)	(1)	(2)
U.K., Canada	−0.001	−0.001	−0.012	−0.005	−0.01
	(0.09)[b]	(0.07)[b]	(1.91)[b]	(0.91)[b]	(2.06)[b]
Europe	−0.001	0.023	−0.001	−0.023	−0.002
	(0.16)	(4.72)	(0.03)	(6.12)	(0.57)
Japan, Korea, China	−0.034	−0.024	−0.041	−0.033	−0.049
	(2.76)	(1.92)	(3.34)	(5.47)	(8.33)
Indochina	c	c	c	−0.169	−0.115
				(13.12)	(9.02)
Philippines	0.109	0.081	0.080	0.160	0.095
	(5.77)	(4.30)	(4.31)	(22.20)	(13.35)
Mexico	−0.103[d]	−0.020	0.003	−0.130[d]	0.001[d]
	(11.29)	(2.16)	(0.37)	(33.36)	(0.11)
Central America	0.151[d]	0.156[d]	0.129[d]	0.047[d]	0.106[d]
	(7.05)	(7.34)	(6.12)	(5.70)	(13.02)
Middle East, Other Asia	-0.051	−0.056	−0.064	−0.131	−0.142
	(2.82)	(3.11)	(3.60)	(17.12)	(18.79)
Caribbean, Africa, Oceania, S. America	0.125	0.119	0.080	0.047	0.042
	(11.44)	(13.8)	(9.42)	(9.20)	(8.40)
Native-Born Black	0.107	0.143	0.161	0.044	0.074
	(36.24)	(48.29)	(54.78)	(23.03)	(39.27)
Native-Born Hispanic	−0.063	−0.009	0.007	−0.089	−0.026
	(13.33)	(1.85)	(1.54)	(24.96)	(7.40)
Native-Born Other	0.021	0.023	0.021	0.012	0.041
	(12.88)	(13.82)	(12.69)	(4.17)	(14.38)
Control Variables					
Quartic in age?	Yes	Yes	Yes	Yes	Yes
Quadratic in education?	No	Yes	Yes	No	Yes
Children ever born?	No	No	Yes	No	No
English skills dummies?	No	No	No	No	No
Observations		468,095		723,772	

[a]Model 4 is not estimated for 1970 because information on English language skills was not obtained in the 1970 census.

[b]Absolute value of t-statistics in parentheses.

[c]Indochinese excluded from the analysis for 1970 because there were too few observations.

[d]Statistically significant difference between Mexicans (Central Americans) and native-born Hispanics at the .05 level. Native-born Whites are the reference group.

Table A.3—continued

1980 (continued)		1990			
(3)	(4)	(1)	(2)	(3)	(4)
−0.021	−0.021	−0.022	−0.030	−0.041	−0.039
(5.34)[b]	(4.10)[b]	(4.48)[b]	(6.23)[b]	(8.56)[b]	(8.39)[b]
−0.020	−0.025	−0.056	−0.043	−0.056	−0.044
(5.34)	(6.06)	(16.06)	(11.89)	(15.78)	(11.50)
−0.073	−0.070	−0.097	−0.095	−0.110	−0.083
(12.41)	(11.34)	(20.85)	(20.78)	(24.13)	(16.94)
−0.104	−0.098	−0.232	−0.117	−0.101	−0.067
(8.26)	(7.67)	(36.90)	(18.80)	(16.24)	(10.32)
0.092	0.088	0.122	0.085	0.086	0.095
(13.03)	(12.29)	(23.29)	(16.50)	(16.78)	(17.95)
0.018[d]	0.025[d]	−0.123[d]	−0.010	−0.004	−0.033[d]
(4.65)	(5.27)	(41.06)	(3.37)	(1.31)	(9.79)
0.096[d]	0.098[d]	0.023[d]	0.094[d]	0.089[d]	0.116[d]
(11.83)	(11.87)	(4.79)	(19.65)	(18.85)	(23.56)
−0.151	−0.153	−0.145	−0.149	−0.149	−0.132
(20.06)	(19.84)	(28.87)	(30.07)	(30.50)	(25.62)
0.022	0.023	0.018	0.015	0.001	0.016
(4.39)	(4.53)	(4.74)	(4.06)	(0.24)	(4.12)
0.090	0.090	−0.005	0.027	0.036	0.035
(47.77)	(47.71)	(2.69)	(13.08)	(21.87)	(21.29)
−0.011	−0.015	−0.058	−0.011	0.001	0.009
(3.20)	(3.94)	(29.49)	(5.73)	(0.56)	(3.99)
0.053	0.050	0.004	0.006	0.013	0.014
(18.81)	(16.92)	(1.25)	(2.06)	(4.17)	(4.81)
Yes	Yes	Yes	Yes	Yes	Yes
Yes	Yes	No	Yes	Yes	Yes
Yes	Yes	No	No	Yes	Yes
No	Yes	No	No	No	Yes
723772 (continued)				882,475	

language skills was not obtained in the 1970 census. The change across models in the coefficient on the dummy variable for whether the women are immigrants indicates the degree to which the controls can account for the differences in the labor-market outcomes between immigrant and native-born women.

In tables A.3, A.4, and A.5, we report a series of models identical to those reported in table A.2, but instead of including an indicator for whether the women were immigrants, we include indicators for each of the nine country/region of origin groups and each of the four racial/ethnic groups among native-born women, with native-born Whites serving as the reference group.

Table A.4

Coefficient on Country/Region of Birth Indicator Variables in Models of Annual Hours with Various Controls, 1980 and 1990

Country of Birth/Race	1980				1990			
	(1)	(2)	(3)	(4)	(1)	(2)	(3)	(4)
U.K., Canada	−32.6	−34.8	−56.5	−55.8	−14.5	−18.5	−42.5	−42.6
	(3.20)[a]	(3.42)[a]	(5.60)[a]	(5.53)[a]	(1.51)[a]	(1.93)[a]	(4.48)[a]	(4.49)[a]
Europe	−2.6	12.8	−23.2	−14.3	−3.8	6.2	−22.1	−20.5
	(0.34)	(1.68)	(3.08)	(1.74)	(0.51)	(0.83)	(2.99)	(2.61)
Japan, Korea, China	56.7	63.4	25.8	36.5	45.5	50.3	24.2	41.6
	(4.87)	(5.44)	(2.24)	(3.04)	(4.80)	(5.32)	(2.58)	(4.18)
Indochina	−38.9	−20.9	−15.2	−3.1	55.7	99.7	95.9	113.9
	(1.34)	(0.72)	(0.53)	(0.11)	(3.85)	(6.88)	(6.69)	(7.68)
Philippines	167.2	152.8	151.2	159.5	144.1	121.6	128.8	129.5
	(13.20)	(12.04)	(12.04)	(12.46)	(14.75)	(12.47)	(13.33)	(12.89)
Mexico	−103.0[b]	−22.1[b]	5.3[b]	18.0[b]	−149.5[b]	−67.4[b]	−39.9[b]	−14.2[b]
	(12.51)	(2.53)	(0.61)	(1.83)	(23.29)	(9.96)	(5.96)	(1.96)
Central America	58.2[b]	97.8[b]	79.8[b]	91.0[b]	-13.7	41.2[b]	38.3	61.8[b]
	(3.75)	(6.28)	(5.18)	(5.72)	(1.40)	(4.17)	(3.92)	(6.10)
Middle East, Other Asia	0.1	1.37	−22.8	−12.7	-45.0	−56.9	−64.5	−60.0
	(0.01)	(0.08)	(1.41)	(0.77)	(4.14)	(5.24)	(6.00)	(5.36)
Caribbean, Africa, Oceania, S. America	36.5	40.1	2.8	10.8	19.5	20.5	−5.9	3.59
	(3.72)	(4.09)	(0.28)	(1.07)	(2.56)	(2.69)	(0.78)	(0.46)
Native-Born Black	64.9	74.2	102.9	102.4	40.7	54.7	80.4	79.7
	(18.07)	(20.6)	(28.7)	(28.54)	(12.31)	(16.57)	(24.52)	(24.29)
Native-Born Hispanic	−2.2	22.0	39.1	46.3	−17.81	8.7	28.4	27.9
	(0.29)	(2.96)	(5.31)	(5.92)	(4.49)	(2.19)	(7.19)	(6.15)
Native-Born Other	6.2	18.3	37.4	41.5	34.7	34.5	44.4	43.9
	(1.12)	(3.29)	(6.79)	(7.21)	(5.65)	(5.6)	(7.32)	(7.21)
Control Variables								
Quartic in age?	Yes	Yes	Yes	Yes	Yes	Yes	Yes	Yes
Quadratic in education?	No	Yes	Yes	Yes	No	Yes	Yes	Yes
Children ever born?	No	No	Yes	Yes	No	No	Yes	Yes
English skills dummies?	No	No	No	Yes	No	No	No	Yes
Observations	474,830				661,976			

[a] Absolute value of t-statistics in parentheses.

[b] Statistically significant difference between Mexicans (Central Americans) and native-born Hispanics at the .05 level. Native-born Whites are the reference group.

Table A.5

Coefficient on Country/Region of Birth Indicator Variables in Models of Log Weekly Earnings with Various Controls, 1970, 1980, and 1990

| | 1970 | | |
Country of Birth/Race	(1)	(2)	(3)
U.K., Canada	0.062	0.071	0.046
	$(4.23)^a$	$(4.98)^a$	$(3.28)^a$
Europe	0.095	0.167	0.128
	(8.07)	(14.72)	(11.39)
Japan, Korea, China	−0.069	−0.042	−0.058
	(2.24)	(1.42)	(1.99)
Indochina	b	b	b
Philippines	0.091	−0.090	−0.038
	(2.23)	(2.32)	(2.14)
Mexico	−.198	0.065^c	0.085^c
	(8.38)	(2.80)	(3.74)
Central America	0.057^c	0.088	0.053
	(1.25)	(2.00)	(1.21)
Middle East, Other Asia	0.073	−0.015	−0.023
	(1.61)	(0.34)	(0.54)
Caribbean, Africa, Oceania, S. America	0.132	0.125	0.070
	(6.83)	(6.69)	(3.77)
Native-Born Black	−0.267	−0.154	−0.124
	(41.46)	(24.53)	(19.93)
Native-Born Hispanic	−0.148	−0.001	0.013
	(12.23)	(0.09)	(1.14)
Native-Born Other	0.051	0.054	0.053
	(13.12)	(14.36)	(14.27)
Control Variables			
Quartic in age?	Yes	Yes	Yes
Quadratic in education?	No	Yes	Yes
Children ever born?	No	No	Yes
English skills dummies?	No	No	No
Observations		255,299	

[a] Absolute value of t-statistics in parentheses.

[b] Indochinese excluded from the analysis for 1970 because there were too few observations.

[c] Statistically significant difference between Mexicans (Central Americans) and native-born Hispanics at the .05 level. Native-born Whites are the reference group.

Table A.5—continued

	1980				1990		
(1)	(2)	(3)	(4)	(1)	(2)	(3)	(4)
0.042	0.039	0.019	0.018	0.140	0.121	0.096	0.096
(3.81)[a]	(3.67)[a]	(1.84)[a]	(1.72)[a]	(13.26)[a]	(12.13)[a]	(9.66)[a]	(9.65)[a]
0.023	0.059	0.026	0.015	0.044	0.066	0.036	0.045
(2.85)	(7.45)	(3.39)	(1.77)	(5.35)	(8.52)	(4.70)	(5.50)
0.017	−0.013	−0.048	−0.045	−0.022	-0.033	−0.062	−0.015
(1.37)	(1.10)	(3.94)	(3.59)	(2.16)	(3.38)	(6.28)	(1.41)
−0.070	−0.017	−0.012	−0.010	−0.126	0.027	0.023	0.076
(2.25)	(0.56)	(0.43)	(0.34)	(7.91)	(1.83)	(1.55)	(4.94)
0.236	0.067	0.065	0.055	0.138	0.013	0.020	0.026
(17.40)	(5.06)	(5.01)	(4.16)	(12.91)	(1.24)	(2.02)	(2.53)
−0.194[c]	0.057[c]	0.083[c]	0.088[c]	−0.290[c]	−0.039[c]	−0.010[c]	0.046[c]
(21.92)	(6.36)	(9.16)	(8.53)	(41.08)	(5.59)	(1.48)	(6.10)
−0.165	-0.029	−0.045[c]	−0.044	−0.280[c]	−0.115[c]	−0.118[c]	-0.063[c]
(9.90)	(1.81)	(2.82)	(2.66)	(26.10)	(11.18)	(11.60)	(6.04)
0.082	0.017	−0.005	−0.013	0.029	−0.060	−0.068	−0.052
(4.61)	(0.99)	(0.29)	(0.79)	(2.42)	(5.28)	(6.07)	(4.43)
0.062	0.058	0.025	0.024	0.017	0.000	−0.028	−0.003
(5.86)	(5.70)	(2.43)	(2.32)	(2.05)	(0.03)	(3.52)	(0.38)
0.002	0.059	0.085	0.085	−0.009	0.060	0.088	0.086
(0.40)	(15.61)	(22.63)	(22.69)	(2.58)	(17.45)	(25.62)	(25.18)
−0.129	−0.022	−0.007	−0.018	−0.035	0.083	0.104	0.106
(16.20)	(2.92)	(0.96)	(2.24)	(8.17)	(15.18)	(25.29)	(22.59)
0.023	0.069	0.087	0.079	0.105	0.097	0.108	0.108
(3.91)	(11.98)	(15.11)	(13.22)	(15.56)	(15.18)	(17.02)	(17.01)
Yes	Yes	Yes	Yes	Yes	Yes	Yes	Yes
No	Yes	Yes	Yes	No	Yes	Yes	Yes
No	No	Yes	Yes	No	No	Yes	Yes
No	No	No	Yes	No	No	No	Yes
	468,387					655,914	

This specification allows us to compare all racial/ethnic and country/region of birth groupings.

The objective of the multivariate analysis is not to estimate a structural model of labor-market outcomes, but to examine the degree to which this limited set of characteristics (i.e., years of completed education, number of children ever born, and English language skills) can explain the disparities in outcomes. These characteristics may influence outcomes through a variety of channels, including wage offers to women, the value of women's leisure time

(Ben-Porath, 1973), and the labor-market outcomes of husbands throughout the marriage market (Lam and Schoeni, 1993).

The model of labor-force participation is a linear probability model; estimates from a probit model lead to the same substantive conclusions, and the linear probability estimates are more easily interpreted. We used ordinary least squares for the models of annual hours and log weekly earnings. In the models of hours and weekly earnings, we are interested in explaining how the factors (i.e., education, children ever born, English language skills) explain the differences among women who are in fact working; therefore, we are not concerned about selection into the labor force in these models.

Notes

1. Specifically, the data are from the 1 percent sample of the 1970 5 percent county-group file, the 1 percent sample of the 1970 state file, the 5 percent 1980-A sample, and the 5 percent 1990-A sample. Both the state and county-group files in 1970 were used to increase the number of immigrants in the sample, and the sampling weights used for 1970 reflect this fact. The sample weights are used in all descriptive analyses but not in the regression analyses. Immigrants who did not know their dates of entry or countries of origin were eliminated, which affected no more than a few percent of immigrants in any census year. The top-coded reported earnings are used in each year. Borjas (1995) examined the sensitivity of the top-coding and found that the relative wages of immigrants and natives "barely changed" (p. 7) when an imputation scheme was used for top-coded earnings. Therefore, we do not anticipate that top-coding by the census altered our substantive findings.

2. For the 1970 Census, the number of weeks worked was reported in six categories, or brackets: 13 or fewer, 14–26, 27–39, 40–47, 48–49, and 50–52. To calculate weekly earnings in 1970, we used the median of each of the intrabracket distributions for weeks worked reported in 1980. These values are, respectively, 7.818, 21.044, 32.926. 42.310, 48.200, and 51.769 weeks. For 1970, when we report weeks worked during the year, we use these imputed values.

3. For 1970 and 1980, education is reported in completed years of schooling and the classification into categories is straightforward. The question in the census on educational attainment changed in 1990 by (among other things) asking for explicit degrees beyond high school, as opposed to years of completed education. In constructing the education categories with the 1990 data, we included individuals with a General Education Degree with those having 12 years of schooling; we coded individuals with some college or associates degree as having 13 to 15 years of schooling; we coded individuals with bachelors degree as having 16 years of schooling; and we coded individuals with advanced degrees as having 17 or more years of schooling. For analyses in which we distinguish women with more than 16 years of schooling, we include those with advanced degrees in this highest category.

Abbreviations

AFDC	Aid to Families with Dependent Children
BLS	Bureau of Labor Statistics
CETA	Comprehensive Employment and Training Act
DED	Defered Enforced Departure
FIRE	Financial, insurance, and real estate
IIRIRA	Illegal Immigration Reform and Immigrant Responsibility Act of 1996
ILO	International Labour Office
INS	U.S. Immigration and Naturalization Service
IRCA	Immigration Reform and Control Act of 1986
JTPA	Job Training and Partnership Act
LAW	Legally Authorized Workers program
NCES	National Center for Education Statistics
PROWRA	Personal Responsibility and Work Opportunity Act of 1996
PRUCOL	Permanent Resident Under Color of Law
PUMS	Public Use Micro Samples
SAW	Supplemental Agricultural Workers program
SIPP	Survey of Income and Program Participation of the U.S. Bureau of the Census
SSI	Supplemental Security Income program
TANF	Temporary Assistance for Needy Families program
TPS	Temporary protective status
WIC	Women, Infants, and Children program
WIN	Work Incentive program

References

Baker, M., and D. Benjamin (1994). "The Performance of Immigrants in the Canadian Labor Market." *Journal of Labor Economics* 12 (3): 369–405.

Bean, F. D., J. V. W. Van Hook, and J. E. Glick (1996). *Country-of-Origin, Type of Public Assistance and Patterns of Welfare Recipiency among U.S. Immigrants and Natives.* Austin, Tex.: Population Research Center, University of Texas.

Bean, F. D., G. Vernez, and C. B. Keely (1989). *Opening and Closing the Doors: Evaluating Immigration Reform and Control.* Santa Monica, Calif.: RAND, JRI-01; and Washington, D.C.: Urban Institute.

Ben-Porath, T. (1973). "Labor Force Participation Rates and the Supply of Labor." *Journal of Political Economics* 81 (3): 697–704.

Borjas, G. J. (1997). "The Earnings of Mexican Immigrants in the United States." *Journal of Development Economics* 51 (1): 69–98.

———. (1995). "Assimilation and Changes in Cohort Quality Revisited: What Happened to Immigrant Earnings in the 1980s?" *Journal of Labor Economics* 13 (2): 201–245.

———. (1993). "Immigration Policy, National Origin, and Immigrant Skills: A Comparison of Canada and the United States." In *Small Differences That Matter: Labor Markets and Income Maintenance in Canada and the United States*, edited by D. Card and R. B. Freeman. Chicago: University of Chicago Press.

———. (1987). "Self-Selection and the Earnings of Immigrants." *American Economic Review* 77 (4): 531–553.

———. (1985). "Assimilation, Changes in Cohort Quality, and the Earnings of Immigrants." *Journal of Labor Economics* 3 (4): 463–489.

Borjas, G. J., R. B. Freeman, and L. F. Katz (1996). "Searching for the Effects of Immigration on the Labor Market." *AEA Papers and Proceedings* 86 (2): 246–251.

Borjas, G. J., and L. Hilton (1995). "Immigration and the Welfare State: Immigration Participation in Means-Tested Entitlement Programs." *Quarterly Journal of Economics* 3 (2): 575–604.

Boyd, M. (1996). "Female Migrant Labor in North America: Trends and Issues for the 1990s." In *International Migration, Refugee Flows and Hu-*

man Rights in North America: The Impact of Free Trade and Restructuring, 193–213, edited by Alan B. Simmons. New York: Center for Migration Studies.

————. (1992). "Gender, Visible Minority, and Immigrant Earnings Inequality: Reassessing an Employment Equity Premise." In *Deconstructing a Nation: Immigration, Multiculturalism, and Racism in the 1990s Canada*, 279–321, edited by V. Satzewich. Halifax: Fernwood Press.

————. (1989). "Family and Personal Networks in International Migration: Recent Developments and New Agendas." *International Migration Review* 23 (3): 638–670.

Brettell, C. B., and R. J. Simon (1986). "Immigrant Women: An Introduction." In *International Migration: The Female Experience*, edited by R. J. Simon and C. B. Brettell. Totowa, N.J.: Rowman & Allanheld.

Card, D. (1996). *Immigration Inflows, Native Outflows, and the Local Labor Market Impacts of Higher Immigration*, Princeton, N.J.: Princeton University Press, Working Paper #368.

Cardoso, L. A. (1980). *Mexican Immigration to the United States 1897–1931*. Tucson, Ariz.: University of Arizona Press.

Center for Continuing Study of the California Economy (CCSCE) (1996). *California Economic Growth*. Palo Alto, Calif.: CCSCE.

Chiswick, B. R. (1980). "An Analysis of the Economic Process and Impact of Immigrants." Washintgon, D.C.: U.S. Department of Commerce, National Technical Information Service, PB80-200454.

Clark, R. L. et al. (1994). *Fiscal Impacts of Undocumented Aliens: Selected Estimates for Seven States*. Washington, D.C.: Urban Institute, UI/PR-94-1.

Cobb-Clark, D.A. (1993). "Immigrant Selectivity and Wages: The Evidence for Women." *The American Economic Review* 83 (4): 986–993.

Crane, K., and B. J. Asch (1990). *The Effect of Employer Sanctions on the Flow of Illegal Aliens to the United States*. Santa Monica, Calif.: RAND, JRI-03; and Washington, D.C.: Urban Institute.

DaVanzo, J., J. Hawes-Dawson, R. B. Valdez, and G. Vernez, (1994). *Surveying Immigrant Communities: Policy Imperatives and Technical Challenges*. Santa Monica, Calif.: RAND, MR-247-FF.

Diner, H. R. (1984). *Erin's Daughters in America: Irish Immigrant Women in the Nineteenth Century*. Baltimore, Md.: Johns Hopkins University Press.

Donato, K. M. (1993). "Current Trends and Patterns of Female Migration: Evidence from Mexico." *International Migration Review* 27 (4): 748–771.

Duleep, H. O., and S. Sanders (1994). "Empirical Regularities across Cultures: The Effect of Children on Women's Work." *The Journal of Human Resources* 29 (2): 328-347.

————. (1993). "The Decision to Work by Married Immigrant Women," *Industrial and Labor Relations Review* 46 (2): 67–80.

Ewen, E. (1985). *Immigrant Women in the Land of Dollars: Life and Culture on the Lower East Side 1890–1925*. New York: Monthly Review Press.

Fernandez, E. W., and J. G. Robinson (1994). *Illustrative Ranges of the Distribution of Undocumented Immigrants by State*. Washington, D.C.: U.S. Bureau of the Census, U.S. Department of Commerce, Technical Working Paper #8.

Fernandez-Kelly, M. P., and A. M. Garcia (1990). "Power Surrendered, Power Restored: The Politics of Work and Family Among Hispanic Garment Workers in California and Florida." In *Women, Politics, and Change*, edited by L. A. Tilly and P. Gurin. New York: Russell Sage Foundation: 130–149.

Friedberg, R. M. (1991). "The Labor Market Assimilation of Immigrants in the United States: The Role of Age at Arrival." Cambridge: Massachusetts Institute of Technology. Unpublished paper.

Frey, R. (1995). "Labor Market Participation of Immigrant and Native Men." Washington, D.C.: Division of Immigration Policy and Research, U.S. Department of Labor, Working Paper (mimeograph).

Funkhauser, E., and S. Trejo (1997). "Female Immigrants in the United States." Santa Barbara, Calif.: University of California, Unpublished paper.

Gabriel, S. A., J. P. Mattey, and W. L. Wascher (1995). *The Demise of California Reconsidered: Interstate Migration over the Economic Cycle*. San Francisco, Calif.: Federal Reserve Bank of San Francisco: 30–45.

Galarza, E. (1964). *Merchants of Labor: The Mexican Bracero History*. Charlotte, Va.: McNally & Loftin.

Gilbertson, G. A. (1995). "Women's Labor and Enclave Employment: The Case of Dominican and Colombian Women in New York City." *International Migration Review* 29 (3): 657–670.

Grasmuck, S., and P. Pessar (1991). *Between Two Islands: Dominican International Migration*. Berkeley: University of California Press.

Ho, C. G. T. (1993). "Internationalization of Kinship and the Feminization of Caribbean Migration: The Case of Afro-Trinidadian Immigrants in Los Angeles." *Human Organization* 52 (1): 32–40.

Holzer, H. J. (1996). *What Employers Want: Job Prospects of Less-Educated Workers*. New York: Russell Sage Foundation.

Hondagneu-Sotelo, P. (1994). "Regulating the Unregulated? Domestic Workers' Social Networks." *Social Problems* 41 (1).

Houston, M. F., R. C. Kramer, and J. M. Barrett (1984). "Female Predominance in Immigration to the United States Since 1930: A First Look." *International Migration Review* 28 (4): 908–963.

Huang, F. Y. (1993). *Migration Patterns and Labor Force Participation: An Analysis of Asian and Hispanic Immigrant Wives in the U.S.* Paper presented at annual meeting of Population Association of America, April 1–3.

Huddle, D. (1994). *The Costs of Immigration.* Washington, D.C.: Carrying Capacity Network.

Hune, S. (1991). "Migrant Women in the Context of the International Convention on the Protection of the Rights of All Migrant Workers and Members of Their Families." *International Migration Review* 25 (4): 800–817.

Johnson, H. (1996). *Undocumented Immigration to California: 1980–1993.* San Francisco, Calif.: Public Policy Institute of California.

Johnson, H. P., and R. Lovelady (1995). *Migration between California and Other States: 1985–1994.* Sacramento, Calif.: California State Library and California Department of Finance, CRB-IS-95-006.

Katz, R. (1982). "The Immigrant Woman: Double Cost or Relative Improvement." *International Migration Review* 16: 661–677.

Keeley, C. (1995). "The Effects of International Migration on U.S. Foreign Policy." In *Threatened Peoples, Threatened Borders: World Migration and U.S. Policy*, edited by M. Teitelbaum and M. Weiner. New York: W. W. Norton, 215–243.

LaLonde, R. J., and R. H. Topel (1992). "The Assimilation of Immigrants in the U.S. Labor Market." In *Immigration and the Work Force,* edited by G. J. Borjas and R. B. Freeman. Chicago: The University of Chicago Press.

Lam, D., and R. F. Schoeni (1993). "Effects of Family Background on Earnings and Return to Schooling: Evidence from Brazil." *Journal of Political Economy* 101 (4): 710–714.

Ley, K. (1981). "Migrant Women. Is Migration a Blessing or a Handicap? Situation of Migrant Women in Switzerland." *International Migration* 19 (1–2): 75–82.

Long, J. E. (1980). "The Effect of Americanization on Earnings: Some Evidence for Women." *Journal of Political Economy* 88 (3): 620–629.

MacPherson, D., and J. Stewart (1989). "The Labor Force Participation and Earnings Profiles of Married Female Immigrants." *Quarterly Review of Economics and Business* 29 (3): 57–72.

Massey, D. S., J. Arango, G. Hugo, A. Kouaouci, A. Pellegrino, and J. E. Taylor (1994). "An Evaluation of International Migration Theory: The North American Case." *Population and Development Review* 20 (4): 699–751.

McCarthy, K., and G. Vernez (1997). *Immigration in a Changing Economy.* Santa Monica, Calif.: MR-854-OSD/CBR/FF/WFHF/IF/AMF.

Mishel, L., and J. Bernstein (1994). *The State of Working America, 1994–1995.* New York: Economic Policy Institute, M. E. Sharpe, Inc.

Morokvasic, M. (1984). "Birds of Passage Are Also Women. . . ." *International Migration Review* 18 (4): 886–907.

Murnane, R. J., and F. Levy (1996). *Teaching the New Basic Skills: Principles for Educating Children to Thrive in a Changing Economy.* Boston: The Free Press.

Nakamura, A., and M. Nakamura (1985). "Dynamic Models of the Labor Force Behavior of Married Women Which Can Be Estimated Using Limited Amounts of Past Information." *Journal of Econometrics* 27 (3) :273–98.

National Research Council (1997). *The New Americans: Economic, Demographic, and Fiscal Effects of Immigration.* Washington, D.C.: National Academy Press.

Ong, P., and A. Valenzuela, Jr. (1996). "The Labor Market: Immigrant Effects and Racial Disparities." In *Ethnic Los Angeles*, 165–192, edited by R. Waldinger and M. Bozorgmehr. New York: Russell Sage Foundation.

Pedraza, S. (1991). "Women and Migration: The Social Consequences of Gender." *Annual Review of Sociology* 17: 303–325.

Perez, L. (1986). "Immigrant Economic Adjustment and Family Organization: The Cuban Success Story Reexamined." *International Migration Review* 20: 4–20.

Piore, M. (1979). *Birds of Passage: Migrant Labor and Industrial Societies,* Boston: Cambridge University Press.

Ranney, S., and S. A. Kossoudji (1984). "The Labor Market Experience of Female Migrants: The Case of Temporary Mexican Migration to the U.S. *International Migration Review* 18 (4): 1120–1143.

Reichert, J., and D. S. Massey (1980). "History and Trends in U.S. Bound Migration from a Mexican Town." *International Migration Review* 14 (4): 475–491.

Reimers, C. (1985). "Cultural Differences in Labor Force Participation among Married Women." *American Economic Review, Papers and Proceedings* 15 (2): 251–255.

Reimers, C. W. (1984). "Wage Determination Among Hispanic, Black, and Anglo Women." In *Hispanics in the U.S. Economy*, edited by G. Borjas and M. Tienda. Academic Press.

Repak, T. A. (1994). "Labor Recruitment and the Lure of the Capital: Central American Migrants in Washington, D.C." *Gender & Society* 8 (4): 507–524.

Romero, P. J., A. J. Chang, and T. Parker (1994). *Shifting the Costs of a Failed Federal Policy: The Net Fiscal Impact of Illegal Immigrants in California.* Sacramento, Calif.: Governor's Office of Planning and Research.

Rothman, E., and T. Espenshade (1992). "Fiscal Impacts of Immigration to the United States." *Population Index* 58 (3): 381–415.

Sassen, S. (1991). *The Global City: New York, London, Tokyo.* Princeton, N.J.: Princeton University Press.

Schoeni, R. F. (1998a). "Labor Market Assimilation of Immigrant Women." *Industrial and Labor Relations Review* 51 (3): 483–504.

————. (1998b). "Labor Market Outcomes of Immigrant Women in the United States: 1970 to 1990." *International Migration Review* 32 (1): 57–77.

Schoeni, R. F., and G. Vernez (1997). *The Economic Progress of Immigrant Women*. Santa Monica, Calif.: RAND, DRU-1705-AMF.

Schoeni, R. F., K. F. McCarthy, and G. Vernez (1996). *The Mixed Economic Progress of Immigrants*. Santa Monica, Calif.: RAND, MR-763-IF/FF.

Schwartz-Seller, M. (1981). *Immigrant Women*. Philadelphia: Temple University Press.

Segura, D. A. (1992). "Ambivalence or Continuity? Motherhood and Employment among Chicanas and Mexican Immigrant Women Workers." *Aztlan* 20 (1 & 2): 119–150.

Silvestri, G. T. (1993). "Occupational Employment: Wide Variations in Growth." *Monthly Labor Review* 116 (11): 58–86.

Simon, R. J., and M. DeLey (1984). "The Work Experience of Undocumented Mexican Women Migrants in Los Angeles." *International Migration Review* 18 (4): 1212–1229.

Stier, H. (1991). "Immigrant Women Go to Work: Analysis of Immigrant Wives' Labor Supply for Six Asian Groups." *Social Science Quarterly* 72 (1): 67–82.

Stier, H., and M. Tienda (1992). "Family, Work, and Women: The Labor Supply of Hispanic Immigrant Wives." *International Migration Review* 26 (4): 1291–1313.

Sullivan, T. A. (1984). "The Occupational Prestige of Women Immigrants: A Comparison of Cubans and Mexicans." *International Migration Review* 18 (4): 1045–1062.

Tienda, M., L. Jensen, and R. L. Bach (1984). "Part III: Census-Based Quantitative Analyses of Female Immigrants and Their Labor Market Characteristics: An International Comparison. Immigration, Gender and the Process of Occupational Change in the United States, 1970–80." *International Migration Review* 18 (4): 1021–1044.

Tyree, A., and K. Donato (1986). "A Demographic Overview of the International Migration of Women. In *International Migration and the Female Experience*, edited by R. J. Simon and C. B. Brettell. Totowa, N.J.: Rowan and Allanheld.

United Nations (1995). *International Migration Poles and the Status of Female Migrants*. New York: United Nations.

U.S. General Accounting Office (1995). *Illegal Aliens: National Net Cost Estimates Vary Widely*. Washington, D.C.: U.S. Government Printing Office, GAO/HEHS-95-133.

Vernez, G., and A. Abrahamse (1996). *How Immigrants Fare in U.S. Education*. Santa Monica, Calif.: RAND, MR-718-AMF.

Vernez, G., and K. F. McCarthy (1996). *The Costs of Immigration to Taxpayers: Analytical and Policy Issues*. Santa Monica, Calif.: RAND, MR-705-FF/IF.

Vernez, G. (1993). *Increased Soviet Emigration and U.S. Immigration Policy*. Santa Monica, Calif.: RAND, DRU-190-FF.

———. (1994). "The United States Immigration Reform and Control Act of 1986: Implementation and Effects." In *Migration Policies in Europe and the United States*, edited by Giacomo Luciani. Dordrecht, the Netherlands: Kluwer Academic Publishers; and Santa Monica, Calif.: RAND, RP-265.

Waldinger, R. (1996). *Still the Promised City? African Americans and New Immigrants in Post-Industrial New York*. Cambridge, Mass.: Harvard University Press.

Weinberg, S. S. (1992). "The Treatment of Women in Immigration History: A Call For Change." *Journal of American Ethnic History* (Summer): 25–69.

Zucker, N. L. and N. F. Zucker (1991). "The 1980 Refugee Act: A 1990 Perspective." In *Refugee Policy: Canada and the United States*, edited by Howard Adelman. Staten Island, N.Y.: Center for Migration Studies: 224–252.

Index

immigrants over time, 176–78;
participation by elderly
immigrants, 168–70;
participation by nonelderly
immigrants, 166–68;
participation data by family
income, 172; participation data
by racial/ethnic groups and
immigration status, 176;
participation rates of
immigrants in, 167, 171–72,
178. *See also* federal programs
SAW. *See* Supplemental
Agricultural Workers program
Schoeni, R., 129n1, 131, 152n1
school breakfast and lunch
programs, 157, 177
sectors of the economy. *See*
employment sectors; individual
sectors
self-employment, 125–27;
defined, 192
service industry sector, 54, 88–90,
105–8; in California, 110;
characteristics of, 106
services. *See* public services
SIPP. *See* Survey of Income and
Program Participation of the
U.S. Bureau of the Census
skill level: changes in occupations
by, 77; occupational
distribution by, 72
social safety net programs. *See*
safety net programs
Social Security, 169–71, 173
sociodemographic characteristics
of immigrant women, 33;
generalizations about, 47; in
high-immigration states, 45
sources of funding. *See* funding
sources
sponsorship, by immigration
status, 165

SSI. *See* Supplemental Security
Income program
states of immigrant residence. *See*
residential concentration;
individual states
Supplemental Agricultural
Workers (SAW) program, 15
Supplemental Security Income
(SSI) program, 154, 156, 168–
76, 180, 189
Survey of Income and Program
Participation (SIPP) of the U.S.
Bureau of the Census, 155,
162–63, 181n2

Temporary Assistance for Needy
Families (TANF) program,
154, 156
Temporary Protective Status
(TPS), 154
Texas, 8, 40, 46–47, 183
textile and apparel industry, value
added and capital investments
in, 101
Title IV federal loans, 157
TPS. *See* Temporary Protective
Status
trade sector, 53
training: of immigrant women,
163–66; received by the more
educated, 163–64; types of,
164–65. *See also* education in
U.S.; job training
transportation sector, 55
trends: in female immigration, 25,
184; in labor-market outcomes,
114–17, 116–17, 184–86; long-
term, 49

unemployment insurance, 156,
173
U.S. Bureau of the Census, 191,
199n2

About the Author

Dr. Georges Vernez is nationally recognized for his objective approach to the study of immigration. In 1986, he became the founding director of RAND's Center on Immigration Policy, which he continues to direct. He has also directed RAND's Institute on Education and Training. To his research and analysis, he brings six years' experience implementing and overseeing the delivery of services to immigrants and to other disadvantaged populations.